Corsica

Corsica made to measure

Corsica à la carte

Contents..15

NATURE   16

A TASTE OF CORSICA   28

RECOMMENDED EATING   38

REGIONAL HISTORY   42

CHARMING VILLAGES, BEAUTIFUL CHURCHES   52

TRADITIONAL ARTS AND CRAFTS   64

SPORTING ACTIVITIES   70

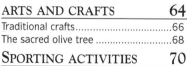

BEACHES   74

HIKING IN CORSICA   78

FAIRS AND FESTIVALS   86

Corsica in detail

Contents..............................89
Map of the region....................90

AJACCIO AND THE WEST COAST   92

BASTIA AND CAP CORSE   102

BALAGNE AND NEBBIO REGIONS   110

IN THE MOUNTAINS   132

CASTAGNICCIA REGION   144

EAST COAST   152

SOUTHERN CORSICA   158

ALTA ROCCA   178

INDEX   186

Getting there

Whether you arrive by boat or plane will very much depend on where you're travelling from and the length of your stay. Sea and air connections to the island are good but, once you land, you'll find that a car – or some means of transport – is essential for getting around.

Four-wheel freedom

Public transport on the island is poor. Buses run infrequently and the only railway line is more of a sightseeing jaunt than a way of getting around. Beaches and scenic spots are often far from the main roads and many isolated villages are only accessible by car. So, if you want to explore this beautiful island, you'll need your own transport. You can hire a car or bring your own. It's possible to find good rental deals (around 1,800F a week in the summer season) and this also saves you having to fork out for the cost of bringing your car over on the ferry as well. Do your sums! Alternatively you might prefer the freedom of travelling around on a motorbike – in some places two wheels are

better than four. Whatever you choose, be prepared for quite a few hairpin bends and roads that seem to cling on to the mountainsides by their fingernails – especially on the west of the island – and try not to have a heart attack each time a local overtakes you on a blind corner, as they sometimes will.

Where to land

While Corsican roads are often good, they are also rather tortuous, so it's more realistic to think in terms of travelling time than distance. The journey from Ajaccio to Calvi is around 105 miles (170 km) by the coast road, but takes more than 5 hours. So it's wise to choose a gateway not far from your final destination. The island's main entry points are Ajaccio, Calvi, Bastia, Île Rousse, Porto-Vecchio and Propriano.

Sea connections

SNCM Ferryterranée operates services to all of the island's ports from the French ports of Marseilles, Nice and Toulon (in season). In winter, there are no services to Propriano and Porto-Vecchio. Contact SNCM for the latest information – departure times and scheduled frequency (from one to four daily) vary according to the day. Although ferries from mainland France are increasingly comfortable, crossings can be affected by the weather and sea conditions. On-board activities and amenities are now more varied, but day crossings can still be a drag

(13 hours from Marseilles to Porto-Vecchio, half that from Nice to Bastia). Night crossings are more expensive, but worth it for the extra day spent on the island.
SNCM: 12, Rue Godot de Mauroy, 75009 Paris. Information and bookings:

☎ 08 36 67 95 00.
Website: www.sncm.fr

Fast boats

SNCM also operates fast NGV boat services, for the same price as the ferry, which connect Nice with the Corsican ports of Calvi, Île Rousse and Bastia in just 3 to 3.5 hours. However, note that services (and travellers) are delayed when conditions are windy or choppy. Make sure you phone in advance (NGV last-minute information: ☎ 08 36 64 00 95). For bookings, contact SNCM (see above).

Air connections

Air travellers arrive at one of Corsica's four airports: Bastia-Poretta, Ajaccio-Campo dell Oro, Calvi-Sainte-Catherine and Figari-Sud Corse. Depending on the day and the time of year, each airport has between one and five daily flights to the continent. There are direct flights from Paris, Nice, Marseilles, Lille and Lyon in France, to Ajaccio, Bastia and Calvi, with either Air France or Corse Méditerranée. Ollandini Voyage operates charter flights from Paris to each of the island's four airports and from various other French cities to Ajaccio, including weekends and public holidays from mid-April to the end of September. Packages inclusive of accommodation and car hire are also available. Figari is the most convenient airport if you're holidaying in southern Corsica, including Propriano, Bonifacio, Porto-Vecchio and Alta Rocca. Apart from charter flights, Figari is served exclusively by Air Liberté, with direct flights from Paris, Nice and Marseilles.

Air France/Corse Méditerranée
(information and bookings):
☎ 0 802 802 802.
Website: www.airfrance.fr

Air Liberté
(information and bookings):
☎ 0 803 805 805.
Paris departures:
☎ 08 03 09 09 09.
Website: www.air.liberte.fr

Ollandini Voyage
(info.): ☎ 04 95 23 92 92.
Bookings through agreed travel agents.

ITALIAN SEA CONNECTIONS

Italy is much closer than mainland France to Corsica, so crossings are shorter and cheaper. Ideal if you tend to get seasick.
Corsica Ferries operates traditional ferry services from Savona (100 miles/ 160 km from Nice by motorway) to Île Rousse (6 hours) and Bastia (4 hours). There are also fast boats from Nice and Savona to Bastia and Calvi (3-3.5 hours). In summer, Corsica Marittima, part of SNCM, operates the routes Bastia/Porto-Vecchio to Livorno and Bastia to Genoa. Moby Lines also has daily crossings between Bastia and the Italian ports of Genoa, Livorno and Piombino from mid-June to early September. Contact the companies for information on crossings at other times of the year.

Corsica Ferries
(information and bookings):
☎ 04 95 32 95 95.
or 0803 095 095.
Website:
www.corsicaferries.com
Corsica Marittima/ SNCM:
(see opposite).
Moby Lines/CIT
(information and bookings):
☎ 01 44 51 39 54.

A weekend in
Corsica

A weekend won't be enough to explore inland Corsica – travelling by road takes too long. Visit some of the coastal towns, which are also the chief points of entry to this beautiful island. Spring and autumn are the ideal times to go.

A weekend in Ajaccio

It's impossible to be in a hurry on this island, which is the home of the siesta. However, if you have only two or three days, go straight for the essentials – the port, Sainte-Marie de l'Assomption cathedral (where Napoleon was baptised) and, in-between, the narrow streets of old

Ajaccio, which open onto the beaches and the old citadel. These streets are a veritable maze of ochre and earth-coloured houses and artisans' leather, weaving and wood workshops (see p. 92). At lunchtime why not try the **Restaurant de France**, 59, Rue Fesch, ☎ 04 95 21 11 00, which specialises in generous servings of charcuterie for less

than 100F per head). In the afternoon try a visit to the interesting **musée A. Bandera** (1, Rue du Général Lévie, ☎ 04 95 51 07 34. Closed Sun. Nov.-Mar. Open Sat. 9am-noon and 2-6pm all-year round. Open Mon.-Fri. 9am-1pm and 3-7pm (2-6pm in winter. Admission charge). Here you'll find maps, illustrations and Corsican artefacts from the Middle Ages to the present day which bring the history of the island to life. Bandera's particular contribution was to have a permanent exhibition on particular aspects of Corsican life, including pirates, island cuisine, and Genoese influences. If you're a museum junkie you might also like to visit the musée nationale de la maison Bonaparte, where the future emperor was born. After this, you'll have just enough time for a pedalo trip around the bay (**Saint-Antoine beach**, *La Déferlante*, ☎ 04 95 21 11 38. Open July-Sept. Admission charge 50F). In the evening, don't miss the dramatic sunset over the **Sanguinaires islands**.

The following day, venture inland to the spectacular **Gravona gorges** (*see* p. 140).

A weekend in Bastia

Choose a weekend in spring or autumn, when there are fewer tourists. Get up early and watch the sun rise over the old port. Nearby, the Hôtel Posta-Vecchia (Quai des Martyrs de la Libération, 20200 Bastia, ☎ 04 95 32 32 38. Around 300F a night) is located right at the heart of the town. After a hearty breakfast, embark on a tour of Bastia. Follow Boulevards Paoli and Augustin Gaudin

to the Romieu gardens and take a romantic stroll around the heights of the town. In the afternoon you'll find lots to see, from the Place du Donjon to the Rue de la Chartreuse and the citadel itself. There's a lively atmosphere in the streets, which are shaded by

the high grey and yellow facades of the houses, where washing blows in the breeze between the windows. Bastia is known as 'Bastia la Génoise' because of its Italian atmosphere. Once night has fallen, Place Saint-Nicolas beckons. Try some of the local specialities, such as sea urchins or squid salad. You'll be spoilt for choice. The following day, prepare a picnic and escape to the small, tranquil ports of **Cap Corse** – Erbalunga, Sisco, Rogliano, Nonza – whose tall granite houses and Genoese towers reflect the island's turbulent past (*see* pp. 106-109).

A weekend in Bonifacio

Save time by going straight to Figari (*see* p. 168). Book a room in the higher part of the town, perhaps at the Royal hotel (Place Bonaparte, 20169 Bonifacio, ☎ 04 95 73 00 51. Under 300F in low season. At least double that price in summer), and take a leisurely stroll along the narrow streets to visit the luxurious mansion located to the southwest of the town. In the afternoon, you can choose to visit either the **caves** or the **Lavezzi islands**. You'll need to allow at least three hours for either trip, or you might like to visit **Santa Amanta bay** instead. Here, a network of paths lead from the beach through the broom and the scrub. This area is very busy in summer, but more peaceful from September onwards. In the evening, don't miss a trip to the naval cemetery to watch the sun set over the **Madonetta lighthouse**. On Sunday, visit the famous **Roccapina lion**, to appreciate the attractive Roccapina beach with its small, neighbouring coves (*see* p. 171). Not many people know about these nearby coves, so pay them a visit if you really want to find some peace and quiet.

Three or four days
in Corsica

There are two options for a three or four-day stay in spring or autumn, avoiding the peak season. You'll need to allow at least this amount of time to really make the most of the island.

A gastronomic weekend

Allow around 1.5 hours for the drive from Ajaccio to the Hôtel du Tourisme in **Zicavo** (☎ 04 95 24 40 06. Around 200F for double room. Open all-year round). Suddenly, you're in a different world. Before dinner, you can take a stroll in the surrounding forest or even climb to **Arleda point** (follow the path) and enjoy the view over the sea. For your

first taste of Corsican cuisine, try **Le Paradis** (Zicavo, 20132, ☎ 04 95 24 41 20. Open all-year round). For less than 100F a head, you can wash

down a range of delicious starters with orange or cherry wine. Louise Pirany does nearly all the cooking herself – the bread, the charcuterie (try the wild boar or chicken liver pâtés, or the Corsican pork rillettes), the jams and preserves, and the delicious chestnut and cinnamon marble cake. The following day, after a tour of the **Cozzano baths**, visit the Gîte de Cozzano (☎ 04 95 24 41 59.

CORSICA'S GOURMET SPECIALITIES

Prized for its charcuterie, cheeses and desserts, Corsica has many delights to offer the gastronome (see pp. 28-41). As well as pâtés, and sausages flavoured with herbs from the island's scrub, you can sample a range of delicious cheeses such as the local *brocciu*, as well as jams, honeys and traditional desserts, such as *fiadone*. Why not check out the Saint-Roch cheese fair in mid-August, which will also give you the chance to sample the local wines.

Open all-year round, but telephone in advance in low season). Here you can have a tasty family meal for around the same price. If you want to visit **Guitera**, you can opt for half board at 150F. On your third day, escape to **Santa-Maria de Siché** where you can then try the kid goat special at the restaurant called '20 123' (☎ 04 95 21 50 05. Closed 15 Jan.-15 Feb.) in Ajaccio. This is a little more expensive at around 130-180F per head, but the pork menu is exceptionally good. Try the chestnut fritters and also leave some room for the *fiadone* (*see* p. 35), a traditional Corsican cake that you'll come across on every menu, but which is particularly good in this restaurant.

Four days of relaxation and culture in southern Corsica

Head straight to Figari and stay in the Zonza or Levie regions in **Alta-Rocca** (*see* pp. 178-181). A visit to the 'old lady' (La Dame de Bonifacio) at the **musée départmental de Levie** is a must (*see* p. 181). Southern Corsica has many souvenirs of the distant past. **Filitosa** (*see* p. 44) and **Cucuruzzu** (*see* p. 181), both date back about four thousand years and make an interesting and pleasant excursion. The standing stones at Filitosa were erected at a time when similar Bronze Age monuments were being put up throughout Europe, and the spirals of stone at Curcuruzzu lead to a panoramic view over the whole of southern Corsica.

A little further off the beaten track, the **Castello de Capula** is one of the best-preserved castles on the island, and boasts a large menhir engraved with a sword. Close by are the **San Lorenzo chapel** and the 12th-C. ruins dating from the later occupation of the area (roughly from the Bronze Age to the Middle Ages). Don't miss one of the most beautiful dolmens in Europe (a large table 14 ft/3.5 m by 12 ft/3 m) at Fontanaccia (signposted from Sartène or Tizzano). Arrive early in the morning and watch the sun slowly rise through the vast opening in the structure. The site is on the **Cauria headland**, nearly 1,200 ft (300 m) above the Mediterranean sea, with a wonderful view over the west coast.

Bronze Age menhir at Filitosa

A week
in Corsica

Explore Alta Rocca, Cap Corse or the island's interior. You won't have time to do the whole island but you can certainly see things in your locality. One week is ideal.

A week
in Alta Rocca

Take your time! This is one of the most beautiful areas of the island. There are some excellent places to stay, including the gîte at **Quenza** (I Muntagnoli Corsi, Centre de Montagne, 20122, ☎ 04 95 78 64 05. Closed mid-Oct. to Jan. Half board under 200F). Alternatively, the gîte at Serra di Scopamène (see p. 181) makes an excellent base from which you can go hiking or walking in the majestic countryside, with its contrasting granite and lush vegetation. Discover the **Bavella needles** and the famous **Trou de la Bombe** sinkhole (see p. 178). The country footpaths are always a good way of getting about (see p. 83). Most gîtes and hotels provide a list of paths, and a map is available from any tourist office. Don't hesitate to ask the knowledgeable locals about places of interest.

The Corsicans know their island like the back of their hand, and are delighted to share their knowledge. One of the most beautiful walks in the region (around 6 miles/ 10 km) takes you from Zonza to the Bavella pass (Col de Bavella) – make arrangements with your gîte or hotel so you don't have to do the return journey on foot. The trail crosses a chestnut grove and then climbs through a pine forest to Bavella, at 4,800 ft (1,200 m). If your children are new to the mountains, enrol them in a mountaineering course. Details at the gîte at Quenza. If you arrange to be in Alta Rocca during the first week of August, you can enjoy

taking part in the **snow pilgrimage** (*pèlerinage des neiges*), a procession to Bavella followed by an open-air mass. It is held each year on 5 August at the foot of the Bavella needles (*see* p. 178).

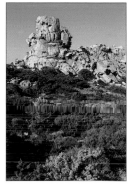

A week in Cap Corse

Strangely, this cape, a narrow outcrop that points in the direction of France – described by some as the thumb on the fist of Corsica – is the only seafaring region in Corsica (*see also* p. 106). It is also a holiday resort, with numerous secluded beaches and coves. Prices peak in summer but are halved in the low season. Whether in spring or summer, **Erbalunga** is an excellent starting point, situated on a schist promontory that juts out into the sea. A good place to stay is the Castel Brando hotel, ☎ 04 95 30 10 30. Closed 30 Oct.-15 Mar. Around 4,500F a week for a double room in summer and

less than 3,000F in low season. Breakfast included. Spend a few days exploring inland. Follow the walking trail through scrub hills and beaches from **Centuri** to **Macinaggio cove** (map available from the tourist office). At **Nonza**, you will find the only black sand beach on the island. This strange phenomenon was caused by an ancient asbestos deposit (don't worry, it's perfectly safe). You'll see an imposing square tower perched on top of the cliffs (*see* p. 106). Sisco is a charming, traditional port and there's an attractive walk from Sisco village to the interior of the cape (5 miles/ 8 km). Romantics and photographers will appreciate the sunset at **Capo Grosso**, at the northwestern tip of Cap Corse.

A week around Corte

This is the geographical and historical heart of the island, the home of Pasquale Paoli, the renowned Corsican freedom fighter. He founded a university here, keen for his

people to be educated. The town and its citadel held out against all invasions throughout the island's history, giving Corte a distinctive atmosphere, which you can savour with a stroll along the Cours Paoli. The surrounding area is good for walking, especially in autumn when the forests turn to gold and ochre. With numerous trails, taking in forests, canyons, gorges, streams and waterfalls, you'll be spoilt for choice. Who knows, you may even come across the rare mountain sheep, the nimble-footed mouflon (*see* p. 25) on one of your walks. A good idea is to arrive at Ajaccio and take the **small train** which crosses the island as far as Corte. The valley and mountain scenery is

unforgettable. Allow at least one day to explore the area on horseback, perhaps the **Tavignano and Restonica gorges**, carved out by the water from the **Lac de Melo**. This area is also renowned for its cuisine. At the shepherd's huts at Grotelle, at the foot of the **Restonica gorges**, you can taste and buy local produce such as *coppa*, *prisottu*, or *lonza* (all different types of cured and smoked cuts of pork) direct from the producers.

A fortnight
in Corsica

A fortnight will give you enough time to enjoy everything Corsica has to offer – sea and mountains, towns and villages, sport and relaxation. The Balagne region and southern Corsica are quieter and make an ideal destination for a holiday that is both active and relaxing.

The Balagne region

May, just before the summer crowds arrive, is the ideal month for exploring this region, which is one of the most beautiful in Corsica and also one of the most varied. Here, you'll find numerous artisans, weavers, sculptors and cabinet and instrument makers, as well as pig farmers and bee-keepers (see pp. 118-121), who have brought life back to the small villages of the region. Explore the

colourful scrubland (*maquis*) around these hamlets, the **Ostriconi** region and the **Agriates** and **Giussani** deserts (*see* p. 83), on foot, horseback or mountain bike. For guided tours from Mach onwards, contact Pierre-Jean Costa at the Ferme-Auberge de l'Ostriconi at Lama (*see* p. 126). He will organise everything and in two weeks you'll learn more about the region than if you had lived there for years. Groups can take a four or five-day horseback trek, with camping and picnics, perfect for discovering the Tartaigne and Pinetu forests, the Asco valleys, the Popolasca peaks,

the deep gorges and the small villages of the interior like Corte and La Restonica. There are many possibilities. In the second week, try cycling. In May the weather is not yet too hot, making it the ideal time to explore **Loto lake** and the unspoilt **Scalavita and Peraiola coves**. At this time of year the snows melt and the famous peat bogs (*pozzine* – *see* p. 23) at the **Lac du Cintu** are spectacular. By the end of your fortnight on the island you will have experienced all this with hardly any travel involved and certainly very little stress. A far cry from work.

Southern Corsica out of season

Be a canny visitor and choose the low season (Mar.-May and

Sept.-Dec.), when Sartène, Bonifacio and Bavella are not overrun by tourists. At this time the businesses and restaurants are more

welcoming and prices are a little easier on the pocket. Bonifacio (*see* p. 162), dramatically sited on a clifftop at the southern tip of Corsica, with a wonderful view of the coast of Sardinia, is a welcoming place to stay out of season. Hotels have double rooms for 200F and campsites cost from 50F a day. The central location of the **A Pignata** farmhouse inn (*see* p. 35) makes it a perfect base from which to explore the south of the island. There's a scenic walking trail from the small village of Tasso, in the Haut-Taravo region, to the summit of Malvesa at 6,400 ft (1,600 m). The walk takes two to three days and is suitable for all abilities (accommodation in the Tasso and Vizzicula refuges, details from the tourist office). The trail crosses a vast forest of chestnuts before reaching the **Bottagio pass** (Col de Bottagio), which offers a splendid panoramic view of the Alta Rocca, and then follows the ridge to the slopes

of Malvesa, part of the *Balcons du Taravo* ('Taravo terraces'). Less well known and quieter than the neighbouring Bavella, the **Velaco range** has an attractive ramble through the Laricio pine forest. The start of the trail, indicated by a wooden sign, is found below the Auberge de Bavella. Follow the red and black signposts of the GR 20, then head for the **Trou de la Bombe,** a huge arch opening onto a sinkhole some 1,600 ft (500 m) deep (*see* p. 179).

Head for Bocca Furesta and you'll reach the **Velaco ridge trail**. To descend, follow the same path but turn right at **Bocca Furesta**, an alternative forest route that rejoins the **Bavella pass**. After an invigorating first week, you can spend the second week relaxing on the southern **beaches**, between the small **Piantarella dock** (from where you can take a magnificent walk along the coast in the direction of Bonifacio) and the white sandy cove of **Petit Spérone**. In spring the water can be a little chilly, but it is just right from September through to mid-November. If you have the time, catch a boat from Bonifacio out to the Lavezzi Islands (*see* p. 166), a little archipelago of attractive islands which are noted for their colourful marine life, with some beautiful dive sites available for those who enjoy exploring the seabed.

Corsica à la carte

Nature

Between the mountains and the sea, discover the varied flora and fauna and the spectacular landscape of this island.

① *Niolo*
Regional nature park.
p. 136

② *Forêt de la Castagniccia*
Chestnut forests as far as the eye can see.
p. 144

③ *Orezza*
Mineral springs.
p. 146

④ *Canaglia*
Manganellu gorges.
p. 143

⑤ *Forêt de Vizzavona*
Wooded waterfalls and gorges.
pp. 142-143

⑥ *Défilés des Strette and de l'Inzecca*
Spectacular gorges.
p. 156

⑦ San Gavino
Macini waterfall and the Abatesco valley.
p. 157

⑧ *Plateau de Cuscione*
Eagles and Corsican wild sheep.
p. 180

⑨ Col de Bavella
Bavella peaks and Alta Rocca mountain panorama.
p. 178

⑩ L'Ospedale
Spectacular Piscia di Gallu waterfall.
p. 161

⑪ *The rocky Îles Lavezzi*
Rocky Lavazzi islands, off the coast of Bonifacio.
p. 167

⑫ *Bonifacio*
Chalk cliffs and caves of Sdragonato.
p. 163

⑬ *Caldane*
Thermal baths – open-air sulphur spa.
p. 183

⑭ *Baraci*
Thermal baths – two naturally hot springs.
p. 175

⑮ *Clue de La Richiusa*
Granite canyons and bathing in the waterfall.
p. 141

⑯ *Névé du Busso*
Perennial snow and glacier.
p. 141

⑰ *Montagnes du Renoso and du Niello*
The island's most beautiful mountains, all year long.
p. 185

⑱ *Gorges du Prunelli and du Val d'Ese*
Prunelli and Ese valley gorges – splendid scenic route.
p. 185

⑲ *Ota*
Spelunca gorges – red canyon, Genoese bridges and swimming.
p. 101

⑳ *Piana*
Rocky coves – some of the most beautiful scenery in Corsica.
p. 101

㉑ *Forêt du Valdo Niello*
Forest and Radule waterfall bathing.
p. 139

㉒ *Popaghjia*
Swimming in Nino lake with views of the Niolo mountains.
p. 139

㉓ *Scala di Santa Regina*
Oldest route to Niolo, and deep granite gorge.
p. 137

㉔ *Gorges de Tavignano*
Near Corte, swimming in the Tavignano gorges.
p. 135

㉕ *Désert des Agriates*
The 'maquis' – wild, deserted scrubland.
p. 126

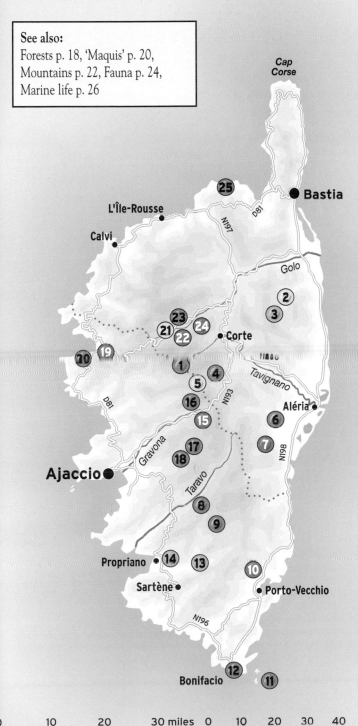

See also:
Forests p. 18, 'Maquis' p. 20,
Mountains p. 22, Fauna p. 24,
Marine life p. 26

Cap
Corse

Bastia

L'Île-Rousse

Calvi

N197

D81

Golo

25

23

21 22 24

19 20

Corte

N193

1

5 4

16

15

Tavignano

Aléria

6

7

N198

Gravona

17

18

Ajaccio

Taravo

8

9

Propriano 14 13

10

Sartène

Porto-Vecchio

N196

12 11

Bonifacio

0   10   20   30 miles   0   10   20   30   40   50 km

In the shade of the Corsican forest

The Corsican forest covers a vast area from the Castagniccia region to the foothills of the Bavella peaks. The Corsicans protect and respect this complex and varied woodland, which includes olive, beech, oak and pine trees. If you want to escape the heat of the beach, it's a great place to escape and relax with a picnic.

On the lower slopes...

Wild boar still roam the oak forest at the foothills of Alta Rocca. Chestnut groves can be found at an altitude of 1,600–2,600 ft (500–800 m), although the Castagniccia forest extends right to the sea. Some pine trees, like those in the Calvi forest, grow at sea level, while the Corsican maritime pine flourishes above 2,600 ft (800 m).

... and high above

Above 3,300 ft (1,000 m), the king of the trees is the famous Laricio pine, almost exclusive to Corsica. Typically, the trunk of this tree is tall and slender, measuring around 160–200 ft (40–50 m) in height and is relatively bare. The most beautiful Laricio pine forests are found in Aïtone, above Evisa, in Valdo Niello in the Niolo region, and in L'Ospedale, above

Porto-Vecchio. At Aïtone and Valdo Niello there are also beeches and other species of pine. The beech is one of the few deciduous trees to have adapted to cold mountainous habitats and its hard wood is used extensively in carpentry.

Trees of life

The forest has for a long time been a source of both food and income. The cork oak of the

fertile lands of the Porto-Vecchio region is a prime example, although the sight of these trees may come as a bit of a surprise to those who normally associate cork

production with Portugal and Spain. You may see many trees stripped of their bark, but this is not a cause for concern as it grows back in about nine or ten years. The second most profitable tree is the chestnut, which was introduced to Corsica by the Genoese. Everything on the tree was at one time put to use. The burs were used to smoke the

SECRETS OF THE FOREST

In the undergrowth you can find **bilberries**, which can be preserved in alcohol or made into jams and preserves. **Arbutus berries** can be eaten raw, but are more tasty when made into jam. **Prickly pears** abound on the slopes (you'll need thick gloves to pick and peel them) and can be eaten raw. **Thyme** is also abundant in clearings and mountain pastures. However, resist the temptation to pluck sweet-smelling plants such as alder, broom, eucalyptus or lavender because this is strictly forbidden.

Prickly Pear

Arbutus

Corsica has many edible **mushrooms** (ceps, chanterelles, horns of plenty, etc.), but also has 12 fatal varieties. You'll need to make sure that mushroom picking is allowed in the particular area that you're staying in and then seek professional advice before you risk eating them – have a pharmacist check them first, for example.

Horn of plenty

Chanterelle

Cep

orchards, dead wood was used for fuel and the wood from diseased trees was used in furniture manufacturing. Even the rotten chestnuts could be used for feeding pigs. The cultivation of the chestnut tree, however, has been progressively abandoned, due to the intensity of the labour involved and the tree's susceptibility to disease.

The danger of forest fires

Don't light fires in the forest and avoid smoking. Although these rules might seem a little obvious, every summer there are catastrophes caused by the carelessness of visitors. If you do feel the need to smoke, please make sure that your cigarette is properly extinguished before you dispose of it. If you travel by car, always use the ashtray and never throw matches or cigarette ends out of the window. In the event of a forest fire, the police and fire brigade always respond quickly. However, the figures are alarming – each year the destruction of trees in Corsica accounts for 75% of the total surface area of French forests lost to fire. On average, 25,000 acres (10,000 ha) are lost each year and an alarming 80% of these fires are due to negligence or malice. The kind of devastation caused can be witnessed on the road from the small village of Ospedale to Porto-Vecchio. After seeing this destruction you'll never want to discard another cigarette carelessly again.

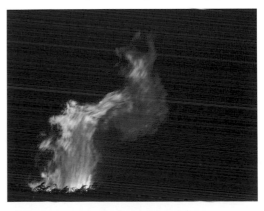

'Maquis' and 'maquisards'

The Corsican *maquis* is an area of thorny scrubland renowned for its dense impenetrability. French resistance fighters in World War II were known as *maquisards*, since they were forced to travel in these remote, inhospitable areas and hide in the undergrowth frm German and Italian troops. If you decide to explore these areas of harsh natural beauty, always remember to stay on the path. It's all too easy to fall and hurt yourself or rip your clothing.

Low maquis...

Corsica has a wide variety of shrub types, including briar, arbutus, mastic and broom. The scrubland varies in composition, according to altitude, position, soil condition and rainfall. While maquis is rarely found higher than 1,600 ft (500 m) above sea level, at the beaches of Balagne (*see* p. 110) it's less than 65 ft (20 m) from the sea. Low-lying maquis is often less dense due to the nature of its sandy soil, and here you can find myrtle and white flowering heather – which should not be picked.

Heather

...and high maquis

Above 1,300 ft (400 m) the maquis becomes taller and thicker and even incorporates species of tree, such as the holm oak or ilex. However, it chiefly consists of 14 to 20-ft (4 to 6-m) high shrubland. Be aware that some cows graze on low-lying maquis. There's no danger unless you have a dog with you, in which case they will not hesitate to charge. The maquis also provides a habitat for wild boar, which feed on the arbutus berry. If you are carrying any food and they sniff it out, you'll need to exercise extreme caution. Give the food to them immediately, as they may otherwise become aggressive. Corsicans make a popular liqueur from the edible but not very sweet arbutus berries, which you can sample at Maison Mattei in Bastia (p. 37). Try a glass of Cap Corse as an aperitif, perhaps with a piece of *finuchiettu*.

Ecology

The maquis was traditionally the hiding place of bandits (p. 62). These days, its water-retentive qualities creates a protective habit for wildlife and prevents soil erosion. The cool shade it provides also slows down evaporation. When Napoleon famously declared that he could smell his way to Corsica, he was, in

Beautiful walks

There are two walking trails suitable for all the family leading directly from the beaches of Balagne (Saleccia, Lotto, Ostriconi). The Désert des Agriates is so-called as it's sparsely populated and crossed by only one path. A riot of colour, it is one of the wildest and most beautiful examples of low-lying maquis. There are also several paths from the Teghime pass (*Col de Teghime*)

between Bastia and Saint-Florent, which lead to more accessible maquis. The best example of high-altitude maquis is found in the foot-hills of the Niolo mountains. There are several possible itineraries, details available from the tourist office in Niolo (p.136). Spring is a wonderful time to enjoy Corsica's scrubland, with its stunning colours and unforget-table scent.

SOME RARE SPECIES

Surprisingly, the pink-flowered butterfly orchid (*orchidée papillon*) can be found in the low-lying maquis, at below 1,400 ft (400 m). A little further up, you can find the beautiful red cyclamen. On the east side of the island, you can find a rare species of *cistus*, namely the 'sage-petalled' cistus or rock rose. In winter, different species of *Erba di Tramontana* ('wine Viburnum') flower abundantly in shades of pink and white. Did you know that praying mantises abound in arid stony areas such as the Désert des Agriates, where they come to flush out the lizards?

Rock rose

fact paying tribute to the many sweet-smelling plants and shrubs that go to make up the maquis, including wild herbs such as marjoram and rosemary, whose scent in spring and summer is carried far and wide on the breeze. Lemon balm and mint can also be found in the scrubland. The herbs used in Corsican traditional cuisine are known locally as *erbiglie*, and they give the dishes their unique flavour. Higher-lying maquis provides an additional source of nutrition for semi-domesticated animals that roam freely (cows, pigs, goats and kids). The maquis still accounts for more than one-fifth of the island's total area, despite frequent damage by fires. Fortunately, maquis is very good at recovering from these disasters and some ecologists even believe they are beneficial, as they kill off old plants and encourage the growth of healthy, new plants.

A mountainous island

Despite Corsica's warm, azure waters and popular sandy beaches, its grand mountain scenery is the very heart of the island. From the foothills of Niolo to the valleys of Monte Incudine, the startling light and colour, the alpine smells and wild landscapes will reveal just why Corsica is known as the *Île de Beauté*.

A choice of mountain scenery

Each micro region of the island has its own attractions. Niolo is one of the most beautiful areas of the island, but Monte Padro and Monte Terello, the Popalasca peaks, the Cinto range (p. 136) and the Alta Rocca (p. 178) all have a distinctive charm. If you have to choose just one, then Monte Rotondo, which towers over the cold, deep, clear green Melo lake, in a setting of alps and snowy peaks, is among the most beautiful landscapes in the world (Venaco, p. 142).

Ski down to the blue sea

Although Corsica doesn't have much in the way of skiing infrastructure (lifts and so on), it does attract a small band of dedicated enthusiasts, and at certain times of the year you can actually go skiing in the morning and swim in the sea in the afternoon. As you ski down the slopes of Renoso, above Ghisoni (which does have ski lifts), you get a

Monte Cinto towers above Corsica at 7,420 ft (2,706 m)

heady view of the small village, the rocky Inzecca gorge, Ghisonaccia beach, the Mediterranean and, in the distance, the coast of Tuscany. Contact the refuge (Refuge d'en Haut. After Ghisoni, turn right before the Col de Verde. ☎ 06 88 21 49 16) or Altore in Saint-Florent (p. 131). There are further skiing opportunities to be had at Padro in the south or Cinto in the north, but you'll need some waterproof clothing for the ascent.

From one end of the island to the other

The Haute Route ('high road'), provides an extra-ordinary skiing experience, but it's only suitable for accomplished skiers. It isn't so much skiing as ski trekking or ski mountaineering, combining rock climbing, snow climbing, cross-country and some downhill. This is a two-week trail that starts at Monte Padro, which overlooks Balagne in the north, and ends at Monte Incadine in the south, taking in the mountains and lakes of Cinto, Renoso and Rotondo on the way. A guide is indispensable, particularly as this is a winter

trail and the shelters are not manned. You will need to be very well equipped. Several expeditions are organised during the year and they are becoming increasingly popular. If you are a sufficiently experienced skier, contact the Corsican tourist agency (**Agence du Tourisme Corse**, 17, Blvd du Roi-Jérôme, 2000 Ajaccio, ☎ 04 95 51 77 77).

LAKES AND *POZZINE*

The Cinto, Niolo, Nino and Melo lakes are all accessible from various local towns or from the GR 20 – head for Albertacce and Casamaccioli for Cinto and Niolo lakes (p. 136) and Venaco for Nino and Melo lakes (p. 142). You can also consult IGN maps or guides published by the nature reserve (p. 80). One of the prettiest lakes, Nino (p. 139), is fabled to be the entrance to hell, but is a wonderful spot for a swim. On the whole, the artificial lakes (including Ospedale and Tolla) are less attractive in summer because the water levels are lower. The numerous gorges and waterfalls are frozen in winter. The *pozzine* (peat bogs) are particularly remarkable in the spring when the snows thaw. As the snow melts, the water floods the flat areas around the lakes and forms small, attractive streams, ponds and stretches of water across the grass. It's possible to walk through the pozzine if you don't mind getting your ankles wet. Those around Cinto lake are typical of the local peatbogs and make a pleasant and easy excursion from Niolo (p. 136).

Fauna

Corsica is home to abundant species of wildlife, even the most timid, such as deer, which were recently successfully reintroduced to the island. The deer were raised in enormous closed reserves and then returned to their natural habitat in the highlands of Alta Rocca. The hard work of the staff at Corsica's nature park has also ensured the survival of hundreds of other species in Corsica, notably a large variety of birds.

Robin

Thrush

Sparrow hawk

Birdland

Corsica is full of birds, from the smallest crossbill to the largest sparrow hawk. In the low-lying scrubland, you can find robins, linnets, thrushes, tariers and blackbirds, as well as partridges, unfortunately threatened by hunting. All these birds depend on the particular ecological balance of the maquis, so it is vital not to disturb the environment. Warblers, jays and goldcrests nest in the oak trees of the high maquis.

Winged hunters

The majestic golden eagle, a consummate hunter of small mammals, nests in the high peaks of Monte Cinto, Monte d'Oro and the Bavella range. It shares its mountain habitat with a type of bearded vulture that Corsicans call the *Altore*. This bird, which has a wingspan approaching 10 ft (3 m) and can dive at speeds of up to 60 mph (100 kph), is also know as the 'bone-breaker' (*casseur d'os*), as it feeds on carcasses, breaking down the bones with its powerful beak. The sparrow hawk and the falcon hunt lower down the mountains, in the forests and the high maquis, feeding on rodents and small mammals. In the northwest of the island, around the coast, you may catch a glimpse of the occasional osprey. Making their nests on the cliffs, these impressive birds, with a wingspan of around 5 ft (1.5 m), live exclusively on

Golden eagle

fish, which they catch with a spectacular feet-first dive, sometimes completely submerging themselves in the process.

Warbler

Bird watching

Apply copious quantities of insect repellent, take a pair of binoculars, find a well-camouflaged spot in the maquis – then don't move! Remember, there's no substitute for patience.

After dark

There are around 30 species of bat in Corsica and, apart from the hedgehog and a few insect-eating falcons that hunt after dark, the night belongs to them. The largest bat is the *Molosse de Cestonie*, which lives in fissures in the coastal cliffs, plunging into the darkness to feed on insects.

Scrubland snakes

Don't panic! The only snakes you'll find in the maquis are a few attractive grass snakes – yellow, green or grey and all completely harmless. There are no poisonous snakes and it's highly unusual (and not dangerous) to be bitten by a grass snake.

Wild pigs or boars?

In Corsica, the two families are close. With their snouts stuck to the ground, sniffing out edible roots and rubbish, wild pigs (*cochons sauvages*) are often seen in

packs, wandering in the forest or on the edge of a village. These animals are semi-domesticated, semi-wild and are easily mistaken for wild boar (restaurants often serve wild pig as though it were boar). The wild boar (*sanglier*) does exist, but lives alone in the depths of the forest. Nevertheless, to get around the law prohibiting the hunting of *sanglier*, the islanders often refer to wild boar as 'Corsican pigs'.

KING MOUFLON

The mouflon, a type of wild sheep, has inhabited Corsica for over 8,000 years and has become the country's emblem. Today, it can only be found high in the mountains, at altitudes of up to 8,500 ft (2,600 m). This is not its natural habitat but it has been forced to take refuge from hunters, poachers and forest fires. Each winter the mouflon comes down from the mountains to avoid the bitter cold and find food. This is the best time to observe the creature, in the vicinity of the Nino or Mela lakes. Without the protection of the island's nature reserve, the mouflon would have long disappeared. Current estimates put their number at 500.

Fish and shellfish

The waters around Corsica are home to over 150 different species of fish. This is a wonderful place for divers, even beginners, since many species favour shallow waters. Although Corsica is agricultural by tradition, fishing provides an additional source of income in the Ajaccio and Valico bays and around Cap Corse.

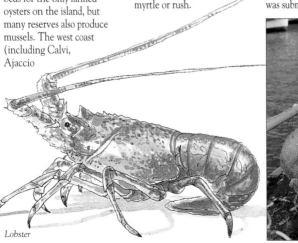

Fishing for shellfish

Diane lake provides suitable beds for the only farmed oysters on the island, but many reserves also produce mussels. The west coast (including Calvi, Ajaccio and Campomoto point) is a source of sea urchins. Fishing for sea urchins is regulated and priority is given to licensed fishermen. Although crabs can be found in the markets of Cap Corse and Bastia, they are not a particular speciality of the island – lobster takes pride of place. It is fished further and further afield and its price varies according to the season (180-240F for 2.2 lbs/1 kg). Corsican lobsters are some of the most prized in the Mediterranean, and are sometimes still fished in the traditional way, using nets made from sprigs of myrtle or rush.

Fish and fishermen

Of the 150 varieties of fish in Corsican waters, around 50 are regularly fished and sold, notably scorpion fish, mullet, sea-bream, bass, sardines and John Dory. Long-line fishing is still practised far out at sea (several vertical lines are joined to a horizontal mother line kept on the surface by means of floats), but drift nets are also used. In former times, the Ajaccio region had its own distinctive method of fishing, with a boat towing a line out to sea while the two ends remained on land. Once the line was submerged, it would be

Lobster

With the exception of trout, the freshwater fish are generally less tasty than saltwater fish, so you won't find them often on restaurant menus. Corsica is the only island in the Mediterranean where you have a chance of seeing the black salamander, with its distinctive yellow markings, which lives near rivers and waterfalls. It's not dangerous but don't touch it

hauled in by men on the beaches. Sometimes more than a thousand fish were caught at a time. This ancient method is still used on occasion on Saint-François beach, and makes for an interesting spectacle for the visitor.

Rare and protected species

Protected species of marine life in the waters around Corsica include the swordfish, grouper, porpoise, moray, dentis and liches. These can be found around the Lavezzi islands and the Scandola reserve. Their activity is monitored by the reserve and deep-sea diving and fishing are strictly prohibited. Numerous excursions can be made from Calvi, Porto or the Île Rousse and occasionally a glass-bottomed boat is available for underwater observation. Details available from the local tourist offices.

Freshwater fishing and salamanders

River fishing on Corsica is considered a sport, and is not done not profit. Waterfalls and rivers are teeming with

GRAB A BASKET

Ajaccio market (*see* p. 92) is one of the most attractive and diverse on the island. It's located between Rue du Roi-Jérôme and the Place du Maréchal Foch. The choice of fish and shellfish is immense and the market's size and the busy tourist trade it attracts keeps the prices at a reasonable level. The sea urchins you will find here are among the largest on the island. Try some with a glass of *pastis* as an aperitif before dinner.

trout, but you can also fish for eels (rarely higher than 3,300 ft/1,000 m) or blenny.

as it can cause urticaria, an itchy skin rash which can last for a few days.

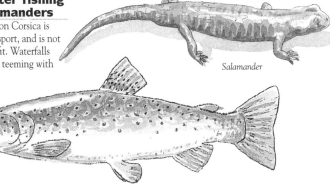

Salamander

Trout

A taste of Corsica

The flavours of Corsica:
Cheese, wine, charcuterie and sweet treats.

① *Cheese shop*
U Grimaldi
in Granaggiolo. Smoked goat's milk cheese.
p. 108

② *Cheese shop*
Philippe Albertini
in Rogliano. Speciality: farm-produced goat's milk cheese.
p. 107

③ *Charcuterie*
U Paese in Bastia. *Coppa*, *figatellu* and *lonzu*.
p. 104

④ *Wine*
Maison Mattel. Speciality: 'Le Cap', a Corsican aperitif.
p. 37

⑤ *Cheese shop*
Xavier Guidicelli
in Ponto Novo, Castello di Rostino area. Speciality: *rustinu* goat's milk cheese.
p. 31

⑥ *Fish and shellfish*
Diane lake oysters in Aléria.
p. 153

⑦ *Local produce*
L'Orriu
in Porto-Vecchio. Donkey sausage, strong cheese and myrtle liqueur
p. 159

⑧ *Charcuterie*
François Urbani in Bastelica. Fresh *prissutu* and smoked *coppa*.
p. 184

⑨ *Cheese shop*
Acciola in Giuncheto. Cheese, wine and farm produce.
p. 172

⑩ *Fish and shellfish*
Ajaccio market.
p. 92

⑪ *Charcuterie*
Jean Acquaviva
in Calacuccia. *Lonzu, figatelli* and other *salsiccia*.
p. 137

⑫ *Confectioners*
E. Fritella
in Calenzana. Corsican speciality biscuits, such as the famous *canistrelli*.
p. 118

⑬ *Local produce*
Domaine Orsini
in Calenzana. Speciality: homemade jams.
p. 35

⑭ *Local produce*
L'Atelier du Village
in Calenzana. Crafts, homemade jam, chestnut-flour cakes, orgeat syrup, myrtle and mandarin liqueurs.
p. 119

⑮ *Wine*
Le Clos Columbu
in Lumin. Large variety of wines at all prices.
p. 119

⑯ *Honey*
Miel de Lozari. Michel and François Gacon.
p. 121

⑰ *Wine*
Domaine de Catarelli
in Farinole. White, rosé and red wines and Muscat.
p. 107

⑱ *Fish and shellfish*
Macciota
in Centuri port. Mullet and lobster.
p. 108

See also:
Cheese p. 30,
Charcuterie p. 32,
Cakes and confectionery p. 34,
Wines and spirits p. 36.

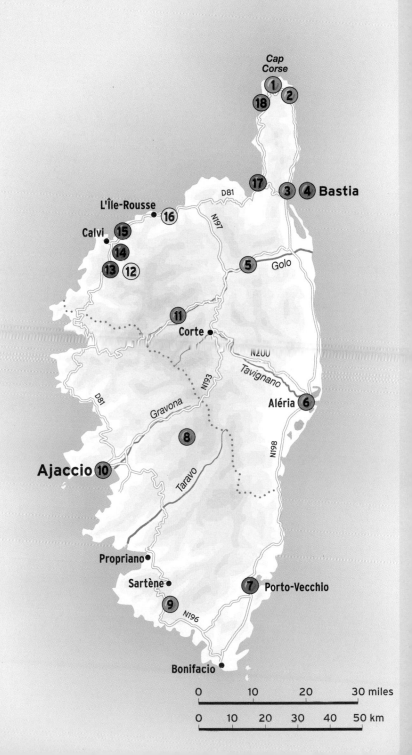

Cap Corse

① ②

⑱

⑰ ③ ④ **Bastia**

D81

L'Île-Rousse ⑯

N197

Calvi ⑮

⑭

⑤ *Golo*

⑬ ⑫

⑪

Corte

N200

Tavignano

N193

Gravona **Aléria** ⑥

⑧

Ajaccio ⑩

Taravo

N198

Propriano

Sartène ⑦ **Porto-Vecchio**

⑨

N196

Bonifacio

| 0 | 10 | 20 | 30 miles |

| 0 | 10 | 20 | 30 | 40 | 50 km |

Cheese,
the taste of the land

After charcuterie, cheese is Corsica's second gourmet speciality and a staple feature of the island's cuisine. All cheeses, whether hard or soft, strong or mild, of goat's or ewe's milk, are made according to a particular method, and the different cooking times, mixtures of various milks and durations of the maturing process are closely-guarded secrets.

Legendary *brocciu*

Legend has it that the secret of making *brocciu* cheese was revealed to local villagers by a starving ogre. Brocciu, usually made with sheep's milk, is not, strictly speaking, a cheese. It's made using just whey and milk and the secret is to stop heating the milk at the precise moment when it starts to solidify. Brocciu is very popular with Corsicans and is used in a variety of dishes, both savoury and sweet (p. 41), and is an essential ingredient in the popular *fiadone* cake (p. 35). It can be eaten fresh (maximum five days old) in spring. In summer it has less flavour, because it is preserved in salt. You will also find it used in the little chestnut fritters (p. 35), where the cheese is combined with chestnut flour and fried in oil.

Soft in the north, hard in the south

In northern Corsica, cheeses tend to be softer and easier to spread than in the south. This is true of many cheeses produced in the Niolo region, which is reputed to be the best gastronomical area on the island. In southern Corsica, cheeses are matured longer and often kept for more than three months in cool cellars,

MEET THE SHEPHERDS

Every year, from 16-18 August, the *Scontru di I Pastori* takes place at Renno, near the Col Saint-Roch. This Corsican phrase translates literally as 'meeting with the shepherds', but this event, also known as the Foire de la Saint-Roch (Saint-Roch fair), is an opportunity to meet the island's cheese makers. The demonstrations of the manufacturing processes of the various cheeses (including *brocciu*), will certainly make your mouth water, but you can easily satisfy your taste buds as all the produce is for sale. This is the most important of all Corsican cheese fairs, so Corsican wine also plays a significant part here for obvious reasons. Further details from **Ajaccio tourist office**, Place du Maréchal Foch, ☎ 04 95 51 53 03.

have been allowed to mature. Conversely, the Galet de San Nicolao, a small sheep's cheese, round and flat with a very runny consistency, is only matured for one month.

Niolo rustinu

Rustinu cheese is the speciality of Xavier Guidicelli, one of the finest cheese makers on the island. At Ponto Novo, in the Niolo foothills, this craftsman welcomes visitors to his workshop where this inimitable soft sheep's cheese is produced. Here you can observe all the stages of the manufacturing process, including the curdling of the milk, maturing, salting and the turning out of the cheeses. If you are unable to visit Ponto Novo, you can also find this cheese in the markets in Bastia, Calvi or Saint-Florent (around 15F a piece). **Fromagerie Guidicelli**, Route du Lento, Ponto Novo, Castello di Rostino commune, ☎ 04 95 38 60 57. Open every day except Sunday, 9am-noon and 2-6pm.

where they are regularly 'turned' to preserve their consistency.

Goat's or sheep's milk?

The taste of the cheese is determined by the maturing process, rather than the source of the milk. For example, Corsican *tomme* cheese is matured for six months, and sometimes even for up to seven or eight months. This gives it a crumbly, parmesan-like texture (it's delicious grated) and a very pungent flavour. Similarly, the consistency of the small goat's cheeses, often rolled in herbs from the maquis, ferns or even heather, will depend on how long they

The distinctive flavour of pork

E very day, Corsicans test the truth of the old saying *'In u porcu tutt' hè bonu!'* (Every bit of the pig is tasty!). The great majority of the island's charcuterie comes from pork meat. The fact is that Corsican pigs are more closely related to boars than to their cousins on the continent and it's this that gives the meat its distinctive and powerful flavour, together with the rather exotic diet enjoyed by the pigs.

A unique flavour

Corsican charcuterie is prized for its flavour and this is doubtless due to the diet and lifestyle of the island's pigs, which you can observe at first hand if you explore the small mountain routes in the centre of the island, where they roam free. These wild pigs can be seen grazing at the edges of forests and the outskirts of villages, feeding on acorns, chestnuts, and roots. Their completely organic diet gives the island's charcuterie its unique quality.

Cured ham

In Corsica, cured ham is known as *prisuttu*, a word reminiscent of the Italian

prosciutto, which it closely resembles. It's particularly tender and tasty and can be eaten on its own, or in omelettes or salads. Grilled chestnuts also make a

particularly delicious accompaniment and complement the subtle flavour of the ham. *Prisuttu* is an essential ingredient of all soups that claim an authentic Corsican heritage. It's generally best eaten raw,

but in the south you may come across a gently-smoked version.

Coppa

The best known Corsican charcuterie, *coppa* is a loin of pork, rolled up and tied compactly. It can be found all over the island but the quality does vary. If you buy it from a local producer, make sure you avoid ending up with a poor quality or badly smoked *coppa*.

Lonzu

Although similar to *coppa* in shape and size, *lonzu* has a different taste. It is smoked in

the same manner, but then seasoned with pepper, which gives it a sharper flavour. It also differs by being made from pork fillet, not loin. Try tasting one after the other and you will soon appreciate the subtle difference in taste.

Salsiccia

This is much the same as the French *saucisson* (spiced dried sausage), although the Corsican version is more chewy, noticeably drier, and benefits from a higher meat and lower fat content. It's often served as an accompaniment to aperitifs, particularly in the open-air cafés of Bastia.

Figatelli

Figatelli are delicious liver sausages which have been infuse the flavours. This is a delicious dish – do try it at least once on your trip.

Traditional side dishes

The perfect accompaniment to the strong flavours of traditional stews or Corsican charcuterie is the famous local *polenta*, which is made from chestnut flour on the island, but can also be made from maize. It's served in a variety of ways and appears on most

marinated in wine, fresh garlic and peppercorns. They can be served cold, sliced ready for tasting. Like *coppa* and *lonzu*, they, too, are smoked. They come into their own, however, when grilled or on the barbecue and are delicious served as a main course, accompanied by marinated peppers, left overnight to restaurant menus. It's a sort of soft chestnut tart. If, however, you're tempted to try some kid goat in a white-wine sauce instead, ask for *a curetella*. In the Vico region, this will be served with *coppa* or *lonzu*, and some barbecued kid's kidneys. With all this mouth-watering choice, you can really indulge yourself!

Sugar mountain

Corsican cuisine is not simply confined to sauces and charcuterie – it's also famous for its cakes and desserts. These sweet delicacies form an integral part of every meal so make sure you leave plenty of room!

A taste of honey

Corsican honey is world famous – make sure you bring some back. At Gaec de Lozari, on the Route des Artisans, you

can buy both runny and set honey from Michel and François Gaco (p. 121), in flavours ranging from maquis and chestnut to arbutus extract. However, the main honey-producing area on the island is the Asco valley. Asco honey is lighter in colour in spring and darker in the autumn and the pollen from which it is made is produced by wild flowers that only grow at high altitudes. Legend has it that its unique flavour is of divine origin. In 1998 the French government awarded a quality-control trademark (AOC) to Corsican honey and to some of its derivatives, such as vinegar and mead.

Jams and preserves

These are also a Corsican speciality. Jams are made from all of the abundant exotic fruits that grow on the island, including clementines, lemons, figs, nuts, melon, peaches and myrtle, as well as classics like quince,

orange and cherry. At Calenzona, Tony Orsini sells all of the above at very fair prices (25-30F for a 17.5 ounce/500 g jar). You can also find pretty baskets of local produce (wine, honey, vinegar and jam), starting at around 100F. There's a very impressive tasting room, so don't hesitate to sample before buying. **Domaine Orsini**, 20214 Calenzana, ☎ 04 95 62 81 01. In addition to finding the local produce turned into jam, you may also come across local farmers setting up their stalls under a tree to sell jars of peeled clementines and other fruits preserved in a light alcohol syrup.

Fiadone
This is a traditional Corsican cake. The essential ingredients are *brocciu* cheese (p. 30), eggs and sugar, and it's eaten at breakfast as well as other mealtimes. You'll find all restaurants have *fiadone* on the menu. Although it's fairly straightforward to make, it does take some time to combine the eggs with the *brocciu* in the proper manner. Occasionally it's flavoured with vanilla, which is quite delicious. On the east coast and at Castagniccia, you'll find a version made with eggs and chestnuts called *castagna*.

Sweets
These are relatively rare on the island. You'll have to

fall back on the famous *canistrelli* (p. 118), dry biscuits made with almonds and nuts flavoured with aniseed, or *panetti*, small sugary cakes which you'll find in any patisserie. Some restaurants, like A Pampana in Ajaccio (set menu from 250F), serve small honey pancakes, heated in the oven, to accompany the dessert. **A Pampana**, 14, Rue Porta, ☎ 04 95 21 19 66.

Golden chestnut fritters
These are often served as a second dessert. Chestnut flour is gently rolled with sugar to form a small ball, which is then plunged into boiling oil. After a few minutes, when they are light, golden and puffy, the fritters are removed from the oil and served

straight away. The Rocca Serra family at the A Pignata farm inn, above Levie, specialise in this delicious dessert. **A Pignata**, Route du Pianu, 20170 Levie, ☎ 04 95 78 41 90.

CHESTNUT TART
This is a very popular cake in the Castagniccia region. It's easy to make and is all the more tasty if you use local produce. You will need 14 oz (400 g) of chestnut flour, 9 oz (250 g) of peeled chestnuts, a tablespoon of olive oil and of milk, salt, water, and one egg. Moisten the flour with some water, then add the salt, the milk and the olive oil. At this stage the mixture should be fairly liquid. Add the egg yolk to this mixture and then fold in the beaten egg white. Add the chestnuts. Turn the mixture out onto a greased baking tray and cook in a hot oven for 20 minutes, taking care that it does not become dry.

Wine country

The island's renowned wines, known as the 'blood of Corsica', can rival any vintage produced on the continent. In ancient times, Corsican wines were appreciated from Athens to Rome and the popes consumed much of this wine, not only for religious purposes. But it was the Genoese who were to give these wines their pedigree and renown by organising viticulture on the island in the 16thC. Strict controls on the production of wine have left the scandals of past decades far behind, although some importers still label Corsican wine, almost apologetically, 'Vin de l'île de beauté'. The wines are 90% reds, but rosé and white wines are also produced on the east coast and in the area of Porto-Vecchio.

Patrimonio, the nectar of Corsica

The small village of Patrimonio produces the best red wines in Corsica. It was the first wine to obtain an AOC trademark, owing to the quality of the grapes and the organisation of the wine makers and, today, Patrimonio is known as the 'village of wine'. After Patrimonio and Ajaccio, the other wines to be recognised with an AOC are Calvi-Balagne, Sartène, Coteaux du Cap Corse, Côte Orientale, Porto-Vecchio and Figari.

On the Corsican wine trail

Cap Corse, where the popular aperitif of the same name is produced, is an obvious starting point. The region also produces an excellent white wine from the Malvasia grape. In Patrimonio, try a white wine from an Italian grape, the Niellucio, which is also produced in Balagne. A little lower down, on the slopes of Ajaccio, you can taste a red wine by the name of Sciaccarello, which rivals the continental Beaujolais. Southern Corsica

produces fine white and rosé wines near Figari and Porto-Vecchio. Crack open a bottle of Vermentino before finishing off your tour of Corsican wines with the tasty and potent Castagniccia, a chestnut-based liqueur. After all that, a siesta under the chestnut trees could be just the thing!

In the heart of the vineyards

On a tour of the Domaine Colombu, one of the largest Corsican estates, you can pretend for a moment that you're the owner of a vast vineyard. On this informative tour you'll visit the wine storehouses and be initiated into all the secrets of winemaking, and then, of course, finish with the traditional tasting session. You can buy wine on the spot or place an order. **Domaine Colombu,** Étienne Suzzoni, RN 197, Chemin de la Chapelle-Saint-Pierre 20260 Lumio. ☎ 04 95 60 70 68. Fax: 04 95 60 63 46.

LEGENDARY CAP CORSE

Exported world wide, often imitated but never equalled, the Cap Corse aperitif – known simply as 'le Cap' on the island – is a Corsican institution. Its bitter and slightly acidic taste is unique. You'll find this aperitif everywhere, but the best place to try it is at the famous Maison Mattei, in Bastia, where it's made. The shop has remained unchanged since the days of Napoleon III. It has a vast red facade, which opens onto a high-ceilinged hall full of pillars, and display counters reminiscent of the late 19thC. Other alcoholic drinks are also on sale and you can sample everything that Corsica has to offer. If you ask at the counter, you can also take a tour of the factory at Furiani. **Maison Mattei,** 15, Boulevard du Général de Gaulle, 20200 Bastia ☎ 04 95 32 44 38.

Other Corsican alcoholic products

Such are the natural riches of the island that all, or nearly all, Corsican produce can be used to make wine. Some winegrowers even make wine from the maquis itself. You can buy an excellent myrtle wine, which also comes in the form of a liqueur, and there's a regional alcoholic beverage made from clementines. In Castagniccia, chestnut liqueur is popular and there's also Pietra beer, which is made from chestnuts, but is good enough to rival any northern beer. A Corsican Schnapps is distilled from the fruits of the arbutus (strawberry tree). In any event, drink it all with a little moderation and remember to toast your health – 'A a saluta!'.

Recommended eating

A selection of good restaurants where you can enjoy
the specialities of the island.

① Erbalunga

Chez Auguste
restaurant.
p. 105

② Furiani

Ferme-Auberge L'Altu.
Mountain and sea
produce.
p. 105

③ Bastia

Chez Huguette
restaurant.
p. 102.

④ Loreto-di-Casinca

U Rastaghju restaurant.
Local cuisine served in a
renovated chestnut-
drying shed.
p. 147

⑤ Piedicroce

Le Refuge restaurant.
Good rural produce.
p. 145

⑥ Pruno

**Chez Antoinette
Don Simoni**
farmhouse inn.
p. 149
Chez Joseph Nasi fish
farm and inn.
p. 149

⑦ San Nicolao

Le Cava restaurant.
Corsican specialities.
p. 151

⑧ Corte

U Spuntinu restaurant.
Corsican specialities.
p. 134

⑨ Zicavo

Le Paradis farmhouse inn
Delicious southern
specialities.
p. 8

⑩ Calacuccia

Le Corsica restaurant.
Local cuisine.
p. 138

⑪ Lévie

A Pignata farmhouse
inn.
Speciality – chestnut
fritters.
p. 35

⑫ Solenzara

**A Mandria di
Sebastien** restaurant.
Local cuisine in a
renovated sheep farm.
p. 154

⑬ Figari

**Ferme-Auberge Pozzo
di Mastri:**
Fresh farm produce.
p. 169

⑭ Bonifacio

Aux Quatre Vents
restaurant.
Traditional Corsican and
Alsatian cuisine.
p. 162
L'Archivolto restaurant.
Local cuisine.
p. 164

⑮ Guincheto

Ferme-Auberge Acciola.
English tarts
and Corsican cheese.
p. 172

⑯ Propriano

L'Hippocampe
restaurant.
Its speciality is
sea urchins.
p. 175
Le Lido restaurant.
Open-air dining on the
beach.
p. 175

⑰ Ajaccio

A Pampana restaurant.
Seafood and market
produce.
p. 94

⑱ Bastelica

U Castagnetu
restaurant.
Local cuisine.
p. 185

⑲ Cargèse

U Rasaghiu restaurant.
Seafood specialities.
p. 98

⑳ Porto

La Tour Génoise
restaurant.
Corsican specialities.
p. 100

㉑ Calvi

Le Cyrnos restaurant.
Seafood specialities.
p. 117
Le Caiellu restaurant.
Seafood specialities.
p. 117

㉒ Lumio

Chez Charles
restaurant.
Corsican specialities.
p. 120

㉓ Lavatoggio

Chez Edgar farmhouse
inn and restaurant.
p. 111

㉔ Pigna

Casa Musicale
restaurant.
Local cuisine
and folk music.
p. 111

㉕ Île Rousse

Chez Paco
restaurant.
Andalucian cuisine
and flamenco.
p. 123

㉖ Lama

L'Ostriconi
farmhouse inn.
Local cuisine.
p. 126

㉗ Murato

Campu di Monte
farmhouse inn.
Local cuisine.
p. 130

28 *Saint-Florent*
La Gaffe restaurant.
Seafood specialities.
p. 128
Le Langoustier
restaurant.
Seafood specialities.
p. 128

Cap
Corse

1

3 **Bastia**
D81 **28**
27 **2**
L'Île-Rousse **26**
25
24 N97
23
Calvi **21** **22**

Golo
4

5 **6**
7

10
Corte **8**
N200
Tavignano
20

19
D81
Gravona N193 **Aléria** ●

18 N198

Taravo **9**

12

Ajaccio **17**

11

Propriano **16**

Sartène ● **Porto-Vecchio** ●
15

N196
13

Bonifacio **14**

0	10	20	30 miles

0	10	20	30	40	50 km

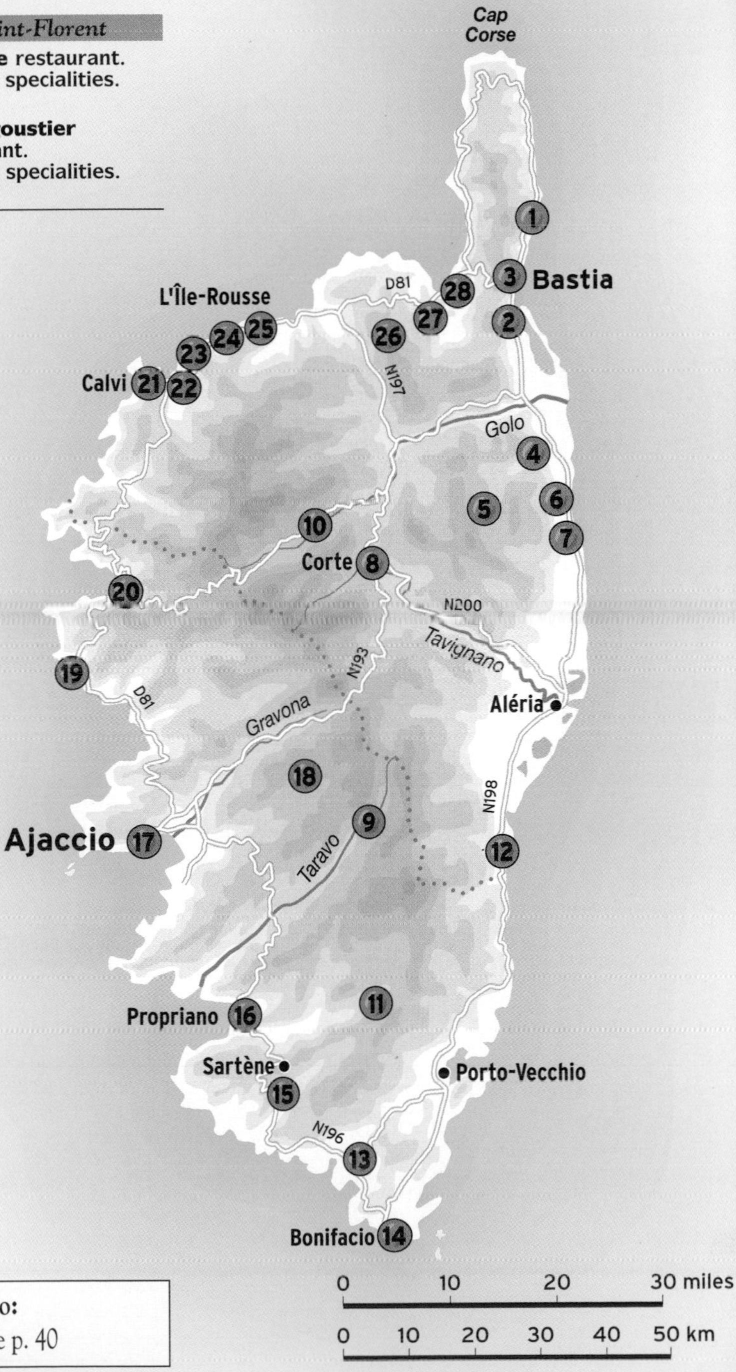

See also:
Cuisine p. 40

Bon' apetittu!

Of course, there are countless variations, but a traditional Corsican meal has some regular features, including soups, charcuterie and cheese. There are also numerous traditional ways of serving game or fish. Similarly, Corsican pies can be based on *brocciu* cheese, myrtle or chestnuts. However, the common denominator in all the various recipes remains the island's excellent local produce.

For starters...

Naturally, Corsican charcuterie (*see* pp. 32-33) is a popular hors d'oeuvre, although the islanders often prefer to eat it as a main dish. Corsican soups, which are good and hearty country fare, appear regularly at both lunchtime and dinner. The vegetable soups are sometimes so thick your spoon will stand up in the bowl.

You won't need to eat much after a bowl of *suppa corsa*, traditionally a main course for the island's country folk. Pasta and white or green beans are its staple ingredients, and chard, and chopped tomatoes and courgettes are often added. *Prisuttu* (cured ham) can also be used, cut into cubes, and herbs from the maquis

always feature. On the coast, seafood often takes the place of soup. Oysters from the Diane lake farm (*see* p. 153) are plumper than the average. Don't leave the island without trying a dozen or so sea urchins at Ajaccio or Porto-Vecchio.

Next course, please!

It's quite common on the island to serve a second starter, often a soufflé omelette flavoured with *brocciu* cheese, or a gratin of pasta, aubergines or chard. Also, the famous Corsican vegetable or *brocciu* pie is often served, with wild herbs from the maquis as an accompaniment (thyme, bay, myrtle and lemon balm). In the mountains and the inland farmhouse inns, typical dishes are boar's liver salad or polenta, a thick amd soft tart made here from chestnut flour rather than the usual maize.

Onto the main meal...

Main courses focus on game or fish – grilled bass, scorpion fish or mullet in sauce, or, further inland, river trout with almonds. In Balagne, try some grilled sardines with

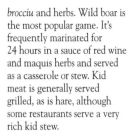

brocciu and herbs. Wild boar is the most popular game. It's frequently marinated for 24 hours in a sauce of red wine and maquis herbs and served as a casserole or stew. Kid meat is generally served grilled, as is hare, although some restaurants serve a very rich kid stew.

... and to follow, cheese and dessert

Try to find a little room for these delights, although you may feel quite full at this stage of a Corsican meal! Although

it's the most famous and widely used cheese in Corsica, brocciu (p. 30) is not in fact a real cheese. It's a type of fromage blanc made from goat or ewe's milk and is preserved in salt – except in springtime, when it can be eaten fresh (maximum 5 days old). Found everywhere on the island, it forms the basis of many dishes. Goats and sheep provide the island with a variety of cheeses, whether hard like Sartène goat's cheese, or soft like the Alta Rocca sheep's cheese, from the Quenza region. You'll often be served cheese with fig jam, a delicious accompaniment – if you've ever eaten deep-fried camembert with gooseberry jam, this marriage of flavours won't come as a surprise. As for desserts, brocciu remains a favourite ingredient for many cakes (p. 35).

BETWEEN MEALS – IF YOU JUST CAN'T WAIT FOR DINNER!

There's a vast choice of snacks. Try some *brocciu* ravioli, or the famous *storzupreti*, Bastia style, which are small balls of spinach, egg and *brocciu* served with kid sauce. If you have a sweet tooth, try some *falculelle* at Corte, a mixture of egg, *brocciu* cheese and lemon, served on a chestnut leaf, or *frappe*, fritters of *brocciu* cheese dipped in honey and sugar. Or how about *pastizzi* – rice cakes with honey and raisins – or then again, go for a big slice of country bread thickly spread with jam made from green tomatoes, figs, grapes or chestnuts. All in all, there's lots to choose from, but whatever you do, make sure you leave room for the next course!

Useful books

If your French is up to it, most of the island's recipes can be found in books. Recommended are: S. Costantini's *La Gastronomie Corse* (U. Muntese, 1968) and M.N. Filippini's *La Cuisine Corse* (Vico la Spusata, 1965). More recent, Paul Sivani's *La Cuisine Corse d'Antan* (La Marge, Ajaccio, 1991) is a comprehensive guide to traditional Corsican cuisine. **Librairie La Marge** (bookshop), 4, Rue Emmanuel-Arène, 20000 Ajaccio ☎ 04 95 51 23 67.

Regional history

A selection of Corsica's most important historical sites, from ancient times to the present day.

① **Bastia**
Citadel, panoramic view of the town and the port.
p. 102

② **Morosaglia**
Home of the Corsican hero Pasquale Paoli.
p. 147

③ **Cervione**
Archaeological museum.
p. 148

④ **Aléria**
Roman site and archaeological museum.
p. 152

⑤ **Pietrapola**
Roman baths.
p. 157

⑥ **Cucuruzzu**
Archaeological site (2000 BC).
p. 181

⑦ **Lévie**
Archaeological museum ('Dame de Bonifacio', 9000 BC).
p. 181

⑧ **Palavesa**
Araghjiu castle, remains of Torréenne civilisation (2000 BC).
p. 160

⑨ **Roccapina**
Genoese tower, magnificent panoramic view.
p. 173.

⑩ **Palaggiu**
Megaliths.

p. 173

⑪ **Spin a Cavallu**
Genoese bridge.
p. 177

⑫ **Filitosa**
Prehistoric site Megaliths.

p. 44

⑬ **Coti-Chiavari**
Capo Muro prehistoric site.
p. 97

⑭ **Corte**
Citadel. Spectacular panoramic view Regional contemporary art foundation.
p. 132

See also:
Archaeology p. 44, Napoleon Bonaparte p. 46,
Foreign influences p. 48,
Famous Corsicans p. 50

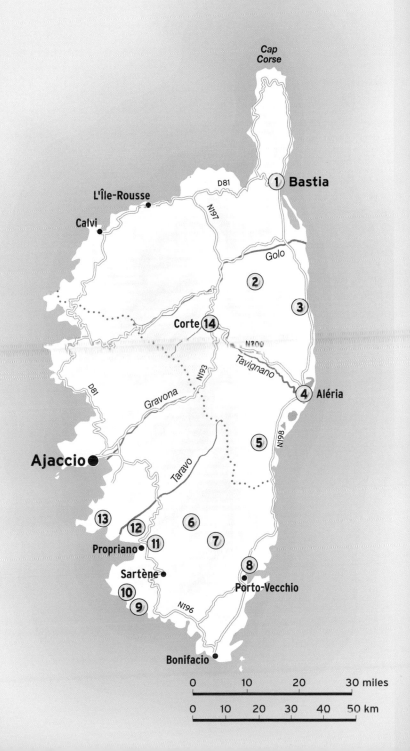

Cap Corse

① **Bastia**

L'Île-Rousse

Calvi

D81

N197

Golo

②

③

Corte ⑭

N200

Tavignano

④ Aléria

N193

Gravona

D81

N198

⑤

Ajaccio ●

Taravo

⑬

⑫

⑥

⑦

⑪

Propriano

⑧

Sartène

Porto-Vecchio

⑩

⑨

N196

Bonifacio

| 0 | 10 | 20 | 30 miles |

| 0 | 10 | 20 | 30 | 40 | 50 km |

Corsica at the time of the Gauls

The famous 'Dame de Bonifacio' (Bonifacio Woman) was discovered on the Araguina site, near Bonifacio, in 1975. Although just 4 ft 10 in (1.49 m) tall, this 8,500-year old skeleton is of huge historical significance, being the earliest evidence of human inhabitation of the island. This exceptional discovery is on display at the Musée Archéologique de Levie (p. 181), along with other exhibits from the same era, notably tools made from obsidian (a hard, glassy black volcanic rock) which are in remarkably good condition.

Menhir at Filitosa, a UNESCO world heritage site

Prehistoric Corsica

The island has a remarkable proliferation of megaliths (menhirs and dolmens).

Filitosa is one of the largest and most interesting megalithic sites in Europe and has been declared a world heritage site by UNESCO.

The Filitosa site is a fortified area on a rocky outcrop at the confluence of two rivers, an ideal location for defence. It's also an extremely scenic area, with the main part of the site set in attractive fields surrounded by woodland. The site offers a insight into the various prehistoric eras of Corsica, from a simple cave shelter (6000 BC) to fortifications, menhirs and stone huts from the Bronze Age (around 1800 BC). This is testimony to the existence of successive civilisations, and their strategic and ritual building practices. Filitosa, signposted from Sartène and Propriano, is a protected area. Open Easter-October, 8am-8pm, winter visits by appointment, ☎ 04 95 74 00 91. Admission charge.

The Torréenne civilisation

The Torréenne, or 'tower' civilisation, is the first known organised civilisation in Corsica. The *torre* (towers) were small, dry-stone dwellings, with roofs made from lauze tiles, constructed using a technique still used by sheep farmers to this day. Grouped together in a *castello*, these huts were built in the

referred to as the 'Shardanes', they were responsible for erecting the fortifications and menhirs at Filitosa.

The arrival of the Greeks

Although the Greeks' main colony was situated further south in Sicily, the Greeks landed on Corsica and founded the site at Alalia, which would later become the Roman settlement of Aleria (p. 152). The Greeks gave three successive names to Corsica – Kalliste ('beautiful'), Tyros and finally Cyrnos, the latter referring to the son of Hercules who, according to legend, chose the island as his homeland. This accounts for

Traces of the Greek civilisation were erased by the Roman invasion

form of a spiral that had a twofold purpose – as a village grouping and as a defensive citadel. The best-preserved examples of these *torre*, dating from 1500-1000 BC, can be found at Cucuruzzu, above Lévie (p. 181). On the mound, the circular construction, designed for defensive purposes, is clearly visible. Today, it's thought that the Torréens, the builders of these villages, came from overseas, perhaps to escape persecution by the Egyptian pharoahs. Their arrival in Corsica ushered in the demise of the megalithic civilisation. Also

the numerous hotels, restaurants and businesses of all kinds that have adopted these names. Some traces of the ancient Greek settlement of Alalia remain, most notably the necropolis. However, the Romans firmly established their presence by transforming and destroying most of the Greek city. In spite of this, some very beautiful ceramic items, originating from the workshops of Ionia or Corinthia, have been found in the vicinity of the necropolis, and these can be seen at the Musée Jérôme-Carcopino in Aléria (p. 152).

Napoleon Bonaparte

There's barely a corner of this island that does not celebrate the most famous Corsican of all, either with a road name or a statue. Napoleon was one of the great conquering heroes of history, likened to Hannibal or Alexander the Great, and he shaped a crucial period of early contemporary European history.

French, but only just

On 15 May 1768, France purchased Corsica from the Republic of Genoa, impoverished and weakened by Paoli's revolt. Napoleon Bonaparte was born just over a year later, on 15 August 1769. Had he been born before the sale, perhaps Genoa, not France, would have dominated Europe for decades. Piqued by Bonaparte's lack of interest in his political writings, Chateaubriand tried to falsify history by spreading the rumour that the emperor had been born on 14 May 1768, just before the annexation of Corsica.

Legendary victories

The Empire was born of a historical coincidence and an extraordinary individual destiny. Soon the whole of Europe would be on its knees before France and all because of the extraordinary achievements of a small, cantankerous, headstrong Corsican. Napoleon's meteoric rise, from artillery captain at Toulon, to first consul after the coup d'état of the 18th Brumaire, to be crowned Emperor in 1802, is testimony to his strength of will, brilliance and political genius. His military victories – the Italian and Egyptian campaigns, Austerlitz, Iéna, Friedland, Wagram – have all become legendary. In France his image remains untarnished to this day, despite the defeats he suffered, which were to leave the country in ruins. The most famous biography of the Emperor Napoleon is by Jacques Bainville, first published in 1931.

Sacre ('Coronation'), painted by Jacques-Louis David between 1805 and 1810, is a striking example of Napoleonic propaganda, trying to popularise his rule by giving him a kind of dynastic legitimacy. Such is the resemblance of Napoleon's coronation to those of the monarchs of the Ancien Régime that in this majestic picture, David seems to have wiped out the 1789 Revolution with a stroke of his brush. The characters and the location are different (this is in Notre-Dame de Paris and not Reims), but the pomp and ceremony are identical. Even the imperial bees, embroidered on the cushions, resemble the royal Fleur de Lys.

The bigger they are, the harder they fall

In October 1805 the English Admiral Nelson humiliated the Emperor at Trafalgar and the French fleet was destroyed. Trafalgar, and Waterloo in June 1815, were Napoleon's most notorious defeats. They overshadow other disasters, such as the loss of the French

A FRENCH PARADOX

Just as dynamite can be used to stop a forest fire, so Napoleon's meteoric rise put an end to the Revolution. All subsequent French history, with its successive uprisings and restorations, can be traced back to the Empire, as France tried to recapture its former glory. The myth and legend of this period has an almost magical attraction and to this day many people ignore the fact that Napoleon left Europe in ruins and France on its knees, weakened by the loss of 1.5 million men – the soldiers of the Grande Armée.

fleet at Aboukir during the Egyptian campaign (1798) and the rout at La Berenzina (1812) or the flight from the Austrians at Leipzig (1813). Exiled on the island of Elba by the English in 1814, the Emperor escaped only to see his army destroyed at Waterloo. Napoleon abdicated four days after this defeat and his imprisonment on the island of St Helena led to his death in 1821. The regional library in Ajaccio, located in a wing of the Fesch palace

(p. 93), built by Cardinal Fesch, Napoleon's uncle, in the early part of the 19thC., has an extensive collection of writings from this astonishing era. **Bibliothèque d'Ajaccio,** 50, Rue Fesch. ☎ 04 95 21 41 61. Open weekdays 2-6pm.

A lasting legacy

The experience of the first Empire gave the French a taste for strong government characterised by charismatic leadership. This explains, perhaps, the quasi-royal status of French presidents to this day. The Empire also saw the establishment of the first real university in France, as well as the Institut de France, where Louis Pasteur, and Pierre and Marie Curie would later work, the Bank of France and, furthermore, the common-law statutes still used in French legal practice.

Foreign influences

The Pisans, the Aragonese, the Genoese, the French… even the English intervened in Corsica at the request of Pasquale Paoli (p. 50). The successive invasions of the island have led to a complex intertwining of

influences, with the islanders themselves most affected. As was the case in Sicily and Sardinia, the native Corsicans were forced to retreat to the clifftop villages of Balagne or Alta Rocca, which led to their agricultural and pastoral lifestyle. The coast was much too dangerous.

The powerful maritime republic of Genoa occupied Corsica for nearly 500 years

Pisan leanings

Around 1000 AD, Corsica emerged from a feudal period that had clashed with the island's clan structures and customs. This had caused innumerable conflicts, which the Tuscan merchants in charge of administration had been powerless to control. At the end of the century, the Pope turned Corsica over to the Pisans, who administered the citadels of Bonifacio and Calvi from afar and traded with the overlords of Cap Corse. This non-intervention suited Corsica down to the ground. However, things were to change when the Genoese captured Bonifacio (1195) and defeated the Pisan fleet at the battle of Meloria (1284). Genoa was to establish a firm grip on the island.

Genoese presence

This was to be the most durable and profound influence on Corsica since the days of the Roman occupation. The Genoese founded two towns around the citadels of Bonfacio and Calvi, while their fleet repulsed barbarian attacks and developed trading routes in the Tyrrhenian sea. By the 14thC. the Italian mercantile republic was in control of the entire island. In spite of numerous insurrections, this occupation was to last for 400 years. In 1420, the Genoese had to repulse an Aragonese attack on Bonifacio and it was during this period that the famous staircase was built (p. 164). In 1453, over-extended and unable to cope, Genoa handed over the administration of Corsica to the Bank of St George, which managed to organise the island and safeguard its defence by erecting the 90 towers which still encircle it. Similarly, the majority of the single-arch, or 'Genoese', bridges are the work of the Bank.

Despite the protection of continental powers, Corsica was subject to pirate attacks over a long period

Genoese were defeated at the Borgo by the insurrectionists. However, the following year, the coalition was to gain the upper hand. This saw the start of a new period of fighting, during which both camps took and then lost strategically important positions, including Bastia and Calvi. In 1753 the French took control, but two years later Pasquale Paoli was declared General of Corsica (p. 50) and signalled the start of a new era of independence.

A time of war

France began to take an interest in Corsica during the second half of the 16thC., taking the island in 1553 with the assistance of Sampiero Corso (p. 184), only to lose it again in the Treaty of Cateau-Cambrésis in 1559. There followed a troubled period during which Genoa was barely able to maintain control and inter-clan warfare caused thousands of deaths. The term 'vendetta' originated from this period (p. 62). In an attempt to achieve independence, Corsicans stepped up their opposition in the 18thC. This was the era of Generals Giaferri and Ceccaldi, whose coups defeated Genoa and lead to the brief reign of King Theodore of Neuhof (1736).

French Corsica

It was the Genoese themselves who requested the help of King Louis XV of France to resist the ceaseless attacks by Corsican independence fighters and re-establish order on the island. At first the French and

General Giaferi helped to free Corsica from Genoese domination

Under the Empire, numerous engravings depicted France's annexation of Corsica

ACQUISITION DE LA CORSE.
en 1768.

YOU'LL FIND CORSICANS EVERYWHERE

Successive wars and invasions, as well as a lack of arable land, has affected Corsican demographics. In 1790 the population of the island was around 150,000. The relative stability of the 19thC., combined with high levels of immigration, particularly from Italy, saw the population increase to 270,000 by 1880. However, a high rate of emigration due to the economic crisis as well as the burden of French interventionism was to reduce this figure to 160,000 by 1950. Fleeing to both shores of the Mediterranean, Corsicans settled in North Africa and France, establishing communities in towns such as Marseille, Nice and Paris. However, the most unusual story must be that of the Cap Corsicans, who emigrated in their tens of thousands to Venezuela. Today, the island has a population of some 250,000 inhabitants.

Famous Corsicans

Colourful Corsican celebrities include warriors, cardinals, singers, actors and bandits, as well as the fictional, such as Mérimée's literary heroine, Colomba, the embodiment of the pride and sense of honour of a people who 'never forget'. Not forgetting Ocatarinetabelatchitchix, hero of the Asterix stories, a classic caricature of the acute loyalty to family and clan for which the island is renowned.

Watercolour by Prosper Mérimée of Colomba and her brother

Cardinal Fesch, uncle of Emperor Napoleon

Cardinal Joseph Fesch
(Ajaccio 1763– Rome 1839)

Having been appointed Archdeacon in 1789, Joseph Fesch, uncle of Napoleon astutely saved his skin by renouncing his vocation. He went on to fight in the Italian campaign at his nephew's side and then took up his ecclesiastical role again, persuading the Pope to proclaim Napoleon Emperor in 1802. However, when his nephew opposed himself to Rome, he withdrew his support and was to die in disgrace and in exile. There's a museum named in his honour in Ajaccio (p. 93).

Pasquale Paoli
(Morosaglia 1725– London 1807)

Even more widely celebrated in Corsica than Napoleon, Paoli was the founder of an independent Corsican state in the mid-18thC. Proclaiming the island's independence in 1755, with Corte as its capital, Paoli left only the coastal areas to the Genoese. When the Genoese ceded control of the island to the French, Paoli suffered a military defeat at Ponte Novo. There followed a 30-year exile in England, interrupted by a failed coup d'état in 1790.

Pasquale Paoli, commander of the rebel forces in the 18thC.

Tino Rossi (Ajaccio 1907 – Neuilly-sur-Seine 1983)

The most popular French singer from the pre-war period to the 1960s, Rossi paid homage to his homeland in his songs. One of his most famous songs, Marinella, refers to a beach at Ajaccio. After his debut at the Casino de Paris in 1934, his fame increased and he regularly appeared at prestigious venues such as Bobino or the Olympia. His most popular song remains 'Petit Papa Noël' ('Dear Father Christmas') which still tops the French charts as Christmas approaches and has done so

for decades. He was always more popular with the general public than the critics and is fondly remembered to this day.

Known as both the 'General of the Corsican state' and 'Father of the Nation', he is Corsica's most famous patriot and the pre-eminent symbol of resistance to oppression.

Antoine and Jacques Bellacoscia (Boscognano ? – Chiavari 1912)

Bellacoscia ('beautiful thigh') was the nickname of the two Bonelli brothers, which they inherited from their father, who had 18 children by 3 sisters! These two bandits murdered, pillaged and kidnapped over a period of 30 years around the end of the 19thC. Their notorious reputation coupled with the half-hearted efforts of the police to arrest them, allowed the brothers to hold court at Ajaccio, along with such guests as Baron Haussmann and the Princess of Saxe-Weimar. One of the Bellacoscia brothers died peacefully in his bed aged 64, after years of crime. The other was eventually imprisoned at Chiavari, with his son-in-law as a bodyguard.

Mari-José Nat (Bonifacio 1940)

Perched on the white cliffs of Bonifacio, her house is one of the most beautiful on the island (p. 162). Mari-José, an actress, visits regularly, though not in high season, to recharge her batteries and remember the times when her mother 'came down barefoot from the mountains to sell baskets of fruit at the market'. 'I often remember', she said, 'when as a young girl it was my duty to watch over the herds of goats'. A star of the Parisian theatre and the French cinema, she is so proud of her native island that she arranged for the bodies of her late parents, who were buried near Paris, to be brought back and reinterred in the graveyard in Bonifacio, close to the sea.

Antoine Bellacoscia, one of the most famous Corsican bandits

Charming villages, beautiful churches

Discover Corsica's picturesque villages and churches, nestling on the mountain slopes.

① *Luri's hamlets*
Seneca tower.
p. 107

② *Sisco*
Santa Catalina church.
p. 109

③ *Piedicroce*
Baroque church.
p. 145

④ *Prunete*
Scupiccia chapel, Statue of the Virgin of the fishermen.
p. 148

⑤ *Prunelli di Fiumorbo*
p. 156

⑥ *Bastelica villages*
pp. 184-185

⑦ *Quenza*
Santa Maria and San Giorgio churches.
p. 57

⑧ *Santa-Lucia-di-Tallano*
Saint-François convent.
p. 182

⑨ *Sotta villages*
'The Man of Cagna'.
p. 161

⑩ *Figari 's hamlets*
p. 168

⑪ *Campomoro village*
p. 177

⑫ *Ajaccio*
Sainte-Marie de l'Assomption cathedral.
p. 57

⑬ *Sagone village*
p. 99

⑭ *Cargèse*
Greek and Latin churches.
p. 98

⑮ *Calvi*
Saint-Jean-Baptiste cathedral.
p. 114

⑯ *Aregno*
La Trinité and San Giovanni churches.
p. 112

⑰ *Pigna village*
p. 110

⑱ *Sant'Antonino village*
p. 113

⑲ *Algajola village*
p. 125

⑳ *Monticello village*
p. 125

㉑ *Rapale village*
p. 131

㉒ *Saint-Florent*
Saint-Florent cathedral.
p. 130

See also:
Tales and legends p. 54,
Traditional architecture p. 56,
Religious customs p. 58,
Corsican culture p. 60,
Corsican bandits p. 62.

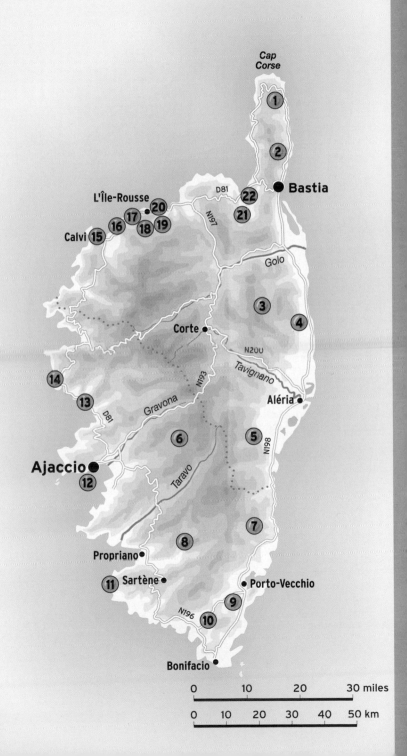

Cap Corse

Bastia

L'Île-Rousse

Calvi

Corte

Golo

N197

D81

Aléria

Tavignano

N200

N193

Gravona

Ajaccio

Taravo

Propriano

Sartène

Porto-Vecchio

N196

Bonifacio

| 0 | 10 | 20 | 30 miles |
| 0 | 10 | 20 | 30 | 40 | 50 km |

Corsican tales and legends

A day-to-day life full of hardship, struggling to work an infertile land, poor standards of education and being forced to retreat in the face of a seemingly endless series of invasions – Corsican history has produced an isolated culture, rich in imaginative tales and legends, steeped in magic and sorcery.

Legendary places

Corsican place names echo with the superstition and wonder of the island's people: the Trou du Diable (devil's hole), Trou de la Sorcière (witch's hole), Montagne du Diamant (diamond mountain), Montagne des Voleurs (robbers' mountain), Cascade du Voile de la Mariée (bride's veil waterfall) and the Coline de l'Homme Mort (dead man's hill) to name just a few. The spectacular nature of the landscape itself also captures the imagination – the rocky coves at Piana, Tafunatu cape, Monte Cintu and Monte d'Oro are all sites which helped to form the imagination of the ancient inhabitants of Corsica.

Witchcraft and healing

Witchcraft is as much a feature of Corsica as its chestnut groves, forests or polyphonic chants. The best reference book on the subject is the *Almanach de la Mémoire et des Coutumes Corses* (Albin Michel, Paris 1986). Each village had – and often still has – a special character credited with supernatural

ALMANACH
de la mémoire et des coutumes

CORSE

par Claire Tiévant et Lucie Desideri

chez Albin Michel, éditeur

powers, capable of healing a variety of afflictions from skin problems to migraines or indigestion. Often this person would be consulted about the weather before embarking on expeditions in the mountains or at sea.

Places of worship

From chapels to churches, from small shrines sheltering a statue of the Virgin to simple crucifixes planted, seemingly by chance, on the side of a mountain, there are plenty of opportunities in Corsica to stop and worship. Note that in the south of the island the Virgin is held in greater respect than the cross.

HOW TO MAKE IT RAIN

'Bull's paw, cow's paw, let Saint Parthée send down water, water and not dew'. At the end of the 3rdC., Bishop San Parteo is said to have used these words to invoke rain to fall on the region of Feliceto. As his prayers were immediately answered, this incantation was used over the centuries whenever drought threatened. It has now fallen into disuse, but is doubtlessly still remembered by some of the older inhabitants. If the summer heat gets a little too much, you could always try it!

Natural and supernatural powers

In the past Corsicans saw the rain as a divine manifestation, washing away the people's sins. It is still said that there can be no *catenacciu* ('penance', see p. 59) without rain. Traditional beliefs and rituals abound on the island. Oracles are consulted before a birth or a harvest and there are still seers who specialise in healing. Hands carved from coral are placed round a baby's neck to ward off the 'evil eye'. Certain plants are also credited with supernatural or mystical powers, including olive, asphodel and green mint.

The Bishop and the grape picker

E Pagliazze, an ancient and insalubrious marshland, was cleared and drained in the middle of the 19thC. and a small vineyard, with a low yield, was planted. At the end of the 19thC., at harvest time, a young girl asked a visiting bishop for permission to try on his episcopal ring. As the young grape-picker slipped it onto her finger, it fell to the ground and was lost. Everybody searched for it, but in vain. The next day, the beautiful vineyard was flooded and reclaimed by the swamp. As is often the case, the legend has some basis in reality. In autumn, heavy storms flood the area, which has only recently been artificially drained and reclaimed from the marshes.

The evil spirits of Zicavo

Agramonte was a warrior who fought for the Italians against the Saracens. During his absence, his wives protected their virtue by sleeping armed with a scythe. But lurking *streghe* ('witches') made off with their children in order to suck their blood. These witches were also said to attack lone travellers, battering their skulls. In the Zicavo region, they are said to haunt the forests after nightfall.

Stone people

By the side of the road, near Sartène, stand two stone pillars, known as *U frate e a sora*. They are said to represent a monk and a nun who were turned to stone (somewhat unfairly in her case), after he had carried her off and ravished her.

Traditional architecture

From Genoese towers to mountain shepherds' huts, Corsican rural architecture is austere but impressive. Largely untouched, weathered by time, it is an integral part of the rural landscape and history. Italian- and French-inspired windmills, bridges and churches can also be found throughout the island. The two earliest architectural legacies were those of the Pisans, responsible for many of the ecclesiastical buildings, and those of the Genoese, who were more interested in defensive military constructions.

Corsican mills

In the mountains there are watermills and in the south, where water has always been a rare, precious commodity, there are windmills. No longer in use, they nevertheless often remain intact. The mill at Bocagnano has exterior horizontal wheels, while the mill at Serra-di-Scopamène (in Alta Rocca) is characterised by a gigantic vertical exterior wheel. The five windmills in the Bonifacio countryside are among the best preserved on the island. Unfortunately, they can only be viewed from the outside.

From winter shelter to summer pasture

Corsica would not be the same without its shepherds and their flocks. Although they are fewer in number today, the island retains its pastoral feel and you will still regularly encounter flocks of sheep and goats on the roads. In the summer, the flocks head for the pastures at Bitalza (p. 61), Naseo (p. 169) or Basseto. The *bergeries* (shepherds' huts) are generally constructed from heavy blocks of stone, without mortar, with small flat stones wedged into the cracks. Those in the north of the island have a double-sided tiled roof. In the south, the same techniques were used as for the rock shelters in the Sotta region (p. 169). In the

limestone area of Bonifacio, you can still find examples of *baracconi* – small, round, stone buildings with arched roofs of dry lauze stone, which date back to the Bronze Age. The top slab closes off the structure, giving it solidity. The same technique was used for the *teghie* (Corsican barns) at Cap Corse.

Genoese heritage

A single, narrow arch made from granite slabs and two strong supports at each side are the chief characteristics of the Genoese bridges built at the end of the 18thC. Some bridges that have been attributed to the Genoese are, in fact, Pisan, as at Giussani for example (p. 112). The oldest Genoese bridge, built at

the beginning of the 18thC., is the Spin at Cavallu, on the Rizzanese river between Propriano and Sartène (p. 177). The famous coastal towers (p. 48) also bear witness to the Genoese occupation. They all have a watchtower, a communal hall and cellars where water, food and weaponry were stored. Around 90 of these towers remain, dotted along the length of the coast.

Romanesque and Baroque churches

There are two examples that epitomise architectural development in Corsica from the 12th to the 15thC. At Quenza, in Alta Rocca, there are two churches which are entirely Romanesque in style. Santa Maria de Quenza is an

HOMES AND STRONGHOLDS

The massive tall, grey houses typical of Corsican villages, with a *perron* (raised porch) and stone stairway, are all based on the same model. Two or three storeys high, they are immense buildings, as several related families would all live under the same roof. Some of these granite houses (limestone in the Bonifacio region and shale in the north) are veritable strongholds, the former homes of local rulers.

austere building of heavy granite, with few apertures, dating from the beginning of AD 1000. San Georgio, the parish church, dates from the 12thC. The facade is more ornamental, the apertures are larger and the famous green serpentine stone from Fium'orbo valley gives the church a more decorative air. At Ajaccio, Sainte- Marie de l'Assomption cathedral is typical of Baroque architecture influenced by 16th-C. Venice, while on a smaller scale, a good example of a Baroque church is Saint Jean Baptiste de la Porta, which can be found in Castagniccia.

Sainte-Marie de l'Assomption cathedral in Ajaccio, a masterpiece of Baroque architecture

Religion, Corsica and all the saints

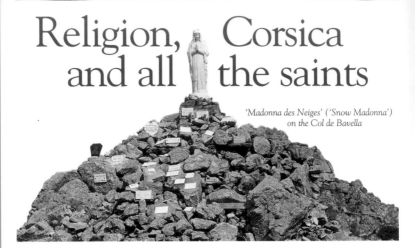

'Madonna des Neiges' ('Snow Madonna') on the Col de Bavella

The religious fervour of Corsicans is more than simple worship. Religion is an integral part of Corsican tradition and daily life, and although the advent of tourism has brought some beliefs into question, religious worship and sentiment remain strong, especially among the older generation.

Churches and crosses

Each region has a parish church where mass is celebrated. These parish regions are often spread over a large area (Sartène, Sotta, Levie). However, Corsicans don't wait for Sunday to worship. Every village has its own chapel or small church and if you visit these places of worship, you'll be surprised at the number of people coming and going. In the bigger towns, churches and cathedrals are filled to capacity every Sunday. If you are invited into a Corsican home, have a look at the walls, where you're bound to see a crucifix or an effigy of the Virgin, adorned with a garland of olive or boxwood.

Patron saints

Each village has its own patron saint, often in commemoration of a miracle in centuries past, which has

Sainte-Marie chapel, perched on the mountainside in the Calvi region

permanently linked the saint to the area. In the Place du Maréchal Foch in Ajaccio, a niche built into the outer walls shelters the *Madanuccia* ('Madonna of mercy'), who protects the town from invasion with the following inscription: *Posuerunt me custodem* ('I have been placed here to guard you'). Corsica is referred to as 'St Peter's island', and has been under papal protection since the 8thC.

CATENACCIU

At nightfall on Good Friday, in the Place de la Libération, at the Sainte-Marie church in Sartène, the priest appears in front of the church, followed by the *catenacciu* (the Corsican word for 'penitent'). As thousands of onlookers, both Corsicans and foreigners, throng on the church steps, the catenacciu, who wears a red hood and carries a cross weighing 66 lbs (30 kg) and 33 lbs (15 kg) of chains, sets off to follow the Stations of the Cross. In imitation of Christ, he will fall three times, closely surrounded by the fervent and somewhat suffocating crowd, before this reconstruction of the Passion concludes with the catenacciu receiving absolution from the priest. Henceforth, he is a new man, cleansed of all his sins. The catenacciu is selected each year by the abbot of Saint-Damien from a group of volunteers. Rumour has it that some of the most infamous bandits, cut-throats and criminals in the world have taken on this role, but it is not possible to confirm this since the abbot alone keeps the list of penitents, seen by no-one else. Apparently the waiting list is 25 years long.

Parish priests

To this day, Corsican parish priests command great respect in their communities. In the 19thC., the priest was the equivalent of a mayor and was consulted on all important local issues, his opinion carrying the most weight. Corsican priests were said to be Corsicans first and priests second and some did not hesitate to provide shelter for runaways and known bandits. Others even brandished weapons, like the celebrated priest of Olmeto, at Valinco bay, who resisted the gendarmes, musket in hand.

Holy Week

This pre-eminent Christian festival is celebrated in earnest all over the island. On Good Friday, in Bonifacio, the five religious orders parade with banners (p. 164). At Levie, a penitent carries the cross through the streets, while at Cargèse, the Greek Orthodox Church organises a huge penitent procession, punctuated by salvos of gunfire. But the biggest and most spectacular of all Holy Week celebrations, the renowned *Catenacciu*, takes place at Sartène.

Granitula

A religious procession observed annually throughout Corsica, in which members of the order of St Anthony and St Erasmus parade bare-footed wearing penitential cowls.

Culture and tradition

Corsicans have a very strong sense of identity, based on a love of their island and a history of resisting invasion and enduring harsh agricultural conditions. This identity is so strong that it sometimes gives rise to the exclusion and rejection of other cultures. Napoleon once famously said, 'I recognise Corsica by its smell', but Corsica's culture and traditions are also highly individual.

Corsican is recognised as a distinct language, taught at the University of Corsica. Never refer to it as a dialect, unless you want to make some enemies! On the contrary, if you want to make friends, make an attempt at Corsican pronunciation.

An island of many voices

Corsica has a unique polyphonic choral tradition and its musical chants, rediscovered in the 1980s, are now famous world wide. Comprising at least three voices, they are often sung a cappella. However, they can also be accompanied by a *cistre* (a musical instrument with eight strings, similar to a guitar), a flute, or an accordion. Hectore Zazu, Michel Rafaelli and Marcel Péres are among the best known polyphonic singers on the island. They have succeeded in adapting this

Corsican, a language apart

As in Brittany, where it was once forbidden to 'spit on the ground or speak in Breton', the Third French Republic tried to stamp out the Corsican language in the name of centralisation. As a result, regional culture in France was severely damaged. This policy, however, failed in Corsica, and the Corsican language is still spoken, although almost everyone is able to speak French. Today,

I Muvrini group in concert

traditional ancestral chant to contemporary tunes and modern rhythms.

Corsican literature

From Homer's *Odyssey* to Maupassant's *Une Vie*, many famous works have celebrated Corsica's beauty and charm. The island's two most prominent authors stand at opposite ends of the spectrum. Angelo Rinaldi, a novelist

Walls of houses are used as political billboards

and literary critic, is harsh in his judgement, particularly in respect of his native Bastia, which he considers suffocating, with a vain and small-minded bourgeoisie in decline. On the other hand, Marie Susini, in *La Renfermée*, is gentler in her appraisal of the island's inhabitants, particularly with regard to the woman's place in the family. She believes that contrary to opinion on the continent, it is in fact the woman who is the most powerful member of the family.

Spirit of independence

In 1914 French nationals of fighting age were not sent to the front if they had more

than four children – with the exception of Senegalese and Corsicans. History testifies to the sacrifices made by the Corsicans for the good of continental France and anger at such discrimination fuelled the Corsicans' desire for independence, a desire which has been ever-present since the island was first inhabited. Local independence movements were encouraged and in 1967 the Front Régional Corse (FRC Corsican Regional Front) and the Action Régionaliste Corse (ARC – Regional Corsican Action) were established. Ten years later, the Front de Libération Nationale Corse (FLNC – Corsican Liberation Front) was born.

Ideals and isolation

Now fragmented into various groupings, including the A Cuncolta and the FLNC Canal Historique, the Corsican independence movement often used legitimate arguments (against isolationism, for example, to encourage industrial or service-industry development) to justify Mafia or criminal activity. This was rapidly condemned by public opinion

SOME RULES OF PRONUNCIATION

Corsican pronunciation is difficult to understand. It comes directly from medieval Tuscan, with some Pisan and Genoese influences. There are, however, some basic rules. 'U' at the end of a word is 'swallowed' and not pronounced. As in Italian, the emphasis is usually on the penultimate syllable. Two 'c's followed by an 'i' are pronounced 'tch', as in *castagniccia* which is pronounced 'castagnitchia'. If followed by another vowel or by 'h', two 'c's are pronounced 'k', as in *Porto Vecchio*. In the south of the island, a final 'e' is often replaced by 'i' to indicate the plural, as in *baracconi*.

N196

PROPRIANO
PRUPRIA

SARTENE
SARTE'

BONIFACIO
BUNIFAZIU

and today the Corsican independence movement is marginal. There is little concrete support on the island, although there may have been some sympathy in the past. The assassination in 1988 of Préfet Claude Erignac was the mark of a movement that had become more and more politically isolated, with the island's population increasingly tired of these acts of desperation.

Corsican bandits, myth or reality?

Certainly a reality, Corsican banditry was born out of the clan structures and traditions of rural Corsican society, although many of the facts have been embroidered by legend. The term 'vendetta' originated in the 17thC., but Roman authors such as Polybus, Pliny and Seneca had already recorded the rivalry that existed between clans. It's important to understand that on the island, most locals feel under as much obligation to comply with Corsican customs as they do with the law.

The hierarchy of the clans

The clan system, with its chiefs and vassals, still has influence to this day, often remaining beyond the bounds of the law. Stories of bloody revenge have long been preserved, in oral traditions as in literature. Mérimée and the famous vendetta of Columba, the Corsican brothers of Alexandre Dumas, Maupassant's honorable Corsican bandit – all are based on these Corsican traditions of pride and honour.

Common law criminal or honourable bandit?

The word 'vendetta' means revenge, but within very specific bounds. Killing your neighbour because of a boundary dispute was seen as a straightforward settling of scores, but to kill a man because he has shown lack of respect for your clan or one of its members (most often a woman) was a 'vendetta'.

The criminal then became an 'honourable bandit', with no other choice than to seek refuge in the mountains, the forest or the maquis, where the law could take years to catch up with him, if it ever did. A code of silence would ensure that the entire clan and its dependents would protect the perpetrator of the vendetta.

From vendettas to the struggle for independence

At the beginning of the 20thC., the concept of the 'honourable bandit' was applied to those who fought against the laws of the Republic, which were held to be oppressive. A fighter for freedom and independence was, by definition, a man of honour. This tradition, which had long equated hero and criminal, gave a certain kudos to any transgressor or opponent of the law, and probably explains why priests were often prepared to provide sanctuary to bandits.

Women were often the reason for vendettas (19thC. engraving)

The traditions of banditry

One of the first known bandits was Tiadore Poli, who was based in the Aitone forest at the beginning of the 19thC. The head of a small army, he escaped capture by the police until he was killed in 1827. Cappa was a well-known bandit of the late 19thC., pursued by a series of French

The notorious bandit, Antoine Bellacoscia

expeditionary corps. He was finally struck down whilst asleep in his shepherd's hut. Nonce Romanetti, friend of the filmmaker Abel Gance, was killed in an ambush in 1926. Lastly, the notorious Bellacoscia brothers (p. 51), held a 30-year reign of terror around the end of the 19thC. All of these bandits had taken refuge in the maquis because of obscure vendettas, long since forgotten.

Entitled 'Corsican huntsman on the look-out', this picturesque postcard of the 1930s is a reminder that, first and foremost, weapons were used to hunt game

AND TODAY?

Since the assassination of the Corsican Préfet, the population would appear to have formed a united front to reject violence and show its support for the laws of the Republic. However, you may hear the recent story of two families whose vendetta, originating in the theft of a donkey, led to bloodshed on more than 30 occasions. Or that of the young man killed for having gone out with a girl in a neighbouring village. In July 1998, when France won the World Cup, the French flag was waved and car horns were sounded all over France. In Corsica, victory was celebrated by shots being fired into the air, typical of the idiosyncratic nature of the island's people and traditions. Whether marginal or anecdotal, the 'vendetta' will remain part of the island's culture for some time to come.

The craziest bandit

This distinction belongs, without question, to André Spada, nicknamed 'God's madman'. Everyone has forgotten the orignal reason why this outlaw took to the maquis. Nevertheless, he has become a legend, the author of numerous bloody crimes and hold-ups, all supposedly in the name of God. When he was finally caught in 1933, he wore a colossal crucifix around his neck. Although he was incarcerated in an insane asylum, no extenuating circumstances were taken into account and he was executed for his crimes in 1935.

The backlash of the 1930's

Appalled at the lawlessness on the island, the French governor launched a vast clean-up campaign in Corsica in the 1930s. Several expeditions were sent to the island, villages were surrounded, the population was threatened and, as a result, it's believed that since 1936, the Corsican maquis has been 'clean'. Certainly, more than one outlaw was flushed out at the time.

During the Easter celebrations in Cargèse, rifles are displayed at the foot of the Cross

Traditional arts and crafts

If you're looking for a gift or a souvenir, there's plenty to choose from, including knives, jewellery, pottery, leather and olive wood items.

① Bastia

Instrument workshop:
Guitars, *cetera* and traditional musical instruments.
p. 103

② Orezza

Valle d'Orezza pipes:
Handcrafted
from olive wood,
alder wood or briar.

p. 146

③ Corte

Tissage Mariani:
Hand woven shawls,
scarves and Corsican
jackets in wool
or cotton.
p. 134

④ Porto-Vecchio

Taillerie de Corail:
Carved coral jewellery,
set in gold.
p. 160

⑤ Portigliolo

Decorative pottery:
Original ceramics.
p. 95

⑥ Ajaccio

Craft workshops:
All kinds of crafts,
including leather,
pottery and wood.
p. 92

⑦ Calenzana

Atelier de Céramique Raku:
Raku ceramics workshop.
p. 118
Atelier du Village:
Arts and crafts, liqueurs
and confectionery.
p. 119

⑧ Feliceto

Soufflerie de Verre Campana:
Glass-blowing factory.
p. 120.

⑨ Lumio

Atelier du CERM:
Bronze and iron workshop
– shepherd's knives, paper
knives and jewellery.
p. 120

⑩ Pigna

Lutherie Casalonga:
Traditional musical
instruments.
p. 119
Music boxes:
Handcrafted and
painted.
p. 120

⑪ Occiglioni

Pottery workshop:
Stoneware.
p. 121
Leather workshop:
Bags, belts
and wallets.

p. 121

⑫ Palasca

Forges d'Art Broomberg:
Iron, bronze and copper
decorative items.

See also:
Traditional crafts p. 66,
Olives and
olive wood p. 68

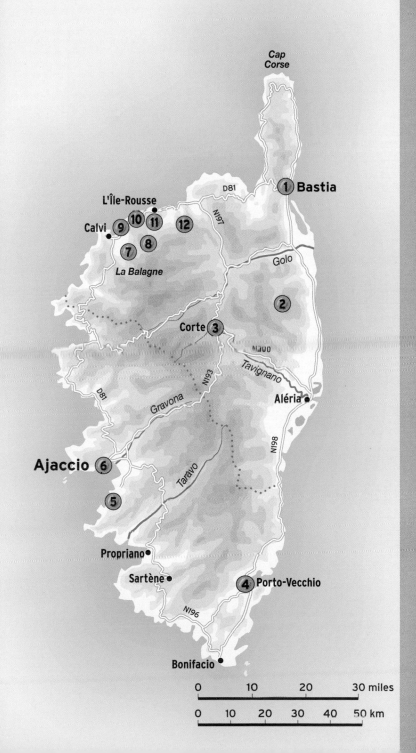

Cap Corse

D81

① **Bastia**

N197

L'Île-Rousse

⑩ ⑪ ⑫

Calvi ⑨ ⑧

⑦

La Balagne

Golo

②

Corte ③

N200

Tavignano

N193

Aléria

Gravona

D81

② **Ajaccio** ⑥

N198

⑤

Taravo

Propriano

Sartène

④ **Porto-Vecchio**

N196

Bonifacio

```
0        10        20      30 miles
0    10   20   30   40  50 km
```

Traditional crafts

Daily life in Corsica is ruled by tradition. This can be seen in all social gatherings (from religious worship to old poachers' reunions), as well as in Corsican cuisine (*see* pp. 40-41) and, of course, in traditional craftsmanship. Here are a selection of Corsican crafts to look out for when you are out and about hunting for souvenirs.

Linen was kept in niches carved into the thick walls, closed off with wooden doors

Chest

Furniture

The chest has always been a staple feature of Corsican furniture and could at one time be found in every home, rich or poor. Although often ornately engraved in wealthier homes, the chest was usually simple in style and and vast in size. It was used to store clothes, both for everyday and 'Sunday best', as well as tools and perishable goods, and would also be used to store a young girl's trousseau. Another indispensable item of furniture found in every home was the kneading trough, generally used on Saturday to prepare the week's bread. Cupboards as such were rare and were confined to wealthier families. Household linen was usually stored in niches carved into the wall, closed off with doors made from oak or beech. The master of the house would have an armchair, while the rest of the family sat on benches.

Tableware

Glass was rarely used, except by wealthy families in Ajaccio or Sarténe – pottery or, more often, wood was used instead.

Kneading trough

Plates and bowls were often made from olive or beechwood. The hearth at the heart of the kitchen would contain a heavy copper cooking pot hanging from a cast-iron rack. You may be able to find some of these items at antique dealers or second hand shops, but Corsicans are aware of the value of items such as these and real bargains are rare.

Working in chestnut

In many regions of Corsica, but especially in Castagniccia

One of the many pottery workshops selling to tourists

(see p. 144), furniture is chiefly made from chestnut wood. The wood can also be used as fuel, but only if the tree is diseased or dead. At Ucciani fair, on 1 May each year, you can see the work of such traditional craftsmen as cutlers, saddlers, weavers, binders and engravers working in wood, wool, leather or iron. There's also a chestnut fair at Bocagnano (see p. 140).

Red coral

Corsica has a tradition of incorporating red coral into jewellery or lucky charms. These days, however, after years of heavy harvesting, the coral used may not originate from the waters around the island.

A Corsican marriage

The traditional marriage ceremony is still respected in the majority of inland villages. According to custom, the bridegroom enters the church first whilst the bride waits patiently, seated alongside the baptismal font, surrounded by women from the village. Beforehand, the two families will have tackled the thorny problem of the dowry. As a general rule, souvenirs of this ceremony will be more authentic if purchased inland rather than at coastal resorts.

'Free' zone

Although this is not strictly speaking a Corsican tradition, you might want to take advantage of Corsica's prices and bring back a few more modern souvenirs. In Corsica tobacco, cigars and cigarettes are around 40% cheaper than in mainland France. Alcohol is more or less the same price, but do try one or two bottles of Pietra, the tasty local chestnut beer. And don't forget to take home a bottle or two for your friends to try.

CORSICAN KNIVES

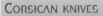

The most authentic souvenir to bring back from Corsica is the famous shepherd's knife. Nearly all Corsicans own one of these. It has a smooth, hard, curved handle, which gives a perfect grip, made from olive wood, beech or heavier oak wood. The blade is concave, which makes 'machete'-like cutting easier. These knives come in all sizes to suit all pockets. Note that if the blade of the knife is longer than the palm of your hand, it's forbidden to carry it back in your hand luggage. If you declare it before boarding the plane, it will be wrapped for you free of charge. Prices range from 200-800F (see p. 120).

The sacred olive tree

Olives and the olive tree are an integral part of Corsican tradition. Recent archaeological discoveries in the Nebbio region have shown that the tree was part of the indigenous flora of the island, together with myrtle, Laricio pine and the maquis. It was the Genoese who developed and organised olive production, as well as the chestnut plantations of Castagniccia (p. 144). The great majority of olive trees in Corsica are therefore over 500 years old and in the south, many trees are more than 2,000 years old.

A truly natural product

Mother Nature takes care of everything. Corsican olive trees are allowed to grow naturally and the majority of olive groves form a source of grazing for cattle. The olives are never actually harvested, the Corsicans simply wait for them to fall off the trees of their own accord! For this reason, huge nets are suspended under the trees, around 3 ft (1 m) above the ground. You'll notice these particularly in the Balagne region. When the olives fall, they are gathered in the nets, just when they are ripe for pressing and storage.

Sabine or Picholine?

Corsican olives are larger than the small Niçoise olives but more delicate than the larger Greek variety. There is little

difference between varieties, the chief criteria for selection being their capacity to produce olive oil. The firm and tasty Picholine variety from the Regno valley produces 15-20% of its weight in oil, whereas the Sabine variety from Balagne produces 30% and the Biancaglijia from the Nebbio region produces 40%. The majority of olives served with an aperitif are of the Picholine variety.

From tree to table

The first cold pressing of the olive harvest is done by 30 or so mills on the island (unfortunately closed to the public). As opposed to grain milling, the procedure is completely mechanised, and no chemicals are used in the process. Once the first pressing is complete, the resulting paste is separated by hand from the uncrushed pips. Over a period of several days, the oil simply separates itself out from this pulp. Olive oil is, in fact, a kind of fruit juice. The traditional process and the scarcity

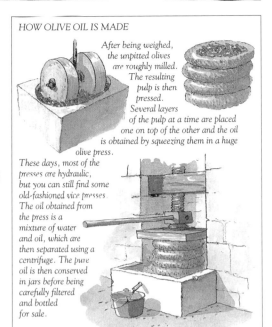

HOW OLIVE OIL IS MADE

After being weighed, the unpitted olives are roughly milled. The resulting pulp is then pressed. Several layers of the pulp at a time are placed one on top of the other and the oil is obtained by squeezing them in a huge olive press.

These days, most of the presses are hydraulic, but you can still find some old-fashioned vice presses. The oil obtained from the press is a mixture of water and oil, which are then separated using a centrifuge. The pure oil is then conserved in jars before being carefully filtered and bottled for sale.

OLIVE OIL AS A BEAUTY PRODUCT

Olive oil has some remarkable cosmetic qualities, and has long been used as an aid to beauty. A facial massage twice a week using a mixture of olive oil and lemon juice is thought to be the best defence against wrinkles. Olive oil, mixed with a few drops of lavender or eucalyptus essence, makes a very potent relaxant in your bath water. For a beautiful smile, gently massage your teeth and gums with a drop of olive oil and leave for several minutes. A recipe for healthy, shiny nails is to soak your fingertips in warm olive oil for 6-8 minutes. You'll definitely see the results after a couple of weeks.

of Corsica's olive groves, means that the island's total production is 110,000 gallons (500,000 litres) from 100,000 trees. In comparison, Spain has a total of 200 million trees and Greece 80 million. Nevertheless, Corsican olive oil is world famous as it is one of the most naturally produced.

Olive festival

Olive cultivation is one of the major agricultural activities of the Balagne region. Each year, producers, craftsmen and buyers meet in the town of Montenaggiore, in the heart

of the region, for a two-day festival, entirely dedicated to the tree and its fruit. There are conferences and presentations on the various uses of olive oil and also olive wood, one of the most hardy varieties, much admired by Corsican craftsmen. The high point of the fair is a regional competition to find the best olive oil. The fair takes place on the first weekend after 14 July. **Foire de l'Olivier**, Details available from the rural information centre at Montemaggiore, ☎ 04 95 62 81 72.

Sporting activities

From paragliding to kayaking, Corsica offers a wide choice of sports for an active holiday.

① **Sea kayaking**
Club Azimut,
Barretali.
p. 109

② **Paragliding**
Cap Corse Parapente,
Canari.
p. 108

③ **Horse riding**
Association de Tourisme
Équestre, Erbalunga.
p. 109

④ **Water sports**
Windsurfing, dinghy
sailing, catamarans and
deep-sea diving, Club
Nautique Bastiais, Bastia.
p. 104

⑤ **Horse riding**
Centre Équestre Soliva,
Poggio de Croce.
p.146-147

⑥ **Diving**
Club de Campoloro,
Valle di Campoloro.
p. 149.

⑦ **Flying**
Aéroclub de Corte.
pp. 134-135

⑧ **Water sports**
Canoeing, kayaking,
hydrospeeding and
rafting, Club de l'Ernella.
p. 153

⑨ **Canyoning**
A Muntagne Corse,
Liberta á la Richiusa.
p. 141

⑩ **Canyoning**
I Muntagnoli Corsi,
Quenza.
p. 181

⑪ **Horse riding**
Jalicu village
equestrian centre,
Quenza.
p. 180

⑫ **Water sports**
Windsurfing, dinghy
sailing, canoeing
and catamarans,
Club Nautique de Santa
Giulia, Porto Vecchio.
p. 160

⑬ **Horse riding**
A Staffa equestrian
centre, Porto Vecchio.
p. 160

⑭ **Quad bikes**
Quad Aventura,
Rondinara (Bonifacio).
p. 167

⑮ **Water sports**
Windsurfing and
funboarding,
Santa Manza bay.
p. 167

⑯ **Water sports**
Windsurfing,
surfing and jet-ski,
Tam-tam Location,
Bonifacio.
pp. 166-167

⑰ **Golf**
Petit Sperone,
Bonifacio.
p. 166

⑱ **Diving**
Barakouda Club,
Bonifacio.
p. 166

⑲ **Water sports**
Windsurfing
and dinghy sailing,
La Tonnara beach,
Bonifacio.
p.165

⑳ **Horse riding**
A Madudina equestrian
centre, Sartène.
p. 172

㉑ **Horse riding**
Equestrian farm,
Baraci.
pp. 176-177

㉒ **Water sports**
Windsurfing
and dinghy sailing,
Nautic Club de Porticcio.
p. 97

㉓ **Diving**
Club des Calanques,
Ajaccio.
p. 95

㉔ **Horse riding**
Poney Club, Campo
dell'Oro (Ajaccio).
p. 95

㉕ **Diving**
Centre Subaquatique
de Sagone.
p. 99

㉖ **Horse riding**
Albadu farm,
Corte.
p. 135

㉗ **Diving**
Club Le Stareso, Calvi.
p. 116

㉘ **Paragliding**
Calvi beach.
p. 116

㉙ **Boat hire**
CCI Yachting Plaisance,
Calvi.
p. 116

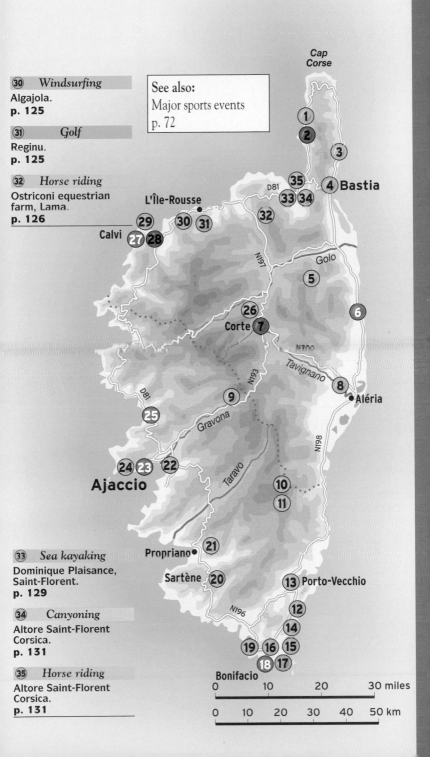

30 *Windsurfing*
Algajola.
p. 125

31 *Golf*
Reginu.
p. 125

32 *Horse riding*
Ostriconi equestrian
farm, Lama.
p. 126

See also:
Major sports events
p. 72

33 *Sea kayaking*
Dominique Plaisance,
Saint-Florent.
p. 129

34 *Canyoning*
Altore Saint-Florent
Corsica.
p. 131

35 *Horse riding*
Altore Saint-Florent
Corsica.
p. 131

Cap
Corse

Bastia
L'Île-Rousse
Calvi
Golo
Corte
Tavignano
Aléria
Gravona
Ajaccio
Taravo
Propriano
Sartène
Porto-Vecchio
Bonifacio

D81
N197
N200
N193
N198
N196

0   10   20   30 miles

0   10   20   30   40   50 km

Major sports events in Corsica

Corsica hosts a whole range of sporting events, from sailing to swimming and from horse racing to car racing. More and more people are getting involved in events like the Tour de Corse, the Corsica car rally, or the

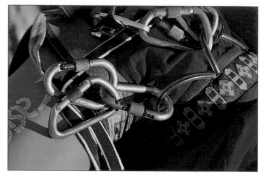

Mediterranean Trophy sailing race, as well as competing in such tests of endurance as the triathlon and the Inter-lacs mountain race. So if you are in the vicinity when one of these events is taking place, don't miss out.

The Tour de Corse car rally

Spectators throng to watch the racing cars hurtle along the highways and byways of the island at break-neck speeds. The Corsica rally is in fact the French stage of the world rally championship and therefore attracts some of the best drivers in the world to take part in this breathtaking race. The competition is fierce. For three days, the drivers are tested to the limit over some 250 miles (400 km) of roads, including the narrow, winding lanes of the Alta

Rocca hills. Don't be tempted to imitate these professionals – even the best drivers come to grief here and crash from time to time. The rally takes place every year, contact the information line for exact dates and further details: ☎ 04 95 23 62 60.

The Corsica triathlon

The island makes an ideal venue to stage a triathlon. Athletes, in teams of five to seven, cycle between the villages of Saint-Florent, Tucci and Île Rousse, and at each stage they compete in a triathlon event – cycling, swimming and running. In

1999, the third time this event was staged, participants came from all over the world.

The Mediterranean Trophy race

This is an international sailing race open to cruisers, single-hull sailboats, IOR, IMS and CHS boats. The race starts and finishes in Corsican waters, often with a stage at Sardinia. The start of the race is a particularly impressive sight, with the brightly coloured sails billowing in the wind. This event takes place in the second week of July. Although the departure venues vary, boats regularly weigh anchor at locations

such as Bonifacio, Propriano or Calvi. Further information: ☎ 04 95 21 40 43.

The six-day cycle race

The *Six Jours Cyclotouristes* event takes place in May and September each year. Around 150 amateurs, split into two groups, take part. The race covers a distance of around 370 miles (600 km), half of which is mountainous terrain, with each group following a different route so that the maximum number of spectators can watch the event. Information can be obtained from the Vivre la Corse à Vélo association: ☎ 04 95 21 96 94.

The Grand Raid Inter-lacs mountain race

The *Grand Raid Inter-lacs* is an endurance race, run on foot, taking competitors to seven

Corsica, a playground the size of an island

THE CORSICA RAID AVENTURE

This is a formidable test of endurance and team spirit. Each year towards the end of May, 30 or so teams each made up of 4 members test their skills at orienteering, mountaineering, kayaking, mountain biking and rock climbing. The challenge takes place over

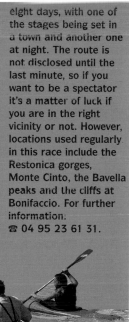

eight days, with one of the stages being set in a town and another one at night. The route is not disclosed until the last minute, so if you want to be a spectator it's a matter of luck if you are in the right vicinity or not. However, locations used regularly in this race include the Restonica gorges, Monte Cinto, the Bavella peaks and the cliffs at Bonifaccio. For further information.
☎ 04 95 23 61 31.

of the most spectacular high-altitude lakes on the island, at the heart of the Corsican regional nature reserve. Having established itself as a classic of its kind, the race is now an annual event. The 18-mile (29-km) course involves close to 20,000 ft (6000 m) of ascents and descents overall, and takes place in two stages on or around 15 and 16 July. There's also a huge 'pasta party' in Corte on the eve of departure, when competitors fill up on as much of the high carbohydrate food as possible to prepare them for the gruelling days ahead. For the third running of the race, in the year 2000, the number of participants was restricted to 300 by the Fédération Française de la Montagne, the governing body responsible for sanctioning the race. For further information:
☎ 04 95 46 12 48.

Beaches

The following are some of the best beaches in Corsica,
whether of sand or pebble, out in the open or hidden in secluded coves.

① *Barcaggiu*

Barcaggiu beach,
one of the few large
sandy beaches
on Cap Corse.
p. 108

② *Bastia*

Marana beaches,
especially pleasant
before 3pm.
p. 104

③ *Prunete*

Beach (no lifeguard)
surrounded by
eucalyptus trees.
p. 149

④ *Moriani*

Alistro beach, 8.5 miles
(14 km) of fine sand.
p. 150

⑤ *Aléria*

Many pretty sandy
beaches.
Quite popular.

p. 153

⑥ *Favone*

Canella cove. Exposed
to the east wind.
p. 155

⑦ *Porto-Vecchio*

Palombaggia beach:
fine sand and pink
rocks. Well equipped
and very popular.
p. 160
Santa-Giulia beach,
well equipped
and very popular.
p. 160

⑧ *Santa Manza*

Santa Manza bay
beaches.
p. 167

⑨ *Bonifacio*

Petit Sperone, beaches
and small creeks.
p. 166
Lavezzi islands: small,
unspoilt beaches.
p. 167

⑩ *Figari*

Figari point:
many coves and
secluded beaches
(sometimes quite windy).
p.168

⑪ *Roccapina*

Roccapina beach:
huge rock
in the shape
of a sleeping lion.
Many secluded coves.
p. 173

⑫ *Baraci*

Baraci beach:
sunset views.

p. 176

⑬ *Portigliolo*

Well-situated beach.
Be careful of waves.
p. 176

⑭ *Porto-Pollo*

Porto-Pollo point:
many quiet,
fine-sand beaches.

p. 176.

⑮ *La Castagna*

Chiavari, Verghia
and Portiglio beaches.
Quieter than the
Porticcio beaches.

p. 96

⑯ *Porticcio*

Viva beach: popular,
well equipped, lifeguard
Agosta beach: white
sand, well equipped,
lifeguard,children's play
area.
p. 96

⑰ *Ajaccio*

Scudo and Saint-Antoine
beaches: pink sands,
no lifeguard.
Vignola beach:
lifeguard.
p. 95

⑱ *Sagone*

Santana beach:
no lifeguard.
p. 99

⑲ *Porto*

Porto's pebble beaches.
p. 100

⑳ *Calvi*

Alga beach
and some secluded
coves around
Revellata point.
p. 116
Calvi beach: well
equipped, lifeguard
p. 116

㉑ *Île Rousse*

Old town beach:
family atmosphere.
Many isolated coves
(nudist beaches)
accessible by sea.
p. 122.

Saint-Florent

㉒ Loto beach:
accessible by boat,
no lifeguard.
Roya beach:
below the citadel,
lifeguard.
p. 129.

㉓ Saleccia beach:
azure sea and white
sands, no lifeguard.

p. 129

See also: Dream beaches p. 76

Cap Corse

Bastia

L'Île-Rousse

Calvi

Corte

Aléria

Tavignano

Ajaccio

Gravona

Taravo

Propriano

Sartène

Porto-Vecchio

Bonifacio

N197

D81

Golo

N200

N193

N198

D81

N196

0	10	20	30 miles

0	10	20	30	40	50 km

Dream beaches

Corsica is paradise for sea and sand lovers, from the wide stretches of sand of the east coast to the small, secluded coves at Bonifaccio and the town beaches of Bastia and Ajaccio. The sun shines on Corsica for six months of the year, the Mediterranean is warm and calm and the waters all around the island are pure and clean and ideal for diving. Take the plunge!

The best in the west

It's hard to decide which are the best beaches on the island. The west coast has an abundance of secluded coves which are often difficult to reach, like those along the Désert des Agriates. On the whole this coast is quite rocky, with precipitous cliffs plunging straight into the sea in many places, but there are also some lovely bays with soft, golden sand. Many beaches, such as Loto or Saleccia, can only be reached by sea (unless you're a world champion mountain biker!), but there is a shuttle service that runs from Saint-Florent. Information from the Agriates tourist office (20246 Santo Pietro di Tinda, ☎ 04 95 37 09 86).

La Tonnara beach, near Figari

The beautiful shell-shaped beach at Rondinara

The eastern plain

Extending for around 62 miles (100 km), the eastern plain stretches from south of Bastia to Conca. The beaches of Moriani, Ghisonaccia, Solenzara and Favone are all similar – huge stretches of white sand protected by a ridge of dunes. The terrain can be marshy, as at Ghisonaccia, but never unpleasant. The main attraction of these beaches is that they are well equipped and have lifeguards, unlike many of the beaches to the west. A green flag (safe bathing) or red flag (bathing prohibited) flies on all these beaches. Decked terraces, little restaurants, ice cream vendors and children's play areas are the order of the day.

Porto's shingle beaches

Corsicans, particularly the inhabitants of Porto and

The clear blue sea is an invitation to swimmers

Piana, regard this as the world's most beautiful bay, and who's to say that their opinion is wrong? Decide for yourself. Caspio and Bussaglia beaches lie at the end of the bay and are the most beautiful shingle beaches on the island. They are more suitable for walking (so keep your shoes on) than for sunbathing, but the sound of the sea rushing over the smooth pebbles is a delight. Take a stroll as the

sun goes down and don't forget to take your camera – the sunsets over the bay are quite breathtaking.

Naturists

Although topless bathing is permitted practically everywhere (although be cautious on family beaches such as Bastia or Ajaccio), naturism is not very popular in Corsica, where a certain religious puritanism is still prevalent. Beaches that permit nudism are concentrated in the Linguizetta commune (Aléria tourist office, ☎ 04 95 57 01 51). There are even small villages dedicated to nudism, the most famous of which is Riva Bella, where you can hire bungalows right beside the sea. Note that in peak season you will need to book several months in advance. Prices vary according to season, from 275F to 495F per day for two people. If Riva Bella is full, try Bagherra, which has comparable prices and facilities. The national federation can provide further information.

Village de Riva Bella
RN 198, north of Aléria.
☎ 04 95 38 81 10.
Village de Bagherra
RN 198, north of Aléria.
☎ 04 95 38 83 20.

TAKE SENSIBLE PRE-CAUTIONS

Watch out for the heat. Drink plenty of water and avoid prolonged exposure to the sun at the hottest time of day (noon-3pm). Use plenty of high-factor sunscreen lotion and always re-apply after swimming. All beaches have areas specifically set aside for water sports, so make sure you give these a wide berth when swimming. Avoid direct contact with the hot sand – use a towel and wear beach sandals or shoes. Animals are prohibited on almost all beaches, but you can obtain more information from the tourist offices. Note particularly that rocky coastlines are littered with minute sea urchins, so be prudent on the west coast. You are more likely to encounter jellyfish on the east coast.

Fédération Nationale de Naturisme
65, Rue de Tocqueville,
Paris 75017. ☎ 01 47 64 32 82.

Is it the Seychelles? No, it's the Lavazzi islands

Hiking in Corsica

Discover Corsica on foot – the beaches, the 'maquis',
the forests and the mountains.

① **Castagniccia**

Waterfalls,
steep gorges
and chestnut forests.
pp. 144-145

② **Forêt
de Vizzavona**

Forests, gorges,
chestnut mills
and straw drying sheds.
pp. 142-143

③ **Prunellie gorges
and
the Ese valley**

Beautiful scenic drives.

p. 185

④ **Plateau
de Cuscione**

Eagles and kites, maquis
and wild marshland.
p.180.

⑤ **Mount
Cagna**

Forest and rocky
hiking terrain.
Shepherd's huts
at Naseo and Bitalza.
p. 169

⑥ **Capo d'Orto**

Scenic limestone coves.
One of the prettiest
coastal walks.
p. 101

⑦ **Balagne**

Spectacular Giussani
walking trails.
p. 112

⑧ **Désert
des Agriates**

Many paths through
wild maquis scrubland.
p. 127

⑨ **Niolo and
Mount Cintu**

Crystal clear lakes,
pastures, canyons
and valleys in medium-
and high-altitude
ranges.
pp. 136-137

Ⓐ **Mare e monti
north**

Ten-day coastal
mountain trail between
Calenzana and Cargèse.
p. 83

Ⓑ **Mare e monti
south**

Five-day trail around
the most beautiful bays
of southern Corsica.
p. 83

Ⓒ **Mare a mare
north**

Easy coast-to-coast
walking trail.

p. 82

Ⓓ **Mare a mare
centre**

Fairly easy, coast-to-
coast woodland route.
p. 82

Ⓔ **Mare a mare
south**

Demanding six-day
hike from coast
to coast in wild terrain.

p. 82

Ⓕ **GR 20**

The best-known hiking
trail on the island. Two
weeks of spectacular
scenery from Calenzana
to Conca.
pp. 84-85

See also:
Hiking – a user's guide
p. 80,
Hiking routes p. 82,
GR 20 trail p. 84

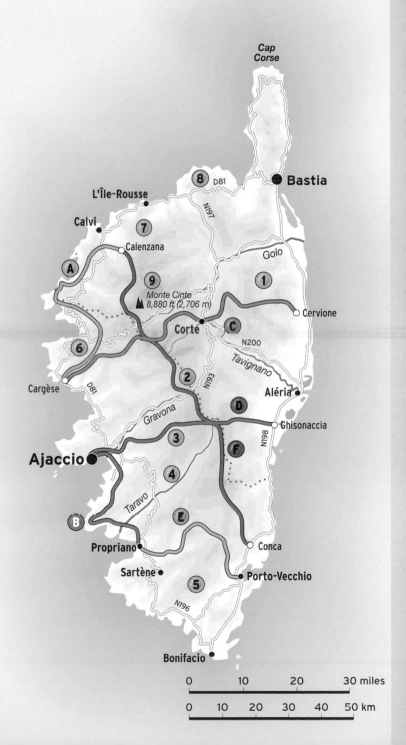

Cap
Corse

Bastia

D81

L'Île-Rousse

Calvi

Calenzana

A

Golo

7

8

N97

9

1

Monte Cinto
8,880 ft (2,706 m)

Corte

C

Cervione

N200

6

Tavignano

2

N193

D81

Gravona

Aléria

Cargèse

D

Ghisonaccia

3

N198

Ajaccio

4

F

Taravo

B

E

Propriano

Conca

Sartène

5

Porto-Vecchio

N196

Bonifacio

0   10   20   30 miles

0   10   20   30   40   50 km

Hiking – a user's guide

O f all the island's attractions, Corsica is particularly suited to hiking. With some impressively high peaks and scenic parks, there's sufficient variety to match hikers of all standards. Here's some advice to make the most of your trip.

Don't forget your bathing suit for a refreshing dip in the many streams and waterfalls

Maps and guides

Start by obtaining the appropriate guide. There is one for the GR 20 and another for the Mare a mare (coast to coast) and the Mare e monti (sea and mountain) trails (p. 82). They cost around 80F each but they are absolutely indispensable. Each route has been divided into sections where any difficult terrain has been

identified.

They also give you an idea of how long each route takes, as well as possible alternatives. Smaller-scale versions of IGN maps are included in these guides, with very detailed information on terrain. If you prefer standard size guides which are easier to read, you'll need 8 maps for the GR 20 (No. 4149 to 4153 OT and No. 4253 and 4254 ET).

Guides and maps are readily available from any bookshop on the island, but you can also obtain them from the National geographical institute in Paris. **Institut Géographique National**, Service de Vente des Cartes, 107, Rue de La Boétie, 75008 Paris, ☎ 01 43 98 80 00.

Be prepared

Don't arrive at the foot of Mount Cinto and discover you haven't got any gloves! Begin by finding a good pair of boots, essential for both comfort and safety. Remember to pack extra layers of

clothing, jumpers, waterproofs, gloves, scarves, sunglasses and a first-aid kit – better safe than sorry. Bring a down-filled sleeping bag as they are light and warm. Always carry a knife and length of rope, and a compass is always a good idea.

Don't get lost!

White and red stripes – as long as you can see these, you know that you're on the GR 20.

The spacing of these markings varies between 330 and 2,000 ft (100 and 600 m) – rarely more, except for mountain ascents, such as Cinto, Rotondo and Incudine. The markings are always clearly visible. This is also true of other routes but the colour is different – they are orange. Routes connecting villages to pathways are marked out in yellow.

Don't panic!

If you get lost, there's no need to panic. Make sure that you have noted down the time

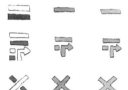

of your departure from the shelter and then work out roughly how far you have travelled per hour. On the flat you can expect a brisk walking pace to be about 5 mph (8 kph), so adjust your estimate according to the terrain. You can then mark out an approximate position on your map. Using your compass or the sun for orientation, go west for 600 yards (1 km), marking the route yourself as you go (with sticks or little piles of stones). If this fails, repeat this procedure but head east, and you'll be sure to come across your path once more.

Friends of the regional nature park

The majority of hiking routes are within the regional nature park (Parc Naturel Régional, ☎ 04 95 51 79 24), which is responsible for the upkeep of the pathways, gîtes, and shelters, and for the protection of Corsican wildlife. When

GÎTES

If you don't want to pitch your tent, you can stay at one of the many gîtes along your hike. However, there is usually an area reserved for campers near the shelters, so that they can use the facilities at less cost. Gîtes provide 20 to 30 beds, but are very busy in summer. All shelters are equipped with showers, kitchen facilities and wood-burning stoves.

However, you will need to provide your own sleeping bag. Some shelters have a radio for use in the event of difficulties, and it might be a sensible precaution to go armed with a mobile phone and local emergency numbers. If you avoid the weekends, you'll have a better chance of finding room at the shelters. They're listed in all the hiking guides. Allow 50F a night per person.

crossing the Alta Rocca you might catch sight of deer. They were reintroduced to Corsica in 1998 by the park. The **Les Amis du Parc** association is for nature enthusiasts and other individuals keen to support the protection of Corsican flora and fauna. It organises around 10 expeditions a year, for both entertainment and education, and welcomes guests. **Le Parc naturel régional et ses amis** 2, Rue du Major-Lambroschini, 20000 Ajaccio. ☎ 04 95 51 79 10.

Hiking routes

A long with its beaches, hiking is Corsica's other major attraction. Each region has a selection of officially signposted trails and the choice is immense. You can even travel the same route over and over again, yet always see something new in the island's ever-changing climate, terrain, flora and fauna. Apart from the GR 20 (*see* p. 84), the Regional nature park also offers another five routes, all of which require overnight stays in tents or shelters.

The *Mare a mare* north route

This 10-day, 'coast-to-coast' hike in Haute-Corse starts on the east coast at Morian (p. 50) and finishes at Cargèse (p. 98), taking in Corte, the traditional capital of Corsica (p. 132). The path winds through the sweet chestnut tree forest of the Castagniccia and round the foothills of the highest mountains on the island, using the paths which lead to the GR 20. This route doesn't present any particular difficulties and is therefore suitable for amateur hikers wanting to gain experience of a long hike.

The *Mare a mare* centre route

This coast-to-coast route extends from Ghisonaccia, on the east coast of the island, as far as Ajaccio, and gives a good taste of hiking either using camp site facilities or shelters. Although this lovely woodland route is fairly easy as hiking trails go, it's one of the most scenic trails on the island, taking you past the Col (peak) de Laparo, Hatu-Taravo, and the Col Saint-Georges.

The *Mare a mare* south route

This six-day, coast-to-coast hike from Porto-Vecchio to Propriano is one of the shortest trails on the island, but it is far from easy. The terrain is varied, crossing the Alta Rocca, one of the best preserved and wildest regions in Corsica (p. 178). At the foot of Alcadina (Incudine), the second highest mountain on the island, it cuts through woodland before climbing to Quenza and Serra-di-Scopamene, where you'll perhaps have the chance to view the spectacular sunrise over the Alta Rocca. It then heads to Propriano via Santa-Lucia di Tallano. It's a simply magnificent walk.

The Mare a mare trail has magnificent views of the coast

The *Mare e monti* north route

This 'sea and mountain' route takes 10 days to reach Cargèse, starting out from Calenzana. From north to south, the trail climbs from sea level to cross the entire Balagne region, the veritable garden of Corsica (p. 110) with its clifftop villages and timeless charm. It then takes in the spectacular Spelunca gorges before descending towards Cargèse. There are *gîtes d'étape* at regular intervals on the walk where you can put up for the night.

The *Mare e monti* south route

This walking trail is an excellent way to discover two of the most spectacular bays in southern Corsica, Ajaccio and Valinco. The six-day hike takes in the Chiavari forest, which shelters the ruins of

the ancient prison, the Capo di Muro (p. 97) and Porto Pollo point. The path then runs along the base of the mountains before descending into the gorges to Olmeto and then gently down to Propriano, with its popular beaches. It's an easy trail, suitable for all the family.

COUNTRY WALKS

There are many country paths and trails on the island that are less demanding than the GR 20 or coast to coast and mountain and sea hikes. Although they are shorter, they do, nevertheless, require careful prior planning of the itinerary in terms of time, distance and difficulty. It's also important to take note of the locations of lookout points, picnic areas, sites of interest, gîtes and restaurants etc. Small information packs are available on the country walks in Alta Rocca (p. 178), Fiumorbu (p. 156), Giusani (p. 112), Niolo (p. 136), Taravo and Venachese. These can be obtained from the relevant tourist offices.

The wild beauty of the Mare e monti trail

GR 20 trail,
the backbone of Corsica

This famous hiking route is well known to both nature and hiking enthusiasts alike. It starts out at Calenzana, in Balagne, and finishes at Conca, near Porto-Vecchio, following the mountain ridges that cut across Corsica from the northwest to the southeast. Although impassable in winter, except by cross-country skiing, it's a popular trail during the spring and summer months. You can see examples of almost all the island's wonderful flora and fauna on this two-week hike.

clusters of wild scrub such as the alder, recognisable by its pungent smell.

The fauna

The maquis is home to the hare and the dormouse, wild pig and boar. Although wild pigs roam in groups, the boar is a solitary beast who is liable to charge without provocation. If either of these animals smell food, be on your guard. If you are camping, protect your provisions carefully, because a hungry boar is well capable of

destroying your tent. If the animal becomes aggressive then leave it some food without delay.

Village pitstops

At some point on your walk you'll need to find a village, to do some shopping, make a phone call or perhaps even ask for some help. The GR 20 goes through Vizzavona, a perfect place to restock your provisions. But there are other possibilities, for example the Vaccaghja shepherd's huts at Corte (allow 8 hours) or the

Flowering rock rose in the maquis

The flora

From the myrtle, arbutus and pistachio and olive trees of the maquis, you'll quickly reach wild forest at 2,000 ft (600 m) above sea level, where there are young oaks and chestnuts. Watch out for the poisonous hellebore that grows at their feet. Higher up, in the Vizzavona and Bocca di Verdi forests, the landscape changes to beech trees and Laricio pines. Finally, at 6,500 ft (2,000 m) you'll see only rare

A mountain grocery shop, often the only source of provisions

Manganu refuge at Soccia (allow 3 hours). The signs from the GR 20 down to the village are in yellow. For everyday provisions, the trail passes numerous shepherd's huts, where you can find cheese, charcuterie and often bread on offer.

Taking the route in stages

The two-week long hike along 124 miles (200 km) of the GR 20 (*Grande Randonnée*) is quite a strenuous undertaking and only 30% of walkers complete the trail from start to finish. The majority take shorter hikes along smaller sections of the route, which can be joined at numerous junctions such as at Monte Cinto, Paglia Orba, Boca Muzzella, Petra Plana, Bavella, Vizzavona and Conca. If you are not a serious or regular hiker, this is a much more pleasant – and sensible – way of enjoying this famous trail. The junctions are all clearly marked in the guides, together with the time between

connections (*see* Hiking – a user's guide p. 80). On some sections, the path even crosses the motorway (Col de Vergio, Col de Bavella). All you need to do is take your car and go on a picnic for just the day, or perhaps a three-day round trip. All the areas in the vicinity of the GR have details of the walks and the terrain. Another way to tackle the GR is to divide it into two sections – Calenzana-Vizzanova, then Vizzanova-Conca. Allow nine and seven days respectively for each part of the route. Further information is available from the Regional nature park (☎ 04 95 51 79 10).

Flowering St John's Wort in the high mountains

SOME USEFUL ADVICE

Keep your eyes open, as the paths can be rocky and are not always clearly visible. Signposts are very clear on the major routes, but more spaced out for smaller pathways. Above 6,000 ft (1,800 m) start out early and make the most of the morning to make good progress. Clouds start to gather at the peaks at around 11am and there are frequent storms in the early afternoon. Avoid exposure to bad weather. Streams can

rapidly become torrents that are impassable for hours at a time. On the other hand, if the weather's fine, you may want to bring your bathing suit for a dip in one of the mountain lakes. Remember, though, that however hot you feel, the water in these lakes is always icy cold, even at the height of summer.

Fairs and festivals

Whether the subject is religion, tradition or culture, there's always something to celebrate in Corsica.

① Bastia

Italian cinema festival. Screenings of films on an Italian theme, from a period in Italian cinema by Italy's foremost directors (January).

p. 105

Cartoon art exhibition (April).
p. 105

Comics festival (April).
pp. 104-105

Maritime festival: week-long gathering of sea enthusiasts (May).
p. 104

Historical re-enactment. (July)
p. 104

Mediterranean film festival: a dozen films compete for the prized 'Olivier d'Or' award (November).
p. 105

② Tavagne region

Folk festival: music and chant (mid-August to mid-September).
p. 151

③ Casamaccioli

Procession of the Saints. The island's oldest pilgrimage (early September).
p. 138

④ Col de Bavella

Snow pilgrimage: procession and open air mass (first week in August).
p. 178

⑤ Bocognano

Chestnut fair: regional arts and crafts (mid-December).
p. 67

⑥ Ucciani

Ucciani bridge fair: Arts and crafts. (1 May).

p. 67

⑦ Golfe de Santa Manza

Funboard championship (May).
p. 166

⑧ Bonifacio

Procession of the Saints by the six Holy Orders (Good Friday).
pp. 59, 164-165

⑨ Alta Rocca

Corsica motor rally (May).
p. 72

⑩ Sartène

'Catanacciu' procession: Spectacular Stations of the Cross (Good Friday).
p. 59

Three-day arts and crafts fair (early August).
p. 170

Comedy festival (around 15 June).
p. 170

⑪ Propriano

Mediterranean Trophy yacht race (second half of August). Departs from Propriano, Bonifacio or Calvi.
p. 72

⑫ Porto

Corsica triathlon (July).
p. 72

⑬ Montemaggiore

Olive fair: conferences and exhibitions on olive oil and wood (July).
p. 69

⑭ Calvi

Contemporary art show (15 June-15 August).
p. 115

Jazz festival: concerts and improvisation (third week in June).
p. 117

Polyphonic chant festival (mid-September).
p. 117

⑮ Pigna

Festival of street theatre and ancient songs (1-15 July).
p. 111

⑯ Île Rousse

Corsican literature fair (mid-July).
p. 124

⑰ Lama

International cinema festival: open-air screenings on the theme of rural lifestyle and traditions (August).
p. 127

Corsica in detail

Ajaccio and the west coast 92

Bastia and Cap Corse 102

Balagne and Nebbio regions 110

In the mountains 132

Castagniccia region 144

East coast 152

Southern Corsica 158

Alta Rocca 178

Corsica in detail

On the following pages, you will find details of the most interesting places to visit in Corsica. The island has been divided into tourist zones, and a colour code enables you to find the area you are looking for at a glance.

Cap Corse

②

● **Bastia**

D81

L'Île-Rousse

N197

Calvi

③

La Balagne

Monte Cinto
8,880 ft
(2,706 m) ▲

*Le
Niolo*

④

Corte ●

⑤

*La
Castagniccia*

N200

Golo

Tavignano

N193

Gravona

● **Aléria**

*Vallée du
Fiumorbo*

①

N198

Ajaccio ●

⑧

Taravo

⑥

▲ Monte Incudine
7,011 ft
(2,136 m)

*L'Alta
Rocca*

Propriano ●

Sartène ●

⑦

● **Porto-Vecchio**

N196

Bonifacio ●

0	10	20	30 miles

0	10	20	30	40	50 km

Ajaccio the capital city

A jaccio is a lively commercial centre, combining the ancient with the modern. The deep waters of the bay accommodate superb yachts as well as the fishermen who still repair their nets by hand. This is a large and imposing city of elegant squares and promenades, overlooking a clear blue sea.

Getting your bearings

The Cours Napoléon and Rue du Cardinal-Fesch are the principal streets of the city, leading through the old town centre to the seafront. Between the two streets, the Place du Diamant is the gateway to the old city, lying in the shadow of the citadel. Here the atmosphere changes, as little avenues and small

workshops and boutiques take the place of the large stores, and typical Corsican houses still hold out against the encroaching modern apartment blocks.

The market, shopping and souvenirs

The market here is one of the most impressive on the island. It's held every morning, except

Mondays, from 8am to noon, between Rue du Roi-Jérome and the Place du Maréchal Foch. Nearby, the old city bustles with workshops of every kind. Here craftsmen work with ceramics, leather, pottery and wood. Take a stroll between Rue Roi-de-Rome and the Quai de la Citadelle and take a look at this veritable hive of industry. At the **Atelier-Galérie A Grotta**, for instance, Patrick Poidvin makes sculptures in terracotta, creating a range of reasonably-priced original pieces (from 200F). Or visit **L'Escarboucle**, where you can watch Nicole working with Corsican leather. Nearby, **U Ghjuvan Chris** is an interesting shop selling a range of souvenirs (cork, olive wood, coral, T-shirts etc.) all at very attractive prices.

Rue Fesch, with its bars, restaurants and shops

Things to do

- Horse riding
- Diving at the Club des Calanques
- Shopping for pottery in Portiglio
- Swimming at Scudo, Vignola or Saint-Antoine beaches

With children

- Easy walks on the Côte des Sanguinaires

Within easy reach

Porticcio (pp. 96-97)
Bastelica (pp. 184-185)
Cargèse and Sagone (pp. 98-99)

Tourist office

Ajaccio:
☎ 04 95 51 53 03

A Grotta and L'Escarboucle
16, Rue Roi-de-Rome
☎ 04 95 21 10 01
and 04 95 25 66 06
Closed Sun. in summer, Sun. and Mon. out of season.

U Ghjuvan Chris
4, Rue Bonaparte
☎ 04 95 21 10 74
Open daily 9am-8pm and 9am-midnight in high season.

As fishermen repair traditional rowing boats or mend their nets, you can sip a pre-lunch aperitif on a quiet terrace and enjoy the scene.

Italian painters
Palais Fesch, 50, Rue Fesch
☎ 04 95 21 48 17
Open 10am-6.30pm in high season, 9.15am-noon and 2-5pm out of season. Closed Mon. am, 15 June-15 Sept. Closed Sun. and Mon. out of season. Open Fri. 9pm-midnight in July and Aug. *Admission charge.*
This museum of Italian painting is very popular, particularly in peak season, so time your visit for the morning, if possible, when it will be less crowded. The major Italian artists are represented here, including Veronese, Raphael, Botticelli and Cosme Tura. This remarkable collection comprises over 200 works and is also housed in a very attractive setting, the splendid palace of Cardinal Fesch. This lovely building merits a visit for itself alone. Situated next door to the Fesch museum you'll find a splendid **Imperial chapel**, containing the tombs of several members of Napoleon's family, though unfortunately

Lamp in the A Grotta boutique

An open-air aperitif
The old port, whose shady terraces overlook the Quai de la Citadelle, is quite charming. Between the two jetties where the boats shelter, the atmosphere is always lively.

AN EASY WALK

This hike, above the winding Côte des Sanguinaires, is suitable for all the family, climbing no higher than 1,200 ft (370 m). There are spectacular views of the bay and particularly of the Sanguinaire islands. The path starts at the Bois des Anglais ('English wood'), near Ajaccio, and finishes at the Plage de Vignola, passing the imposing fountain of Cupetta. From Vignola beach you can easily return to Ajaccio by bus.

Italian primitive painting

not that of Napoleon himself. After your morning of culture, you'll certainly have earned lunch at the **Restaurant de France**, one of the best and most affordable restaurants in this popular area (90-125F per head, wine included). The delicious grilled Corsican pork is highly recommended.

Restaurant de France
59, Rue Fesch
☎ 04 95 21 11 00

Seafood and market produce
A Pampana
14, Rue di a Porta
☎ 04 95 21 19 66
This is a typical Corsican *perron*, set in the old quarter of Ajaccio with a large old-fashioned dining room, fine cuisine and a family atmosphere where you'll receive a warm welcome. The squid salad is highly recommended, but everything on the menu is excellent. The young chef here loves her work and it shows. Seafood, Corsican charcuterie, ragoût of grilled boar or kid – there's an extensive choice which varies according to the time of year. This is one of the finest restaurants in Ajaccio. Prices are around 250F (all inclusive, during the evening).

Nightlife
Santa Lina
Route des Sanguinaires
☎ 04 95 52 05 94
Summer evenings in Corsica are lively. In Ajaccio, the **Santa Lina** bowling alley is open to amateur and professional bowlers alike from 5pm (open weekends only in low season). The alley doubles as a piano bar, where you can listen to quality music in elegant surroundings. If you like to party until all hours, head for the nightclubs, **La Place** (Place du Diamant, ☎ 04 95 51 09 10) or **Week-End** (Route des Sanguinaires, ☎ 04 95 52 06 00).

Above and below the water
Club des Calanques
Hôtel des Calanques,
Route des Sanguinaires
☎ 04 95 52 09 37
Managed by one of the island's most accomplished divers, the **Club des Calanques** can offer an amazing first underwater experience, even to those who have always kept their heads strictly above water. Great emphasis is placed on safety and training, allowing you to explore the treasures of Corsica's colourful marine life in total confidence. So, jump straight in!

Pointe de la Parata
7.5 miles (12 km)
W of Ajaccio
Technicolour sunsets
The sunset at Ajaccio must be experienced at least once. As the sun dips slowly behind the towers of the Îles Sanguinaires ('blood-red islands'), they

The Îles Sanguinaires ('blood-red islands') live up to their name at sunset

really live up to their name. You can see this spectacular sight from the esplanade at the end of the road, but some prefer to climb the rocky promontory of the Tour de la Parata (Parata tower), to be at the same height as the towers behind which the sun disappears so spectacularly every evening.

Campo dell'Oro

6 miles (10 km)
E of Ajaccio

Horse riding

Poney-Club Ajaccio
Route de Sartène, 20000
Campo dell'Oro
☎ **04 95 23 03 10.**
One of the best ways to discover Corsica is on horseback and Ajaccio is no

exception. These horses at this pony-club are used to many different riders and are generally gentle in temperament, and prefer to amble along, particularly when they are in a group. On horseback, you can enjoy a trek through the maquis without mishap. An hour's trek will cost 110F.

TO THE BEACH

The bay has many attractive beaches – at Porticcio, of course (p. 96), but also on the coast of the Sanguinaire islands. Scudo, Vignola and Saint-Antoine are all pink sand beaches that are ideal to visit in the afternoon, when the sun is directly opposite. While all these locations are attractive, please note that only Vignola beach has lifeguards.

Portigliolo

21.5 miles (35 km)
S of Ajaccio

Pottery workshop

Christine and Bernard Isarn
Portigliolo
☎ **04 95 25 59 51**
You won't find Christine and Bernard Isarn's work on sale in the market place. If you want to purchase one of their highly original hand-made pieces you'll need to make an excursion to their workshop at Portigliolo, which is open to the public and where you

can see them make their pottery from scratch. These days, although they have become established potters, their prices still remain reasonable. Items from 30F; 200F for an attractive wine cooler.

EXCURSIONS

Other activities you may like to try while in Ajaccio include boat trips out to the Îles Sanguinaires, just at the mouth of the bay, or further afield, to the nature reserve at Scandola to the north of Ajaccio, or south to the spectacularly sited town of Bonifacio (see p. 162). You can book these trips down at the port. There are also organised coach trips to Bonifacio, which some consider to be Corsica's most beautiful town. The independent-minded might like to consider hiring out their own dinghy for the day.

Potter Bernard Isarn at work

Porticcio,
Ajaccio's popular beach resort

Porticcio is the favourite swimming spot of the inhabitants of Ajaccio. Lying across the bay, facing the capital, Porticcio is not famous for its architecture or its glorious past, but its beaches are really quite superb.

Agosta beach, an ideal day out for all the family

Porticcio's glorious beaches

The most famous and easily accessible of Porticcio's beaches is the **Plage de la Viva**. It's well equipped, with lifeguards on duty to allow bathing in safety and makes the ideal family beach. Further along the bay is the **Plage d'Agosta**, a vast stretch of white sand, which is also well equipped, with lifeguards as well as a children's play area. However, be prepared for plenty of bare flesh during peak season. The **Plages de Verghia**, located beneath the pine groves of Chiavari, and **Portigliolo**, close by the hamlet of Castagna, are a little quieter. Between these two lies the **Anse d'Ottioni**, a secluded cove that might just turn out to be the hide away you have always dreamed of.

La Castagna

10 miles (16.5 km)
S of Porticcio

La Castagna tower walk

This is a pretty half-hour walk from La Castagna village through pine forest and maquis. From the 300-ft (90-m) cliff you can see across to the far side of the bay, as well as the La Prata tower and the Sanguinaires islands. At the end of your walk lies the Genoese Tour de la Castagna, dating from 1584. It's the most solid tower that can be found on the island, due to extensive fortifications made by the Germans during World War II.

Bisinao
15.5 miles (25 km)
SE of Porticcio
A charming escape
A Tramuntana
Bisinao 20166
☎ **04 95 24 21 66**
Open all-year round
Porticcio is busy in summer, so it's best to book in advance. If you enjoy camping and barbecues, the **Camping du Sud** (☎ 04 95 25 40 51) is close to Ruppione beach, in Ottioni cove. The amenities are fairly good (grocery, pizza parlour, toilets etc.) and it's

SAIL AWAY
Nautic Club
Plage de la Viva,
Porticcio 20166
Open May-Sept.
☎ **04 95 25 01 06**
Ajaccio bay is one of Corsica's most sheltered locations and an ideal place for dinghy or yacht sailing. The Nautic Club in Porticcio is one of the best on the island in terms of safety and teaching facilities. Children aged eight and over can participate. The price is around 400F for five hours of sailing lessons (spread over a five-day period) and 900F for ten hours of catamaran instruction.

open all-year round. Prices start at around 700F per week. The very different setting of **A Tramuntana**, between Porticcio and the Col Saint-Georges, has more charm. This well-equipped rustic-style gîte is in the centre of the quiet village of Bisinao, on the southern *Mare e monti* walking trail (p. 83). Several family apartments with balconies are available. They also serve abundant helpings of country cooking, Corsican style. Half board starts at 150-200F per day. Book the restaurant in advance in low season.

Pointe des Sept Navires
9.5 miles (15 km)
S of Porticcio
A scenic walk
The Pointe des Sept Navires ('seven-ships point') has one of the most spectacular views of the bay and is an easy and pleasant walk. The Tour de l'Isoletta, a tower built in 1608, overlooks the point. Turn right onto the path along Agosta beach and you're just a few minutes from the pretty little port of Chiavari with its shady pines, ideal for a picnic.

Coti-Chiavari prison
This penitentiary has been abandoned since 1905, but the remaining ruins testify to the

Spotcheck
A3

Things to do
• Water sports on Viva beach
• Swimming at Verghia beaches
• Portigliolo and Ottioni cove
• La Castagna tower walk

With children
• Dinghy sailing or yachting at the Nautic Club
• Picnic in the pine groves of Chiavari

Within easy reach
Ajaccio (pp. 92-95)
Bastelica (pp. 184-185)
Propriano (pp. 174-177)

Tourist office
Porticcio:
☎ **04 95 25 01 01**
and 04 95 25 07 02

suffering endured here. You'll have to climb high into the maquis (path marked with arrows) to reach the ruins, but it's worth the effort. There's a view over both Ajaccio and Valinco (Propriano) bays. A little to the east is the **Capo Muro prehistoric site**, still under excavation. Close by, on the D55, a Genoese tower overlooks the Mediterranean. These defensive towers, each in line of sight of the other, originally ringed the island. They are gradually falling into disrepair, so take the opportunity to go and see one while you still can.

Cargèse
the Greek city in the gulf of Sagone

Around 1776, Greek refugees fleeing Turkish persecution landed at Ajaccio, from where they were deported by the French to Cargèse. To this day Greek is spoken in this area and Cargèse is home to Corsica's only Greek Orthodox community. The area's beaches are some of the most popular on the island.

A town with two churches

The Catholic and the Greek Orthodox communities live together in harmony in Cargèse. In fact, their respective churches face

one other across the small village square. The Catholic church is resolutely Baroque in style, whereas the Greek Orthodox church is more classical, and commands a spectacular view of the little port and Sagone bay. Cargèse port at sunset makes a pleasant evening stroll.

Gourmet stop
U Rasaghiu,
Marine de Cargèse
20130
☎ **04 95 26 48 60**
Open 1 May-20 Sept.
Visit the terrace of this pleasant restaurant in the marina and try the grilled fish or the house speciality – *spaghetti à la langoustine* (lobster). On Wednesday and Saturday evenings there's Corsican song and guitar music. Set menus 95-145F.

A scenic walk to the waterfall

Allow six to eight hours for this hike to the attractive Piazzilellu waterfall. Pack a picnic and set out early in the morning from Cargèse. Make for the village of Revinda, signposted on the right, 4.5 miles (7 km) along the road to Piana. From

Revinda, visit the abandoned village of E Case (only one gîte remains – bed and evening meal for around 150F. ☎ 06 08 16 94 90). From E Case there's a **superb panorama** of the little coves of Chiuni and Pero. You can then continue to the **Suelloni copper mines**, finally reaching the cool **Piazzilellu waterfall** (Cascade

The abandoned village of E Case

de Piazzilellu), a refreshing climax to your walk. Return via the mountainside path towards the Cargèse road (signposted by a pile of five stones). Further information available from **Cargèse tourist office**, Rue du Docteur Dragacci, ☎ 04 95 26 41 31. Open daily June-Sept. 9am-noon and 4-7pm, Mon.-Fri. 3-5pm, rest of the year.

Sagone
8 miles (13 km)
E of Cargèse

Sagone and its beaches

The tiny village of Sagone, at the far end of the bay, is the site of one of the most beautiful Genoese towers on the island. However, this is not its only attraction – its beaches are very popular with tourists. At one time the low-lying land along the coast here was the breeding ground for malaria-carrying mosquitoes, but fortunately, malaria is now a thing of the past. **Santana beach** (Plage de Santana) is attractive, sunny and sheltered but beware of the strong currents, which frequently carry unsuspecting bathers out to sea. Moreover, there are no lifeguards on duty. The port and village of Sagone are not particularly attractive, due to the uneasy combination of traditional stone architecture and ugly modern construction. Nonetheless, the balcony of **La Marine** hotel is a pleasant place to stop for a drink (rooms 200-300F depending on the season).

Hôtel La Marine
Marine de Sagone 20118
☎ **04 95 28 00 03**
Closed during the Christmas holidays.

Spotcheck
A3

Things to do
• Hike to the Piazzilellu waterfall
• Swimming (no lifeguards) at Santana beach
• Scuba-diving at Sagone

Within easy reach
Porto (pp. 100-101)
Bocognano (pp. 140-141)
Ajaccio (pp. 92-95)

Tourist office
Cargèse:
☎ 04 95 26 41 31
Sagone:
☎ 04 95 28 05 36

DIVER'S PARADISE
Centre Subaquatique de Sagone
Hôtel Cyrnos 20118 Sagone
☎ 04 95 28 00 01
Open 1 May 30 Sept.
Sagone bay, Trio and San Giuseppe points and the Licciola plateau are all highly prized by divers. The underwater landscape is quite magnificent, even in shallow waters (14-20 ft/4-6 m), and ideal for beginners. Corsica is well known for the rich and varied sea life around its shores, and if you're lucky you might see some impressive fish and even some rare red coral. All dives are made from a boat in the company of an instructor and very high standards of safety are observed. Prices are around 300F for half a day (concessions for groups).

Santana beach

Porto a bay of beauty

Each coastal village claims to have the island's prettiest bay. Porto, however, claims to have the most beautiful bay in the world. It's certainly a strong contender. The deep cove, overlooked by the Piana limestone headlands – among the island's true wonders – is truly magnificent. This is a must.

Choosing the right moment

Porto is an old fishing village of entrancing charm, which loses its attraction, however, in peak season. For some reason, Porto seems to attract over-heated, grumbling tourists in greater numbers than any other place on the island. Off-peak, the small port is really quite charming, and you'll meet friendly people who are always willing to help. Like Bonifacio, Porto is much easier to appreciate in low season. With fewer people around, you can explore the inlets of the bay much more readily, and you'll receive much better service in the village's bars and restaurants.

Shingle beaches

The singular feature of all Porto's beaches is the absence of any sand. These shingle

beaches may not be so comfortable for sunbathing, but they are perfect for pre-dinner walks to get the appetite going.

A gourmet stop in Porto
La Tour Génoise
Porto Marine 20150
☎ 04 95 26 17 11
Open daily May-Oct.
Stop for a while in the port and have a meal, perhaps at

La Tour Génoise. For a good meal for under 100F, try a plate of Corsican charcuterie, followed by a wonderfully prepared *pasta au brocciu* (pasta with fresh brocciu cheese), washed down with some Calvi wine. Make sure to visit the tower from which the restaurant takes its name, found at the end of the street.

Piana

7 miles (11 km) SW of Porto
The red needles of Piana
Said to be one of the island's unique wonders, the *calanches*

THE CALANCHES BY SEA

From Porto, a trip to the *calanches* will cost 100-200F – contact the Companie des Promenades en Mer (open Apr.-Oct.) to organise your trip. The trip will also take you to the Scandola marine park, the biggest marine nature reserve in Corsica, classed as a UNESCO natural world heritage site. The route to the rocks will take you via the little village of Girolata – a little village that can only be reached by boat. Girolata is very beautiful in spring, but spoilt in the summer because of its popularity with tourists.

at Piana have a mysterious charm that is hard to put into words. These huge needle-like cliffs, at least 1,000 ft (300 m) high, plunge directly into the calm, crystal-clear water, glowing with a strange red light that is emitted by the natural porphyritic rock. It's best to visit the needles in the late afternoon, when the glow from the setting sun gives them an almost magical quality. Make your way slowly along the open road that joins Porto to Piana, and stop at the various viewpoints on your way.

One of the island's most beautiful walks

It's possible to venture down the *calanches* on foot, but remember you'll have to climb back up. It's much better to take the signposted route to the top of Capo d'Orto (4,250 ft/1,294 m). The walk is not difficult (suitable for all) and the view that awaits you is out of this world. From the top, there's a commanding view of Porto and its bay – behind is a panoramic view of the Corsican mountains and, in front, an extensive view of the Mediterranean. Of all the walks you can take in Corsica, this has to be one of the most beautiful. The walk starts at the Stade Municipal de Piana, the Piana stadium, and is signposted.

....

Ota
3 miles (4.5 km) E of Porto

The Spelunca gorges

The Gorges de Spelunca are among Corsica's most beautiful gorges. A signposted trail takes you from Ota to Evisa in 3 hours (6-7 hours round-trip). The path follows the side of the canyon, which is quite rocky but still fine for a family walk. Look out for the small

Genoese bridges at Pianella and Zaglia, and don't forget your bathing costume. There are a number of pools that you can safely swim in along the way. Just keep an eye on the sky. Heavy rain can suddenly make the path underfoot very slippery, turning little streams into dangerous torrents.

Spotcheck
A2

Things to do

• Walk to the Capo d'Orto
• Car journey to the Piana needles
• Boat trip to the Scandola nature reserve
• Swimming in the Spelunca gorges

With children

• Sea trip to the Piana *calanches*

Within easy reach

Cagèse and Sagone (pp. 98-99)
Niolo region (pp. 136-139)
Calvi (pp. 114-117)
Crafts trail (pp. 118-121)

Tourist office

Porto bay:
☎ 04 95 26 10 55

Old Genoese bridge in the Spelunca gorges

Bastia
the economic capital of Corsica

Bastia resembles Genoa, the town on which it was modelled. This northern Corsican city, huddled between the sea and the wide range of mountains, is an area built-up of several towns, including Furani, Borgo and Biguglia. During the peak season these towns are invaded by hundreds of thousands of tourists, giving the city a cosmopolitan feel. Nevertheless, Bastia still takes pride in being a friendly and harmonious city.

A tour of the citadel
Information from the tourist office, Place Saint-Nicolas ☎ 04 95 55 96 96

The huge citadel looks slightly out of place in Bastia, but it nevertheless has one of the best viewpoints over the town and the port. A picturesque arched stairway leads into the citadel and then through into the Romieu gardens. This same stairway also takes you to the governers' palace (Palais des Gouverneurs), formerly known as the 'bastion' or 'bastille', from which the name Bastia is derived. A tour of the town is also available with an approved guide.

Lunch in the open-air
Chez Huguette
Vieux Port
☎ 04 95 31 37 60
Open 11.30am-2.30pm and evenings (last orders 10.30pm). Closed Sat. lunchtime and Mon.

The old port of Bastia, which is the soul of the city, lies between two piers, nestling among tall houses and dominated by the buttresses of the citadel. Here there are small coloured boats moored in the harbour and terraced bistros dotted around the quay.

THE SWEET FRAGRANCE OF THE CORSICAN MAQUIS

Musée de la Parfumerie Laboratoire Cynarom
29, Avenue Émile Sari
☎ 04 95 31 39 30
In this perfumery M. Cecchini makes and distills all the fragrances himself. Choose from the sweet essences of the maquis – myrtle, Laricio pine, verbena and violet. They make excellent presents and are very good value (from 30F). There's also a small museum that has some very old distilling equipment, perfume-making utensils and a collection of rare perfume bottles. The owner is happy to advise on the best way to look after such plants as lavender, thyme and rose geranium.

The port is the perfect place for a relaxing lunch while watching the boats come in, and **Chez Hugette** is ideal for a sandwich or some lobster.

Coffee in the Place Saint-Nicolas

Not to be missed is the Place Saint-Nicolas – the town's largest square, where the people of Bastia meet up in the shade of the palm trees. This is a popular place to take a leisurely stroll or enjoy a coffee in one of the many open-air bars. Looking out to the port and the sea, the atmosphere is wonderfully relaxed. You'll also find the famous **Maison Mattei** shop here (p. 37).

Beer or pool?
Pub Assunta
5, Place Fontaine-Neuve
☎ 04 95 34 11 40
Open daily 11am-2am (6pm on Sun.).
At the **Pub Assunta** you can choose to drink beer or play pool – or both. Before chalking up, try a Pietra (Corsican beer), perhaps followed by a *grillade de cabri* (grilled goat) or a mixed salad for about 50F. The pub is very popular with Bastia's youth. It's one of their favourite Saturday night haunts. The terrace is also a popular place for a pastis aperitif and olives, and you'll be lucky to find a seat straight away. The little square opposite gives the bar a Mediterranean atmosphere.

Spotcheck
B1

Things to do
• Cyrnarom perfumery and museum
• Nature walks accompanied by guides
• Film festivals

With children
• Cartoon art show

Within easy reach
Cap Corse (pp. 106-109)
Saint-Florent (pp. 128-131)
Castagniccia region (pp. 144-147)

Tourist office
Bastia:
☎ 04 95 55 96 96

Cetera workshop
Christian Magdeleine
2, Place Guasco
☎ 04 95 31 78 993
Open Thurs., Fri. and Sat., 9am-noon and 2.30-7pm.

In this workshop smelling of wood and varnish, nestled within the Bastia citadel, Christian Magdeleine preserves the traditional craft, passed down through his family, of manufacturing musical instruments. As well as being a specialist guitar maker, with several model designs to his name, Christian also promotes the traditional, guitar-like Corsican instrument, the *cetera*. His guitars are true works of art and they promote the good reputation of Corsican instrument makers throughout the world.

Traditional Corsican charcuterie

U Paese
4, Rue Napoléon
☎/fax 04 95 32 33 18
Here, charcuterie reigns supreme. These cold meats, flavoured with herbs from the Corsican maquis, are all organically produced. Before making your choice, try some of the *coppa*, *figatelli* and *lonzu* specialities (*see* pp. 32-33). If you decide to buy some, note that Corsican charcuterie does not like the heat and is kept hung up rather than on the shelf.

Nature hikes

Objectif Nature
3, Rue Notre-Dame-de-Lourdes
☎ 04 95 32 54 34
Put on your hiking boots and sun hat and enjoy a nature ramble. The countryside above the town is home to many treasures – sheepfolds, a Romanesque chapel, an old copper mine, medicinal plants and Corsican scrubland. Objectif Nature organises guided nature hikes (medium difficulty).

Bastia beaches

Club Nautique Bastiais
Plage de la Marana, June-Sept; Vieux Port, rest of the year.
☎ 04 95 32 67 33
or 06 11 83 09 14
It would be a shame to come to Bastia and not take full advantage of the superb coast nearby. If you just want to

At the beginning of spring, crocuses begin to appear

relax, head for the charming Plage de l'Arinella beach, which is open until around 3pm. However, for the more active, the Club Nautique Bastiais, at the Plage de la Marana, offers a full range of water sports activities, including catamaran sailing and diving. You can find out if the oysters are really as big underwater as they are in the restaurants!

Festivals and a touch of history

Bastia stages a number of colourful events throughout the year. In May, the Semaine de la Mer is a week-long **sea festival**. Among the most popular events with tourists are the **Italian film festival**, held in January, and the 'changing of the Governor' ('La Relève du Gouverneur'), a **historical re-enactment** that takes place in July. During this spectacle, the 'new governor' is welcomed to the old port, from where he makes his way through the narrow streets of the old town to the Place du donjon, where the ceremony of the transfer of power takes place. It's a colourful event, with a parade, jugglers and drummers.

However, the prize for the best event has to go to the **cartoon art show** (Salon de la BD), which attracts an increasingly large crowd of young people every April. Further information is available from the tourist office, Place Saint-Nicolas, ☎ 04 95 55 96 96

A cinematic feast

Bastia's film festivals are discreetly taking their place alongside those of Cannes, Venice and Berlin. In January, comedians, producers and critics dock at the old port for the 'Rencontres du Cinéma Italian', a **celebration of Italian cinema**, which is always based on a specific theme or period of Italian cinema. Over 3 days there are 15 public screenings,

including films by the best Italian directors, such as Fellini, Scola, Moretti and Benigni. Further information from the tourist office, ☎ 04 95 55 96 96. The town's **Mediterranean film festival**, the 'Festival du Film des Cultures Méditerranéennes', held in November, is a vibrant cultural forum. Around 10 different films are scheduled each year, one from each of the Mediterranean countries. After careful deliberation the jury decide which film will take home the coveted *Olivier d'Or* ('golden olive tree'). Each year there's a tribute to one of the leading personalities of the world of Mediterranean cinema. There are also exhibitions of books, paintings and photographs, and to round off the festival, a variety of workshops for people who want to try their hand at directing, acting or photography.

Lavasina

4.5 miles (7.5 km)
N of Bastia
Erbalunga, bathed in water
Chez Auguste
Lavasina, Cap Corse
☎ 04 95 33 25 40
Closed out of season.

The old port of Erbalunga is not as busy as it used to be, but there are still boats that use the small picturesque marina. It's worth stopping here for a while to see the village's buildings which perch right at the water's edge, including the ruins of the 16th-C. tower that dominates the village. The local speciality here is fish soup, which you can lap up before your main course of dressed lobster, at the **Chez Auguste** restaurant.

Furiani

4.5 miles (7.5 km)
S of Bastia
A gourmet stopover
L'Altu
Furiani village
☎ 04 95 33 37 67
Closed Mon.
and the whole of Feb.
Gastronomy is one of the main attractions of Corsican tourism, and Bastia is ideally placed for combining the best ingredients from the sea and the mountains. At the L'Altu farmhouse inn, in the little village of Furiani, the Mariani-Maccei family docs just that. You can enjoy traditional Corsican charcuterie as well as fresh fish for 120F.

Evocative ruins of the Genoese tower in Erbalunga

Cap Corse
a region apart

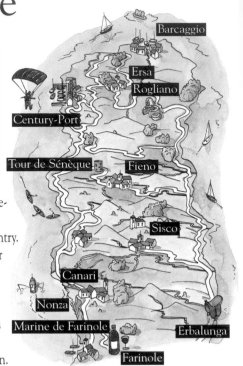

While Corsica is traditionally an agricultural and cattle-breeding island, the Cap Corse headland is staunch fishing country. The region's fishermen travel far out to sea to catch lobsters, and seafood is the region's gastronomic delicacy. The landscape and way of life of this region is much like the French region of Brittany – but with sun.

Barcaggio

Ersa
Rogliano

Century-Port

Tour de Sénèque

Fieno

Sisco

Canari

Nonza

Marine de Farinole

Erbalunga

Farinole

Nonza beach, below the 'devil's hole'

Nonza
20 miles (32.5 km) NW of Bastia
The Devil's hole
The little village of Nonza is typical of Corsica's sentry-like headland. The houses lining the 330-ft (100-m) cliffs face seaward as if hypnotised by the open spaces. On the precipice stands the 550-ft (167-m) Torre di Nonze, built under the orders of Pasquale Paoli, then rebuilt after being destroyed by the Genoese. At the top of the tower there's a spectacular view of the entire headland and at the entrance to the tower the *Trou du Diable* ('devil's hole') gives an impressive view of Nonza marina and the unusual black sandy beach nearly 500 ft (150 m) below.

Laurent Le Stunff shares his passion for winemaking at the Domaine de Catarelli

Farinole

14 miles (22 km)
NW of Bastia
A toast to Cap Corse wine
Domaine de Caterelli
Marine de Farinol
Route de Nonza
20253 Farinole
☎ 04 95 37 02 84
Fax: 04 95 37 18 72

Seneca in exile in Cap Corse

Laurent Le Stunff invites you to visit the Caterelli estate and its wine cellar, located in one of the headland's most beautiful valleys. All his wines are accredited with the Patrimonio AOC trademark. The visit starts with a free wine tasting, where you can try red, white, rosé or Muscat wines (the Muscat has its own AOC, 'Muscat du Cap'). Try to really get a feel for the different flavours. and respect wine tasting etiquette by sampling only a small quantity

at a time. You can buy or order any wine you like while visiting the estate.

Luri

12 miles (19 km)
S of Rogliano
Luri and the Seneca tower
This pretty village comprises of 10 hamlets. In Piazza, the Église Saint-Pierre has a 15th-C. painting on wood, which is well worth seeing. It depicts St Peter and, in the background you can see the fortified chateaux of the Cap, as they would have appeared some 600 years ago. From Fieno hamlet, take the path that leads to the ridge at the centre of the headland. At the pass, you'll come across a little slope that will take you to the top of **Monte Alticcione**, with a wonderful view of the wild northern part of the Cap. From here, there's a path leading to the **Tour Sénèque**

Legend has it that the Roman philosopher Seneca lived in this tower during his time in exile in Corsica.

Rogliano

Gourmet shopping
Phillipe Albertini's Rogliano cheeses
Hameau Olivio
20147 Rogliano
Open Dec.-end Aug.
Although Cap Corse cuisine revolves around fish, the locals really know how to make

Spotcheck
B1-C1

Things to do
- Cap Corse on horseback
- Sea kayaking
- Paragliding in Canari

Within easy reach
Bastia (p. 102-105)
Saint-Florent (p. 128-131)

Tourist offices
Bastia:
☎ 04 95 55 96 96
Port de Toga
(Maison du Cap Corse):
☎ 04 95 32 01 00

GONE FISHIN'
Destination Pêche Cap Corse
20217 Nonza
☎ 04 95 37 84 13
The **Cap Corse fishing centre** allows you to try your luck fishing on the open sea. Here you have the chance to catch red mullet, gurnards, scorpion fish, conger eels and rock lobsters. You can keep what you catch, but even if you come back empty-handed, you'll certainly still have enjoyed a fantastic day at sea, under the watchful guidance of professional fishermen.

cheese. In Phillipe Albertini's cheese shop you'll find soft, hard, mild and strong cheeses – a real treat for all cheese lovers. Phillipe makes a delicious speciality goat's cheese that can be eaten young or when it has matured. An added bonus is that the shop is located in the pretty village of Rogliano, where you can also visit the two castle ruins and the five defence towers.

than 200 inhabitants. At the far north is the small port of Barcaggiu, which was once very busy, supplying fish and rock lobsters, caught as far away as the Tunisian shores, to the Italian town of Livorno. Barcaggiu is also home to one of Cap Corse's few large white-sand beaches, where the Acqua Tignese river reaches the sea.

Canari

23 miles (37 km)
SW of Rogliano
Cap Corse paragliding
Cap Corse Parapente
M. Baldassari
20217 Canari
☎ 04 95 37 84 81
Corsica's headland is even more beautiful seen from the air. Your first paragliding flight will convince you of that. Flights take you along the ridge of Cap Corse and over the villages that cling tightly to the wooded hills and the little ports along the coastline. Flights are by two-seater aircraft with a qualified instructor. Just open your eyes and take in the unforgettable sights. Initial flights, lasting between 30 minutes and an hour, depending on wind and humidity, start at 250F.

Barcaggiu

11 miles (18 km)
N of Rogliano
Ersa, the end of Corsica
Ersa is the Corsica's northernmost point, apart from tiny Giraglia island, which is overrun by hares and Corsican scrub. The region is made up of eleven hamlets, none of which have more

After enjoying the fresh air in Barcaggiu, spend the afternoon enjoying the floral scent of the hamlet of Cannelle, near the village of Camera (about 1 mile/2 km on the way back down towards Centuri). In the hamlet of Granaggioli, you will find some excellent ash-covered goat's cheeses (**Fromagerie U Grimaldi**, Hameau Granaggiolo, 20275 Ersa, ☎ 04 95 35 62 69).

Centuri

10 miles (16 km)
W of Rogliano
Centuri marina
A Macciota
20238 Port de Centuri
☎ 04 95 35 64 12
In Italian, *marina* means 'sailing harbour' whereas *porto* refers to a commercial port.

The timeless charm of Centuri marina

The Italian influence is still much in evidence in Corsica, where a marina is a little port where fishing and pleasure boats sit side by side. The Centuri marina is one of the island's prettiest little ports. Two small stone jetties flank this ideal shelter that harbours about 10 boats that still frequent the deep waters of northern Cap Corse. In the past, Centuri port played a vital role in the export of wine, wood, oil and citrus fruits to Italy. Today it's still the main port of Cap Corse and three tons (3,000 kg) of rock lobsters pass through it every year. The round tower and the chapel located by the port make this place decidedly picturesque. The **A Macciota restaurant** is the perfect place to sample some wonderful seafood, caught by the owner himself.

work of art was moulded directly from the face of the Saint himself.

Erbalunga
6 miles (9.5 km) from Bastia (east coast)
Cap Corse on horseback
U Cavallu di Brandu

Sisco
13.5 miles (21.5 km) N of Bastia (east coast)
Relics of Sisco
People once came from afar to pray in the Romanesque Santa Catalina church, in the little village of Sisco. Just outside the village lies the hamlet of Poggio, home to the Martino chapel, which houses one of the island's most astonishing relics – a detailed mask of St John of Chrysostome. Made from bronze and silver, the sculpture is breathtakingly lifelike in every way – from the hair and the mouth to the expressive eyes, beard and eyebrows. It's amazing to think that this

Association de tourisme équestre
Glacières de Brando
20222 Erbalunga
☎ 04 95 33 94 02
and 06 13 89 56 05
If you enjoy riding, you'll enjoy Corsica, as there are equestrian centres dotted all around the island. Cap Corse is particularly good country for horseback trekking, either from coast-to-coast, across the mountains or through the Corsican maquis. Start your journey in the west and follow the ridge to the north end of the headland. The sun should rise above the mountains just as you reach the west side of the headland, so you'll have the sun behind you throughout the day. So saddle up and set off for a ride you'll never forget. Prices vary depending on the amount of people going on the trek.

SEA KAYAKING
Club Azimut
Marine de Giottani
20228 Barrettali
13 miles (21 km) SW of Rogliano
☎ 04 95 35 10 93,
This is an excellent way to get to know the coast. The sea kayak is easy to control and anybody can use one. You *will* have to paddle though. The flat bottom of the kayak allows you to reach all the smallest inlets, and get close to the untold wonders along the coastline. You can also take part in a sea kayak expedition, under the watchful supervision of qualified instructors who will guide you and give you tips on how to steer your kayak more successfully, how to right yourself quickly if you flip over, and other useful advice. Prices start from 200F per person for half-a-day's kayaking.

Balagne region
once a wheat-gold land

Balagne's reputed agricultural wealth is now ancient history. A combination of rural exodus, drought, and forest and scrub fires decimated the farming and cattle-breeding industries. The people of Balagne, however, have made a comeback, turning their attention to tourism instead. Île-Rousse and Calvi are the most popular destinations, but the central clifftop villages, the region's secret beaches and mild climate are also a strong attraction.

Clifftop village of Sant'Antonino

Citadel villages

Huddled together, built upwards rather than spread out, Balagne's villages have a theatrical air. The houses are veritable towers and the streets are narrow and labyrinthine. Unlike the southern communes (Sartène or Sotta, for example), which occupy large areas of land, Balagne's **clifftop villages** were forced to grow internally. The reason for this was that successive invasions (from Greece, Pisa, Genoa and the Barbary Coast) meant that the inhabitants had to group their buildings close together as a defensive measure. As well as this, in the past, agriculture (olive groves and wheat fields) took up most of the available land, leaving little space for houses.

Pigna
11 miles (18 km)
NE of Calvi
Where time stands still

Pigna is one of the most picturesque villages in Corsica. Its well-established craft industry (p. 119) has helped Pigna retain its early-19th-C.

feel, as have the tall houses of light-coloured stone that nestle in the mountainside and the square orchards, protected from the scrub and the wind by low walls. Pigna is an authentic, well-preserved village, although in high season it gets a little crowded. It's best to visit in the late afternoon as the sunsets are legendary.

Festive dining

Casa Musicale
Pigna
☎ 04 95 61 77 31

On the first floor, every Tuesday evening (sometimes more often during peak season – phone the night before), you can hear Corsican folk music, often performed by musicians in traditional costumes. You should come here at least once during your stay (Admission charge 40F).

Festivoce music festival

Reservations:
Casa Musicale, Pigna
☎ 04 95 61 77 31
From 1-15 July, the village becomes the world centre of **polyphonic and medieval song**, with street entertainers, troubadours, trouvères and storytellers. The *Festivoce* festival is becoming more popular every year, so book several days in advance to be sure of catching a show.

Corsican chant festival in Pigna

Things to do
- Sant'Antonio walk
- Musical dinner in Pigna

Within easy reach
Calvi (pp. 114-117)
Île Rousse (pp. 122-125)
Crafts trail (pp. 118-121)
Saint-Florent (pp. 128-131)

Tourist offices
Calvi:
☎ 04 95 65 16 67
Galeria:
☎ 04 95 62 02 27

Lavatoggio
8 miles (13 km)
NE of Calvi
Chez Edgar
Lavatoggio
☎ 04 95 61 70 76
Closed mid-Oct. to early Apr. Last orders 10.30pm. Open evenings only.
At this **traditional farmhouse inn**, located in the village of Lavatoggio, try the thick *prisuttu* soup, spit-roast pork and flambéed chestnuts, as well as the Calvi wine. Edgar uses only fresh ingredients from his orchards and farm. Before dinner, why not take a stroll in the Lavatoggio hills. The evening light makes the countryside of Balagne look even more beautiful.

Open eves daily.
Closed Jan.-end Apr and restaurant closed Mon. (exc. July-Aug.).
The ground floor of the Casa Musicale boasts a fantastic restaurant, with a menu based around **local ingredients**, such as charcuterie, chestnuts and brocciu cheese tarts. The food is excellent, but not for those watching their figure. Expect to pay around 200F per head.

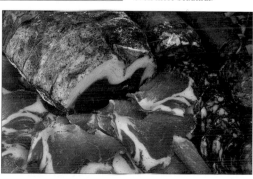

If you forget about lunch, distracted by the region's beautiful scenery, then don't worry. At the Aghjola farm inn at Pioggiola, the food is served from 9am to 11pm. In this pretty ivy-covered inn, the famous *repas du berger* (shepherd's meal) is the most popular choice (about 80F excluding drinks). Consisting of cheese and a selection of cold meats and a dessert, this meal is the perfect tonic for tired legs. The meal will also give you an excuse to have a little siesta by the pool in the afternoon. You can also stay here in one of the ten comfortable rooms, all with bathroom. Rooms cost between 300-375F per night, and half-board (375F) is obligatory in the high season. It makes a perfect base to explore the region, especially the beautiful neighbouring village of Speloncato, with its pretty 18thC. church, and the nearby Tartagin Melaja forest.

Aregno
9.5 miles (15 km)
NE of Calvi
Pagan frescoes
You really mustn't miss Aregno, with its floral square surrounded by dilapidated stone-walled houses, sun-kissed terrace and tall **Baroque church** with its tiny, picturesque cemetery. The Église de la Trinité et de San-Giovanni (mid-17thC.) is one of the oldest churches on the island and the sculptures and frescoes that decorate the inside give it a somewhat eerie feel. A man removing a thorn from his foot, two lions fighting, a woman carrying a jar – not particularly religious subjects – but the work of the Italian architects and sculptors is first-class.

Pioggiola
18.5 miles (30 km)
E of Calvi
A shepherd's meal
Auberge Aghjola
20259 Pioggiola
☎ 04 95 61 90 48
Open 1 Apr.-30 Sept.

Pioggiola
18.5 miles (30 km)
E of Calvi
Giussani walking trails
Improved three years ago, the walking trails around Giussani are some of the most beautiful in Corsica. Giussani, one of the last areas

on the island to undergo modernisation (electricity, road surfacing etc.), is surrounded by mountains, which are home to some of Corsica's prettiest hamlets. Many of these are almost completely deserted, with only two or three families remaining. The locals, renowned for their storytelling, are more than happy to talk to visitors. The winding paths, which cut through the valley of beech and chestnut trees, were for many years the only way to reach the area. You can explore the region on one of several **circular trails** (all of which are easy) starting in Pioggiola and Olmi-Capella. You can get a free, detailed brochure from tourist offices or from the Olmi-Capella town hall (Open Mon.-Fri., 9am-noon and 2-5pm, ☎ 04 95 61 90 17).

Sant'Antonino
13.5 miles (22 km)
NE of Calvi
A scenic view from a charming village
The people of Balagne will tell you that Sant'Antonino, perched high up in the hills, is Corsica's most beautiful village, although the hilltop hamlets of the region are all so charming that it seems an impossible choice to make.

Still, it's certainly worth making a detour, as much for Sant'Antonino's medieval passageways, covered alleyways and unevenly surfaced paths, as for its splendid view over the whole of the Balagne countryside,

Île-Rousse, Calvi and, glittering in the distance, the Mediterranean sea.

Feliceto
6 miles (10 km)
E of Calvi
The notorious falcon's nest
Legend has it that a mayor of Feliceto, in the early 19thC., built a small shelter overlooking the town, hidden in the rocks of Monte Grosso. From this vantage point, the story goes, he used to keep an eye on his people – the ladies, in particular. The *Falcunaghija*, ('falcon's nest') was also used as a hideaway by bandits on the run from the police. A half-hour walk from the village square will take you to the foot of the falcon's nest.

The shadowy alleyways
of Sant'Antonino village

Calvi the faithful

A rriving at Calvi by boat is a delight. From a distance, the blue and white harbour looks like a theatre. The lively port, imposing citadel, long white sandy beach and green pine forest forming the stage, the maquis plains alongside the beaches comprising the orchestra, and the snow-capped summits of the Cinto range in the balcony. The town's motto, *semper fidelis* (always faithful), reflects Calvi's former ties with Genoa, but it could just as easily refer to its attachment to a traditional lifestyle that combines Corsican customs with Italian exuberance.

A peaceful walk around the citadel

For many years this huge construction kept the people of Calvi safe from attack. A maze-like network of alleyways

and high-walled stairways link up the different parts of the citadel. The Governors' palace, the Saint-Antoine oratorium and the Saint-Jean-Baptiste cathedral are the principal places of interest.

A gentle morning stroll is the best way to enjoy the calm majesty of this place, before the throngs of tourists arrive, filling the citadel with noise and bustle. Tourist office, Port de Plaisance (marina)

☎ 04 95 65 16 67. Open daily 9am-7.30pm in summer season. Out of season, 9am-noon and 2-6pm. Closed weekends.

The terraces of the marina

Calvi's Port de Plaisance is one of the most welcoming marinas in Corsica. Here, you can watch the luxury yachts and colourful fishing boats come and go from the popular terraces of the marina's bars and restaurants. Experience the slow evening sunset while sipping an aperitif, before moving on to a restaurant for dinner. There are also many seaside walks from the marina, along the rocky coastline with its charming **hidden coves,** that stretch as far as the Scandola nature reserve. You can also take a boat trip to the Porto coast or Girolata bay (One day trip 280F, half a day trip 230F).

Colombo Line cruises (departures 9am and 2pm, Apr.-end Oct.), Port de Plaisance, ☎ 04 95 65 03 40

Calvi's motto is 'always faithful'

Underwater treasures

Underwater, the scenery around Calvi is just as good. Several companies (all which have offices in the port) can take you out to the best dive sites (Pointe de la Revellata, Punta Bianca and Rocher de Porto-Vecchio). Here, in addition to long shiny ribbons of seaweed, prickly sea urchins

Spotcheck
A2

Things to do
• Walk in the citadel
• Parascending on the beach
• Diving at Revellata point

With children
• Sea trip to the Scandola nature reserve

Within easy reach
*Porto bay (pp. 100-101)
Balagne region (pp. 110-113)
Crafts trail (pp. 118-121)*

Tourist office
**Calvi:
☎ 04 95 65 16 67**

A LIVELY EVENING OUT

In August, Calvi is a prime tourist attraction and the town and surrounding area barely stops to sleep. With a traditional glass of pastis at one of the marina's bars, you can plan the rest of your evening. Why not try some flambéed prawns in the rustic, 16th-C. **San Carlu** restaurant? (10, Place Saint-Charles, ☎ 04 95 65 92 20. Open every evening, Aug.-Oct.). Prices are reasonable and it's open until late. After your meal, head for **Chez Tao** bar in the old citadel.

Then, after knocking back a few tequilas, follow the crowd to one of the town's two nightclubs – **Challenger** or **Acapulco** (80F entrance includes one free drink). The **Acapulco** has a pool, so if you're feeling really brave, you could take a 2am dip. Finally, to clear your head, take a walk around the darkened, atmospheric streets of the citadel, and ponder on the fact that you might be walking in the footsteps of Christopher Columbus.

and the rocks that are dotted along the coast, you'll certainly see a few groupers. You should note, however, that the best dive sites are at a depth of 100 ft (30 m) – too deep for a first dive. You have to complete around five dives in shallow water, accompanied by an instructor, before you're ready to go to this depth.

Stareso
Club corse scientifique,
plongée et biologie
sous-marine,
Pointe de la Revellata
☎ 04 95 65 06 18

Calvi's unspoilt beaches
These beaches could be just what you're looking for – beautiful long stretches of white sand, punctuated by small, secluded inlets. Calvi's main beach,

Revellata lighthouse

which stretches along the entire bay, has lifeguards and good facilities (picnic areas, snack bars, etc.). The **Plage de l'Alga**, near Revellata point, is a lot less busy, even in the height of summer. However, if you really love the sea you might prefer to hire a small boat and play Robinson Crusoe for a day at one of the small, isolated inlets further away.

Corse Loisirs
location
Boat rental,
Port de Plaisance
☎ 04 95 65 21 26

Calvi from the air
From the air, Calvi bay is a work of art. You can see the slopes of Mount Cinto, the broken coast as far as Île-Rousse and, on the other side, the massive citadel takes centre stage. The parallel bands of turquoise and white at the bottom of the bay are very striking. The time to go **parascending** is in the late afternoon, when the sun is in the west, to get the best views of the surrounding landscapes. Introduction 100F; one ride 220F.

Le Blockaus
parascending,
Plage de Calvi
☎ 04 95 65 11 20

Seafood delights
Le Cyrnos restaurant
Quai Landry,
20260 Calvi
☎ 04 95 65 06 10
Closed Feb. and Mar.

Nestling in the marina, Le Cyrnos' terrace overlooks the bay and the mountains. You won't find a better place for seafood. The *menu de la mer* (seafood menu – about 100F) offers fresh red mullet, sardines and rockfish, depending on the catch of the day. Another speciality is the wrapped sea bream, which is quite delicious. The meat dishes are accompanied by a tasty potato gratin. Le Cyranos also offers a fine selection of Corsican wines, a perfect opportunity to taste some of the best products of the sea and vine that the island has to offer.

Nelson's eye

It was here, in the sight of Calvi's walls, that Admiral Nelson lost his right eye. In 1794, the English fleet had been attacking the town for nearly 40 days when grapeshot from one of his own men hit Nelson in the face. It was almost as though Corsica was taking early revenge for the two famous defeats that the Admiral would later inflict on the French navy and the islanders' own 'Little Corporal', Napoleon. About twenty years ago a bust of Nelson, originally presented by him to a Corsican family, was rediscovered in a garage in Calvi, and is now housed in the palace formerly occupied by the Bishop of Genoa. One of his fleet's cannons can be seen outside the police station.

Jazz and polyphonic music festivals

One annual event not to be missed is the **Festival de Jazz**, which takes place

CALELLU FISH RESTAURANT

The owner of this excellent restaurant apparently once turned away Sylvester Stallone for not booking in advance. If you are more sensible and make a reservation, you'll be treated to a fabulous meal that will set you back no more than 100F, which is very rare inb this day and age. Not only that, the fish – red mullet, sea bass and scorpion fish – are all caught the same day, so it really couldn't be any fresher. Instead of taking a table inside, try to get a table outside on the terrace, from where you can enjoy a great view of the port and the citadel.

Le Calellu
Quai Landry
☎ 04 95 65 22 18
Open daily in season.
Closed Mon. in Apr., May, Sept. and Oct

in the third week of June. The people of Calvi spend the week of the festival jiving to the sounds of such jazz impressarios as Ella Fitzgerald, Duke Ellington and Charlie Parker, and there are numerous street concerts and solo performances staged in the nightclubs, bars and restaurants. None of the musicians are paid – they come to party, to play and hopefully to be discovered. In September, however, the scene is radically different for the **Rencontres Polyphoniques**. Corsica's unique polyphonic chants (*see* p. 60), consist of at least three voices and are often sung a cappella. During this festival the people of Calvi dress in black and red – black in Corsican tradition and red in honour of the old Red Army, whose famous choirs perform alongside the local soloists and choral groups who sing songs from the Corsican tradition of polyphonic music. The mix works very well. The concerts often take place in the Cathédrale Saint-Jean-Baptiste. For further information contact the Calvi tourist office, Port de Plaisance, ☎ 04 95 6516 67.

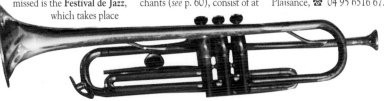

Crafts trail
the traditional skills of Balagne

Route des Artisans
Strada di l'Artigiani

The famous *Strada di l'Artigiani* ('crafts trail') couldn't have a better location. The Balagne region's clifftop villages and old houses perched on rocky outcrops have preserved a timeless charm. The people along the crafts trail feature beekeepers, furniture makers, ironmongers and potters and the journey offers a fascinating insight into the traditional life of this Corsican region.

Calenzana
**7.5 miles (12 km)
SE of Calvi**
E Fritelli biscuit shop
Tiassa Longu,
Calenzana
☎ 04 95 62 78 17
Here they still make biscuits the old-fashioned way – by hand, slow baked and traditionally presented. Christian Perrin perpetuates Corsica's biscuit-making tradition, which is gradually fading. Only Corsican specialities are sold here, including the best *canistrelli* on the island. These are dry biscuits made with almonds and nuts and flavoured with aniseed. They cost from 20F for 3.5 oz (100 g), depending on the shape and size (you can buy them in animal shapes, for example).

Raku ceramics workshop
**Paradella
Route de l'Aéroport,
Calenzana**
☎ 04 95 65 13 61
Mireille Gurfinkel makes ceramics which, in itself, is not amazing. However, she uses an ancient Japanese technique, dating back to the 13thC., which involves taking the pots out the kiln when they are still hot – at 900°C (1,650°F)! This ensures the glazes are bright and shiny, and very striking. You may well be tempted by a little salt pot for 30F.

Traditional ceramic art at the Raku workshop

Village workshop
Place Commune
Haut du Village, Calenzana
☎ 04 95 62 75 83

Everything the island produces is sold at this workshop, including **cakes**, **sweets** and

liqueurs. The workshop specialises in almond-based products, such as amaretti, and other crunchy biscuits, as well as pralines, orgeat syrup, cakes made from chestnut flour, and homemade jams. It also sells aperitif wines and myrtle and mandarin liqueurs.

Pigna
15.5 miles (25 km) N of Calenzana
Casalonga instrument makers
Pigna
☎ 04 95 61 77 15
Professional visits arranged by appt.

You may have thought the Italians were the masters of instrument making, but Corsica comes a close second. Ugo Casalonga puts his heart, soul and considerable expertise into the design and manufacture of guitars and harpsichords. He has also branched out into repairing old and modern stringed instruments.

Spotcheck
B2

Things to do
• Lumio wines
• Colette Clément leather workshop
• Casalonga instrument makers

With children
• Visit the biscuit shop
• Campana glassblowing

Within easy reach
Balage region (pp. 110-113)
Calvi (pp. 114-117)
Île Rousse (pp. 122-125)
Lama (pp. 126-127)

Tourist offices
Calvi: ☎ 04 95 65 16 67
Lama: ☎ 04 95 48 23 90

Lumio
8 miles (13.5 km) N of Calenzana
Clos Colombu wines
Étienne Suzzoni
Propriétaire-récoltant
Chemin de San Pedro, Lumio
☎ 04 95 60 70 68

MUSICAL BOXES

Pigna
☎ 04 95 61 77 34
If you can't make it to a concert of polyphonic choral music, to hear traditional tunes such as *Ciucciarella* or *Muresca*, then this is the place to visit. The splendid musical boxes on sale here are designed and created in traditional fashion by Marie-Claire Darnêal. They are beautifully coloured, expertly carved and finely decorated.

Étienne Suzzoni's fine Calvi AOC wine is remarkably good value (from around 18F a bottle). Restauranteurs know their stuff and more and more are offering the Clos Colombu, a dry, fruity wine that's a treat for the palette. You can also see where and how this wine is made.

A treat for food-lovers

Chez Charles restaurant
At the entrance to Lumio village
☎ 04 95 60 61 71
Reservation advisable. When you've worked up an appetite, head for Chez Charles where you can admire a panoramic view over Calvi bay before diving into a succulent fisherman's salad, followed by rack of lamb with garlic confit or the regional speciality, swordfish escalope. For dessert, the famous nougat

ice cream is unsurpassed. The restaurant terrace is one of the best places in the bay to watch the sunset.

Calvi

Iron and bronze workshop

Atelier du CERM
Formozzelo Calvi
☎ 04 95 65 32 54
The CERM (centre for ethnography and metallurgical research) is a group of craftspeople working with iron and bronze, which are mined in Corsica. The group's workshop produces traditional shepherds' knives, letter openers and jewellery, which are works of art. As well as working in metal, they also use olive, beech and oak wood in their pieces. All the work is carried out using traditional methods, the steel being heated with Corsican charcoal and shaped with a mallet,

before being left to cool down naturally. The traditional shepherds' knives cost around 400F apiece, but they are real masterpieces. As a gift, you may prefer to buy a bronze pendant made by Patrick Martin. This piece of jewellery features a man with his arms in the air and is aptly titled 'free man' – 140F with the chain. You can also visit the forge and see how the pieces are made, from the extraction of the raw materials to the finished item.

Feliceto

NE of Calenzana
Campana glassblowing

Verrerie Corse
Feliceto
☎ 04 95 61 73 05
The superb blue hand-engraved carafes on sale at the Verrerie Corse are made entirely from blown glass. They will cost you upwards of 300F, but each one is inspected by the **master glassblower** for quality. The craft of glassblowing involves mastering the right combination of blowing and heating to produce the final product. Given the amount of effort required, it's easy to see why this traditional craft is dying out.

Clos Reginu and E Prove wines
Domaine Maestracci
Route de Santa Reparata
☎ 04 95 61 72 11

The vineyards of Monte Grosse already produced a wine with a good reputation (*U vino di prove*) before Roger Maestracci, a doctor, replanted the estate in 1945. At Clos Reginu, you can taste Calvi AOC wines, including some full-bodied reds, well-rounded rosés with fruity and slightly spicy aromas, and fresh white wines with delicious floral fragrances (sold in bulk or by the bottle).

OCCIGLIONI LEATHER WORKSHOP
☎ 04 95 60 51 53.

Collette Clément sells all types of luxury leather goods in her workshop, all made the traditional way from sheep and cow hide. Especially good are her collection of bags, belts and wallets made from soft but strong leather. Wallets cost 250-300F, bags from 300F. It is also possible to order your own design.

Occiglioni
N of Feliceto
Occiglioni pottery workshop
Poterie Occiglioni
☎ 04 95 60 07 04

Palasca
NE of Feliceto
Broomberg craft forge
Forges d'Art Broomberg
Route de la Gare, Palasca
☎ 04 95 61 35 44

At the Forges d'Art Broomberg, you can buy first-class, unique and original pieces of sculpture. Martin Broomberg will also adapt any pieces you bring him and make gates and furniture to order. He works with bronze and copper equally well. Count on three to six months between order and delivery.

Lozari
E of Île Rousse
Lozari honey
GAEC de Lozari
Michel and François Gacon, Route de Belgodere, Lozari
☎ 04 95 60 18 13

If you are feeling a little peckish, this is the perfect place to stop. Here you'll find a huge range of honeys, with such unusual flavours as asphodel, thistle, Corsican maquis, strawberry and chestnut, as well as all sorts of honey-derived products including mead, pollen, and vinegar. Note that the shop is only open between 5-7pm.

A wide range of tasteful objects can be bought here, from tiny salt cellars to huge vases. Marie-France Loddi makes pieces using a blend of clays, coating them in a mottled or ash-based glaze. They make **excellent gift ideas** (from 30F).

Île Rousse
warm and lively

The name 'Île Rousse' means 'red island', although there are, in fact, three islands – Pietra, Brocciu and Piana – which are all connected to mainland Corsica by bridge. When the setting sun casts a distinctive red hue over the rocks, it's easy to see where the name comes from.

Beach life in the centre of town

A distinctive feature of Île Rousse is that it's only a few steps from the sun-drenched café terraces of the town to the hot sands and the sea. The **old-town beach** (Plage de la Vieille Ville), which extends as far as the village of Monticello, has a family atmosphere, with lifeguards in season making it a safe place for children to swim. A little further north are various coves which can only be reached by boat, departing from Île Rousse or Saint-Florent (p. 128). These are much sought after by sunbathers and naturists for their guaranteed peace and tranquility.

Photographic tips

The best place to photograph the daily blaze of light from

the neighbouring islands is from the coast road that snakes towards the mouth of the Ostriconi river to the north. From here, you can see the islands, the old town and the beaches. Don't forget your camera!

Playing boules in the shadow of Pasquale Paoli

As Calvi remained faithful to Genoa, the Corsican independence leader, Pasquale Paoli (p. 50), looking for a route to the sea in the west, chose Île Rousse. Founded in 1758, the port became a French commune in 1805. The Place Paoli has a bust of this Corsican

Pasquale Paoli, founder of Île Rousse

A TRADITIONAL TAVERN

Chez Paco
18, Rue Napoléon
☎ 04 95 60 03 76
Open daily in season. Closed Jan. and Sun. pm in winter.

Right in the heart of the old town, **Chez Paco** is a traditional tavern in the basement of an old bourgeois house. Stone walls and wooden beams give the place a real sense of style and keep the building pleasantly cool in summer. On the menu there's a wealth of sumptuous dishes, including bouillabaisse, fish stew, stuffed mussels and paella – the menu has a decidedly Andalucian flavour. Flamenco music in the background adds to the ambience. They even serve very late if there's a good atmosphere. You can also come just for a couple of drinks. Expect to pay around 100F, wine included.

Spotcheck
B1

Things to do

• Algajola beaches
• Windsurfing and naturism at Bocca di Carbonaghjia beaches
• Balagne train-tramway

With children

• Donkey rides at Île Rousse
• Reginu mini-golf
• Musée Océanographique

Within easy reach

Balagne region (pp. 110-112)
Crafts trail (pp. 118-121)
Calvi (pp. 114-117)
Lama (pp. 126-127)

Tourist office

Île Rousse:
☎ 04 95 60 04 35

hero and is now a focal point for boules players, who meet in the square every afternoon, after their siesta. The game of boules is a highly colourful event, which can involve a few heated exchanges. However, an aperitif after the game allows the players to quickly resolve their differences. You'll have a perfect view of the whole proceedings from one of the terraced cafés that surround the square, which is also home to the island's biggest luxury hotel, the **Napoléon Bonaparte**, ☎ 04 95 60 06 09. Double rooms cost 460-800F a night, depending on the time of the year. Closed October and April.

Like a fish to water

Musée Océanographique
Plage de Ginepara
Open 1 May-30 Sept. Guided visits at 11am, 3pm and 5pm.
☎ **04 95 60 27 81**
Admission charge.
The Île Rousse museum of oceanography is unique,

because the wide variety of sea creatures on show are kept together, interacting in the same water. With three huge glass tanks, the museum offers a **complete view of the underwater world**. You can watch the sea creatures swim about in their recreated natural habitat with rocks, coral and sea anemones in abundance. The museum is also a research centre for oceanographers. Here they study how the sea creatures live together and interact. The results of their research are explained to you in the form of a commentary during the visit.

A Corsican book fair

Even if you don't speak the Corsican language, this book fair, which takes place in June every year, is quite fascinating. The atmosphere is warm and people come from afar to swap and sell all sorts of books. A good number of books are published in Corsican, but there are also many new and old books about Corsica written in or translated into French. In the surrounding area, they also stage a number of other shows and exhibitions

that complement the fair, including Corsican singing, polyphonic chanting, painting exhibitions and street entertainment of all kinds. As you might expect, the local cafés get extremely busy. Further information available from **Île Rousse tourist office**, Place Paoli, ☎ 04 95 60 04 35

Donkey rides

Children love donkeys. Of course, you'll have to be patient and perhaps follow a few steps behind… but it is the holidays, and your children will have so much fun. A guide will escort the children around the streets and squares of Île Rousse for

just 40F. The donkeys are calm and gentle and the walk lasts about 30 minutes, unless they're feeling stubborn – the donkeys, that is! The rides start at the tourist office in the Place Paoli.

The little island train

You can travel from Île Rousse to Calvi and back on the **Balagne train-tramway**. It's a pleasant journey through Corsican scrubland and shaded valleys where you can see some old winding donkey trails. As the little train weaves slowly along the coastline, you have plenty of time to take in the beautiful surroundings and panoramic views of the long beaches, the inlets and the pine forests. The windows of the train also open so that you can take photos. However, this twisting, undulating journey is not recommended for people who suffer from travel sickness. There are about 10 return journeys made each day which cost 50F per person. For **information** contact: Île Rousse station, ☎ 04 95 60 00 50 and Calvi station, ☎ 04 95 65 00 61

Monticello

3 miles (5 km)
S of Île Rousse

The charming village of Monticello

This pretty village is nestled in the mountains overlooking Île Rousse and is well worth the 3-mile journey from the coast. From the little square there is a wonderful panoramic view that extends as far as Calvi. Tiled white and ochre houses blend together

and the narrow cobbled streets are an ideal place for a pleasant stroll. There are also a number of walking trails that you can follow, which will take you into the Corsican scrubland (signposted from

The clifftop village of Algajola

the Place de l'Église). If you're hungry after your walk and fancy dining at a great restaurant, **Pastorella** offers an unusual starter of blackbird pâté followed by a main course of grilled goat for around 150F including wine.

Pastorella
Monticello
☎ 04 95 60 05 65
Last orders 11pm in season. Closed Nov. and Sun. evenings Dec. to end Mar

MINI GOLF WITH A SPLENDID VIEW

There are few golf courses on Corsica, so make the most of the small Golf de Reginu club, 3.5 miles (6 km) from Île Rousse. There are six holes, a putting green and a practice range. Non-players can enjoy a relaxing drink in the clubhouse or, alternatively, walk into the village of Monticello for superb views of the coast, Île Rousse and the islands.

Golf de Reginu
☎ 04 95 61 51 41
Open daily, all-year round.

Algajola

9.5 miles (15 km)
SW of Île Rousse

A clifftop village with sandy beaches

This little village combines the charm of the clifftop villages of the Haute-Balagne area with all the delights of a seaside town. Old Algajola includes the citadel, home of the regional governor in the 17thC. (when the town was the capital of the Balagne region), an attractive fortified church and some narrow alleyways that give the place the appearance of a château fort. There is also an old quarry of yellow- and pink-coloured porphyritic rock, from which the base of Paris' famous Vendôme column was extracted. Arriving at Algajola from Île Rousse, you cannot miss the 'Paperweight', a 300-ton (300,000-kg) porphyry monolith, which has lain here for 165 years. Algajola, the seaside town, has two good beaches, one popular with windsurfers and the other with naturists. Both get crowded during the summer months. You can get to Algajola by train from both Calvi and Île Rousse – it is virtually mid-way between the two. Those who want to get away from it all will prefer the white sandy bays of Bocca di Carbonagjia, 1 mile (2 km) away, at the exit to Île Rousse (take the little dirt track on the right).

Lama back to nature

L ama is the capital of the tiny Ostriconi region and clings tightly to the side of a deep valley that follows the river to the coast. Lama is a tranquil town, with narrow, steep cobbled streets and flower-filled squares that offer excellent views of the whole valley and the Agriates area.

Country comfort

Whether you choose a gîte, rented accommodation or a farmstead, Lama offers real rural comfort. There are many options for accommodation in the surrounding area too. At the **Ostriconi tourist office** (Maison du Pays d'Accueil de l'Ostriconi, ☎ 04 95 48 23 90. Open 9am-noon and 2-5pm; closed Sunday out of season), you can get all the information you need about the region's attractions and facilities. Average accommodation prices for a week range from 1,500F in low season to 3,500F in July and August.

Ostriconi on horseback
Ferme-Auberge Costa
Place de l'Église, Lama
☎ 04 95 48 22 99
Open all-year round. This is quite simply one of the best addresses in Corsica. Firstly, because of Françoise Costa's delicious cooking, using all local produce. The menu includes game terrine, wild-boar stew, tart with maquis herbs and river trout (around 120F per head). Secondly, because the **Costa farmhouse inn** also offers four pleasant guestrooms. Thirdly,

because its location at the entrance to the village has a beautiful panoramic view across the whole of Ostriconi and the Agriates area. And, last but not least, because you also have the opportunity to explore the whole area on horseback by day and by night (with a guide). Prices vary according to requirements.

Pretend you're Indiana Jones for a day

The Désert des Agriates is not quite the Sahara, but it certainly gets hot. Here the sun blazes down on a wild, arid landscape of bushy scrubland and rocky cliffs. The area used to be forested, but the trees were burnt down over time by shepherds who wanted to increase the amount of grazing land for their flocks. There's a coastal path, which you can

The Désert des Agriates has many walking trails in an unspoilt natural environment

Spotcheck
B2

Things to do
• Ostriconi on horseback
• Walking in the Désert des Agriates
• International film festival

Within easy reach
Balagne region (pp. 110-113)
Île Rousse (pp. 128-131)
Crafts trail (pp. 118-121)

Tourist office
Lama:
☎ 04 95 48 23 90

Join from the beach, at the mouth of the Ostriconi river, that takes you some way into this 'Corsican jungle'. Don't attempt to follow the old stony trails in the Désert des Agriates as they are usually overgrown and difficult to make out. There's another beautiful signposted trail that runs from the church in Lama to the neighbouring village of **Urtaca**. This walk takes about three hours. If you're feeling brave, you can try scaling the heights of Monte Asto (5,000 ft/1,535 m – 4 hours from Lama) or the Bocca di San Pancrazio (2 hours from Urtaca). These paths are fine for family walks but don't forget to wear sun hats and carry a good supply of water.

Lama international festival

Amazingly, Lama organises an annual cinema festival that is very much an international affair. Outdoor screenings are open to all (arrive early as the festival is starting to attract large audiences) and the long and short films shown cover issues relating to rural traditions, lifestyle and the countryside in general. The shows end with conferences, discussions, and exhibitions. Information from the local tourist office.
☎ 04 95 48 23 90.

PHOTOGRAPHIC MEMORIES

The former village stables in Lama, a huge rectangular building with narrow doorways, is home to a particularly interesting and ongoing photo exhibition. The displays in the huge pillared hall recount the histories of **traditional Corsican professions** through photos, post-cards and written accounts. These métiers include the work of shepherds, fishermen, olive and chestnut growers – professions which are still very much alive in Corsica, making the comparison of how much, or little, has changed all the more fascinating. The visit is a lot more interesting with a guide (contact the Maison de Pays information centre or the Costa farmhouse inn), who can give you all the background information on the customs and characters of the rural life of the region. The exhibition offers a passionate look at a past which still enthrals Corsicans to this day.

Saint-Florent
just say 'Saint-Flo'

Saint-Florent, or 'Saint-Flo' as it is more commonly known, is the most lively, fashionable resort in Corsica. Although the town's winter population only reaches 1,000, in summer it's a different story. If it's style you're after, then this is the place to come. Don't forget your shades!

Dine on the terrace

Shielded by the start of Corsica's mountainous backbone, Saint-Florent is one of the most popular holiday destinations for pleasure seekers. The Place des Portes is the bustling heart of this thriving resort. The narrow streets of the old town are very stylish, although in summer the marina is the place to be, with its vibrant bar terraces

and crowded quays. The port is particularly busy in the late afternoon. If you can't bear to leave, **La Gaffe** (☎ 04 95 37 00 12, closed 15 Nov.-1 Feb. and Tuesday lunchtime in the summer season) is a good fish restaurant. They serve food until late if you fancy dinner beneath the stars (expect to pay about 150F per person including drinks).

Finding a place to stay

Saint-Florent tourist office,
Route du Cap Corse
☎ 04 95 37 06 04
Open daily 8.30am-12.30pm and 2-7pm (2-5pm out of season). Closed Sat. pm and Sun. out of season.
If you're looking for a hotel or rented accommodation in Saint-Florent for the summer you need to book by January.

It's that popular. And, it may be a little obvious, but the best places do get booked up first. However, it's not essential that you stay right in the centre. The little surrounding villages of Murato, Sorio, San Pietro di Tenda and Rapale all have good guesthouses. The rooms are no more expensive than the hotels and the atmosphere is far more jovial. Expect to pay upward of 250F per night for half board. A list of accommodation in the Nebbio region is available from the tourist office.

Beautiful beaches

The best beaches are only really accessible by sea. There are several boats that leave from the marina, departing at regular intervals from 9am and returning from 4pm onwards, costing around 50F per person. **U Seleccia** (☎ 04 95 36 90 78) has services between 15 June and

RELAXING ON 'D-DAY BEACH'

Plage de Saleccia
6 miles (10 km) from Casta (7.5 miles/12 km NE of Saint-Florent)

It's difficult to imagine 3,000 soldiers landing on this tranquil beach, but all the D-Day scenes in the film 'The Longest Day' were filmed here. Saleccia is heaven on earth – like a Tahitian lagoon with turquoise water and hot white sand, which is peaceful even in the middle of July. Rolling dunes separate the beach from a magnificent pine forest (the only Aleppo pine forest on the island). It's safe to swim, but the beach is not supervised. There's just one forest ranger, living in a small sheepfold overlooking the beach, who patrols the forest making sure the habitat is protected and minimising fire hazards. Although the only track to the beach runs for 6 miles (10 km) from the hamlet of Casta, this paradise is definitely worth the effort. Hire a mountain bike, leave early in the morning with a picnic and don't return before sunset. You'll be able to get a large stretch of beach to yourself, with little chance of another film crew turning up!

30 September. **Vedette Popeye** (☎ 04 95 37 19 07) will take you to the **Loto** and **Saleccia beaches** (p. 76), which are difficult to reach overland. The resort does, however, have other family beaches that are easy to get to. The large **Plage de la Roya**, beneath the citadel, is the only beach with lifeguards in summer. To the north, **Olzu** and **Tettola beaches** have no lifeguard, but are well sheltered and nearer if you're staying on the Patrimonio side.

Boat hire
Dominique Plaisance
Lotissement Saint-Flor
☎ 04 95 37 07 08

Open 1 Apr.-15 Oct., 9am-5pm.
Don't worry if you miss the first boat out to Saleccia beach. You don't need a licence to hire a fishing boat, canoe, sea kayak or motor boat – you can simply take your pick. Hiring a boat will also give you the chance to visit the beautiful western coves on the way. Kayaks or canoes are a good idea, because you can stay very close to the coast and stop wherever you want. If you can get a group of people together, you could hire a six-seater motorised rubber dinghy (about 500F in peak season), with which you get a coastal map.

Spotcheck
B1

Things to do
• Mountain biking to the Saleccia lagoon
• Sea kayaking or canoeing
• Altore Parachuting and canyoning
• Murato gourmet stop

Within easy reach
Bastia (p. 102-103)
Cap Corse (p. 106-109)
Lama (p. 126-127)
Île Rousse (p. 122-125)

Tourist office
St-Florent:
☎ 04 95 37 06 04

Saint-Florent tourist office,
Route du Cap Corse,
☎ 04 95 37 06 04. Open daily
8.30am-12.30pm and 2-7pm.
Closed weekends out of
season.

Dancing the night away

La Conca d'Oro
Route Oletta,
20217 Saint-Florent
☎ 04 95 39 00 46
**Open weekends in June
and every evening in
July and Aug.**

No fashionable resort is
complete without a **stylish
nightclub**. The La Conca
d'Oro nightclub in Saint-
Florent bay is located 3 miles
(5 km) from the town on the
Bastia road, at the exit of the
little village of Orletta. It's
housed in a restored sheepfold,
with an open-air dance floor
looking onto a small garden
of sweet-smelling Corsican
scrub. The atmosphere is that
of a typical seaside nightclub,
with clients sporting shorts
and tanned shoulders.
Admission 70F, includes one
free drink.

Say a prayer for Saint Flor

Saint-Florent is home to one
of the island's most beautiful
cathedrals. A short cultural
and historical tour of the
**Santa Maria Assunta
cathedral** will leave you
enchanted. Built on the site
of a Roman edifice and one
of the last remains of the
ancient town of Nebbio that
existed before Saint-Florent,
the cathedral probably dates
back to the late 12thC.
With its three Romanesque
naves, its highly ornate,
sculpted facade and wings,
the cathedral has an airy and
unusually elegant feel. It's
one of the better examples
of Pisan architectural
development – rejecting the
heavy edifices of the first
Romanesque age in favour
of sculpted buildings. If you
want to light a candle by the
wooden statue of Saint Flor,
which sits enthroned on top
of the altar inside the church,
you'll have to ask for the key
at the tourist office.

Murato

11 miles (17.5 km)
S of Saint-Florent

Traditional farmhouse dining

**Campu di Monte
farmhouse inn**
20239 Murato
☎ 04 95 37 64 39
**Open daily 1 July-15
Sept. Open Fri., Sat.
and Sun. lunchtime out
of season. Reservation
required.**

The Ferme-Auberge Campu
di Monte has long enjoyed a
good reputation on the island,
so make sure you book. With
its traditional living quarters,
grange, chestnut drying sheds
and old-fashioned oven, the
farm (although renovated)
looks as it did in the 18thC.

ADVENTURE SPORTS
Altore
Saint-Florent
☎ 04 95 37 19 30

After a week of beaches, bars, sun and relaxation, why not try something a little more adventurous, such as hang-gliding, diving, horse riding or horse jumping. At Altore you'll see Corsica from an entirely different angle – the sky. You can take your first parachute jump, with

lessons for beginners and those who want to improve their skills. From the sky, the bay looks more beautiful than from any other vantage point. Back on the ground, you can visit the rocky canyons or go rock climbing south of Saint-Florent. You'll be harnessed and very carefully supervised, so you needn't worry about safety. If these high adrenaline activities make your hair stand on end, maybe you'd prefer a night-time horse-trek instead, to explore the rocky hinterland of Nebbio. Around 200-300F for each activity. A week-long parachuting course, with qualified instructors, costs 2,400F.

Inside, there are a number of small separate dining rooms, some with magnificent stone walls – perfect for dining with friends or for more intimate candlelit dinners. You might even get to sit by the fireplace, which is a beautiful wooden gem, more than 300 years old. As for the menu, your hosts Pauline and Henry, certainly know how to look after their guests, offering soup, a fine selection of cold meats, courgette fritters, lasagne, farm veal in sauce, stuffed vegetables and *fiadone*. Their food is masterful in every way. Make sure not to miss out on their wonderful assortment of cheeses, especially the Casgiu Minatu cheese – a small goat's cheese finished with eau-de-vie, served with dried figs. Up in the Murato highlands, Pauline and Henry keep traditional Corsican hospitality very much alive – you can eat as much as you like of each dish. Minimum 200F per head.

Rapale
12 miles (19 km)
S of Saint-Florent
A picturesque village

Rapale is one of the few Corsican communes not to have a coastline. Nevertheless, the village is one of the most charming in the Haute-Corse region. There's a delightful half-hour walk, leaving from the little village square, that heads across the Corsican scrubland, chestnut forest and white rocks, up to the Nebbio highlands and finishing up at the San Cesario chapel. From here, the magnificent **panoramic view** takes in the whole of the coastline and most of the Balagne region. The chapel is of little architectural interest, but the building's combination of green and white stone is certainly highly original. Return to Rapale on the same path (2.5 miles/4 km round-trip).

Rapale, one of Haute-Corse's most charming villages

Corte the soul of Corsica

From Cap Corse to Bonifacio, the town of Corte is renowned and respected like the head of a Corsican clan. Pasquale Paoli made Corte his capital when he declared Corsica's independence. Untamed, rugged and beautiful, Corte is now a student town and a focal point for the whole island.

The piece was sculpted in 1867 by Auguste Bartholdi, who is more famous for the Statue of Liberty in New York.

From the heights of the citadel
☎ 04 95 45 25 45
Open 10am-8pm in season and 10am-noon and 2-5pm out of season.
→ *Admission charge.*

The overhang at the cliff's edge gives this citadel the feel

Cours Paoli street life
Named after the main man himself, this road is the hub of life and commerce in Corte. In summer the atmosphere remains electric well into the night, even if Corte itself is not reputed for its nightlife. The Cours Paoli runs into the quaint little square of the same name, where there's a magnificent bronze statue of the Duke of Padoue.

of a Cathar castle. Enter from the Cours Paoli. The oldest part of the citadel dates back to the early 15thC. A long stairway made of Restonica marble takes you to the tower, from where there's a fantastic **panoramic view** to the distant mountains. The citadel is used as a university annexe and is also the headquarters of the Regional contemporary art foundation (FRAC) and home to an anthropological museum (Museé d'Anthropologie de la Corse, ☎ 04 95 45 25 45. Open daily in season 10am-7.45pm. Out of season, contact the museum for opening hours).

Place Gaffori

This, the second of the town's squares, pays tribute to the Corte's other hero, General Gaffori, who was overthrown in 1753 by the Genoese because of his attempts to free Corsica from Italian control. The General was not only opposed to the Italians, he also despised the French, and thus had enemies on both sides. The Genoese eventually exploited clan rivalries to get rid of him.

Place Poilu

The Place Poilu is a small and very pretty square in front of the entrance to the citadel. The house at No. 1 is a doubly famous birthplace. The General Arrighi de Casanova – known more widely as the

Duke of Padoue and related to the Bonaparte family on his mother's side – was born here in 1778. This general went on to rally the Italian army and follow Napoleon in Egypt, Spain, Wagram and Russia, before later becoming Corsican Senator. Napoleon's older brother, Joseph Bonaparte, was also born here (1768). He went on to become King of Naples and then Spain. Opposite, the Palais National, the old residence of Pasquale Paoli, stages a variety of exhibitions related to the history of the region. For more information contact the **tourist office**, inside the citadel.

The tale of Saint Théophile

Biagio de Signori was born in Corte on 30 October 1676. At the age of 17 he joined the Franciscan order of monks under the name of Théophile. He studied theology in Italy before returning to Corsica. In 1732 he petitioned the Prince of Wurtemberg, who was invading the island at the time, to spare the town of Corte. In the Église de l'Annonciation (under restoration), above Place Paoli, an enormous painting depicts Théophile pleading with the conqueror for the good of his town. This protector of Corte was beatified in 1886 and canonised by Pope Pious XI on 29 June 1930.

Andrei's fabulous wooden toys
1, Place Gaffori
20250 Corte
This is one of the most beautiful wooden toy shops on the island. When wood is

finely carved and polished, it gives a toy a real sense of majesty. These works of art are not just for children but for collectors too. Andrei is also a specialist in wooden puzzles. Here you can find a souvenir to assemble yourself, for example, a map of Corsica, a Moor's head, an animal or a typical landscape.

Traditional Corsican weaving
Tissage Mariani
2, Rue du Docteur-Santiaggi
☎ 04 95 47 05 52
Using wool or cotton, Dominique Mariani makes everything by hand. Her products (on sale in all the region's markets) are really

original – no two pieces are the same. She has worked in Corte for 17 years and has many loyal customers. Whether you choose a scarf, a Corsican wool jacket, a cotton waistcoat or a rug, you're sure to be delighted. Prices start at 200F.

Corte by miniature train
☎ 04 95 46 05 17
(in summer)
and 06 09 95 70 36
(in winter)

Reservation required. The young and young at heart love this little train. U trenu travels the streets of Corte, with a push-button commentary to keep you interested as you go along. It's a simple way to introduce your children to history, culture and traditions that are sometimes difficult to understand. There are several return journeys throughout the day, departing from the town car park.

Spend an evening in Corte
U Spuntinu restaurant
Rue des Deux Villas
(lower town)
☎ 04 95 46 17 04
Here you can have a real Corsican meal for less than 100F. U Spuntinu is a

seductive restaurant, serving traditional Corsican soup, made with beans, parsnips and bacon pieces, as well as charcuterie, grilled goat (considered a delicacy), roasted wild boar and the classic fiadone dessert (p. 35), all washed down with a good Corte wine.

After all this delicious food you'll be in the perfect mood for a Pietra, the delicious local chestnut beer, at **Bip's** bar (Cours Paoli, ☎ 04 95 46 06 26), before dancing the night away at the An 2000 nightclub, located in the same place as the restaurant.

Corsica from the air
Aéroclub de Corte
Aérodrome Centre,
Corse RN200,
20250 Corte
☎ 04 95 46 21 00

With two feet firmly on the ground, Corsica is a magnificent place. But from the air, the view is magical: the mountains curve around gushing rivers, gorges split the cliffs and little villages are perched on the hillsides. The island's contours stand out clearly and it's probably the best way to see Corsica's amazing natural habitat. The Corte flying club offers a variety of flight packages. First flights cost upwards of 200F.

Central Corsica on horseback
Ferme Équestre L'Albadu
Ancienne Route d'Ajaccio
(old Ajaccio road)
☎ **04 95 46 24 55**
The region around Corte probably lends itself to horse trekking better than any other in Corsica. The paths are well organised and the horses are happy to venture through forest, undergrowth and Corsican scrub. At the L'Albadu horse farm, you can pay for treks on an hourly basis (100F depending on the number of people), by the day or for several days. However, if you simply want a typical Corsican meal here, you need to book in advance.

The Restonica refuge
Le Refuge
☎ **04 95 46 09 13**
Open 1 Apr.-30 Sept.
Beside the Restonica river, right in the centre of the valley, Lucien and Angèle Baldacci provide a warm welcome in their wood-furnished restaurant. Here you can try herbed tart, sautéed lamb and Corsican soup – a great traditional Corsican meal for just 100F a head.

After the meal you can take a pleasant walk in the wonderful countryside that surrounds the inn.

A walk through the Tavignano gorges

This splendid walk, suitable for all, starts from Rue du Colonel Feracci and finishes at the citadel. Having walked all the way along the narrow pass and then crossed the valley (there are other places to cross, but make sure to find your way back to the signposted route), you'll come to a fun and easy-to-cross **monkey bridge**. If you fancy a dip, this is the place, so don't forget your swimming costume. However, watch out as the water is quite cold, even in summer. If you want to spend the night in the Gorges de Tavignano, stop at U Tavignanu, which has a few dormitories sleeping up to five, and a campsite. From the bridge, you'll need to retrace your footsteps for about an hour. You can't miss the signs.

U Tavignanu
Vallée de Tavignano
☎ **04 95 46 16 85**
80F a night including breakfast
Further information from the Maison du Parc in the citadel
☎ **04 95 46 27 44**
(in season only).

Niolo region
the land of tall blondes

L egend has it that the inhabitants of this little region, who are generally tall, with blonde hair and pale skin, are direct descendants of the Norman and Breton invaders. This is a magnificently wild and once inaccesible area, wedged in the mountains at the heart of Corsica. Most of the locals are shepherds, and they come together once a year for a big fair and singing competition.

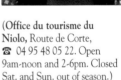

(**Office du tourisme du Niolo,** Route de Corte, ☎ 04 95 48 05 22. Open 9am-noon and 2-6pm. Closed Sat. and Sun. out of season.)

Monte Cinto

Monte Cinto is the highest mountain on the island at 8,900 ft (2,710 m) and dominates the plains of central Niolo. The mountain authorities organise many walks up the mountain, catering for all levels of ability. The 'Genoese bridge' route (*des ponts Génois*) is one of the easiest and best walks. Departing from the centre of the village of Albertacce, this trail takes you on a six-hour round-trip on the old path that the Genoese invaders created to cross the mountains more easily. Don't forget to bring plenty to eat and drink. Departing from Casamaccioli, the 'panoramic' path (*le panoramique*) has wonderful scenery. These two paths are signposted in orange, but please note that the markers are often difficult to locate.

Getting to the region

Until the 1950s, when the Vergio pass was properly redeveloped, it was very difficult to reach the heart of Niolo. The old route, via the Scala di Santa Regina, was often impassable in winter. In summer, however, you can enjoy pleasant walks along the old route. Dark, natural granite corridors dominate the deep canyons. The views are stunning so most visitors come to Niolo to go walking. There are several experts, guides and park staff who lead walks for all levels of ability, stopping over in a hostel for the night. If you want to go on a long hike, it's advisable to go with a group. If there are six or more of you the price is very affordable (about 200F per person). A list of guides is available from the Niolo tourist office.

Spotcheck
B2

Things to do

- Swimming in Nino lake
- Cesta sheepfold walk
- Monte Cinto walking trails
- Charcuterie shopping

With children

- Swimming in Radule waterfall

Within easy reach

Corte (pp. 132-135)
Venaco (pp. 142-143)
Bocagnano (pp. 140-141)
Porto bay (pp. 100-101)

Tourist office

Calacuccia:
☎ 04 95 48 05 22

Those who would like to climb right to the top of the mountain must hire a guide. Paul-André Acquaviva is one of the most experienced. He'll show you all of Cinto's hidden secrets. The climbs are personalised to cater for your own individual requirements. It's advisable to go with a group, and if there are six or more of you the price is very good (around 200F per person). A list of guides is available at the Niolo tourist office.

Scala di Santa Regina

This is the oldest route to Niolo – a huge, natural, deep corridor of granite. There's a path alongside the Scala that goes to Corte, but fans of lunar landscapes will prefer the walk signposted in orange, which follows the sheep route to the summer pastures. The walks are suitable for all.

Calacuccia

The best Corsican charcuterie
Jean Acquaviva
(Producer-charcutier)
Calacuccia
☎ **04 95 48 04 85**
Open daily in season 8am-8pm. Out of season, 8am-5pm.

The fresh air and pastures of Niolo make for first-class cattle. Jean-Pierre Acquaviva inherited this charcuterie business, dating back several generations in Calacuccia. Jean-Pierre is more than delighted to give advice on

the best times to buy the different varieties of *lonzu*, *salsiccia* and other *figatelli* (*see* pp. 32-33). Niolo is also the cheapest place on the island for cured meats. There's even a restaurant where you can eat delicious charcuterie products for a mere 59F.

A gourmet lunch
Le Corsica restaurant
Route du Couvent,
Calacuccia
☎ **04 95 48 01 31**
Open daily. Closed evenings in winter.
This is real, hearty, **traditional Corsican cooking**, using only locally produced ingredients, and excellent value for money. Here they will treat you to *brocciu*, white bean gratin with herbs from the Corsican maquis and a chestnut tart for about 100F. Don't eat too much if you're planning an afternoon walk though, or

you'll regret it. In spring, the *brocciu* omelette is a real speciality but the cheese does not keep well, so if you have it in summer it will not have the authentic taste.

Casamaccioli
3 miles (5 km)
S of Calacuccia
Corsica's oldest pilgrimage
If you're in the area, this event should not be missed. The **pilgrimage of La Santa** (Santa Maria della Stella) takes place each year on 8-10 September. It originates in the legend of a star that appeared above Selva to guide ships in difficulty to the coast. Later, when pirates forced the monks of Selva to take refuge in Casamaccioli, the monks took the statue of Santa Maria, and the tradition, with them. The people of Casamaccioli,

all dressed in white, parade the statue in the village. The festival coincides with the end of summer, when shepherds would traditionally bring their flocks down from the upland pastures as the days started to grow shorter and the sheep needed the long grass of the lowlands. It's also the occasion of Corsica's largest folk festival, with singing competitions in which the shepherds sing tradional songs, make speeches and declaim improvised poems

(who said rap was new!). In former days, gambling was allowed during the period of the celebrations. As recently as 30 years ago, hundreds of

The shepherds' hut in Radule

SWIMMING IN NINO LAKE

Popaghija
8.5 miles (13.5 km)
SW of Calacuccia.
The Lac de Nino is one of Niolo's prettiest lakes. The return journey takes about six hours, but take your time along the rocky path that leads to the lake, as there are wonderful panoramic views of the Niolo mountains, fast-flowing rivers and mountain pastures. Legend dictates that the lake is the entrance to hell, but it's also a lovely spot for swimming. From the Maison Forestière de Popaghja (information centre), between the villages of Niolo and the Col de Vergio, follow the yellow markers along the river. The climb is suitable for all.

thousands of francs would change hands, as the event attracted smugglers and money launderers.

A night at the altar

You might expect some sort of religious experience if you stay at Madame Ingrand's gîte, as it's housed in a converted church, located in the village of **Casamaccioli** (☎ 04 95 48 03 47). Half board can be arranged for groups, and reservations are essential. The place is very picturesque and extremely busy. Its lakeside location is a big attraction. If the gîte is full don't worry, just go back down to the Saint-François convent in Niolo (☎ 04 95 48 00 11), located on the road from Calacuccia to Albertacce. Here they have a few double beds. Prices start at 60F per night in the dormitories.

The Radule waterfall

A pleasant two-hour walk takes you to the Cascade de Radule, one of Corsica's most beautiful waterfalls. You'll come across a few other waterfalls on the way, perfect for refreshing dips in the deep green pools that lie beneath them. Make sure you stop to take a look at the abandoned **Radule shepherds' huts**, whose architecture is very characteristic of rural Corsica.

This easy walk starts at the Fer à Cheval, 2.5 miles (4 km) below the Col de Vergio, and follows the GR 20.

Lozzi
1 mile (2 km)
W of Calacuccia

The walk to the Cesta sheepfold

The walk to this superb dry stone shepherd's hut on the Cinto road is very pleasant and not as hard as the climb to the top of Monte Cinto. If you ask Paul-André Acquaviva (a qualified guide) to accompany you, he'll give you an interesting lesson on the region's plant and animal life. The best piece of advice is not to attempt the walk alone. Get together a group of six to eight people and split the cost of the guided walk (1,000F if you spend the night in a hostel).

The vengeful sister

This is one of the greatest and most revealing of Corsican legends. In the early 19thC., there was a young shepherdess, by the name of Maria Felica, who spent her time in the Calacuccia town square, calling for her brother's murder to be avenged. Marie Felica's fiancé refused to take up her cause and went to spend his time with his animals in the pastures. On his return to the village, he discovered the coffin of his loved one, who had died of grief and shame. He too died soon after. Today, in the shops of the region's bigger towns, you'll find souvenirs that pay tribute to this vendetta, with the following inscription: *Ma per fa la to vindetta stà sicuru basta anch'ella*, which means, 'Your sister will suffer to avenge you, you can be sure of that'.

Bocognano serene Corsica

Bocognano is a traditional but changing town, some way off the beaten track, that has several attractions. It's close to the Vizzavona pass (3,900 ft/1,200 m), wedged between the Migliacello peak (7,395 ft/2,254 m) and Monte Renoso (7,716 ft/2,352 m), where east meets west. It's also the capital of chestnut production. More often than not Bocognano is passed through en route to other, more popular places, but why not break with tradition. You won't regret it.

Traditional chestnut mill, Bocognano

A choice of rural cuisine

A Tanedda
☎ 04 95 27 42 44
Open Apr.-end Sept.

L'Ustaria
☎ 04 95 27 41 10
Open daily July-Aug. Closed Mar. and evenings, out of season.

These two restaurants will make your mouth water. At the **A Tenedda farmhouse inn**, you can enjoy vegetable tarts in summer and wild boar and grilled goat in the spring, all washed down with a red wine from Ajaccio. You'll then be ready for a siesta in the shade of a chestnut tree. The **L'Ustaria restaurant**, in the Place de l'Église, serves even more refined Corsican cuisine. This is your best bet in rural Corsica for sea anemone fritters with myrtle. At either place, expect to pay 120-150F per head, including wine. It's best to arrive before 10pm.

Forest walks

In the surrounding forest and along the River Gravona, which reaches as far as the Ajaccio sands of Campo dell'Oro, a small path winds between the granite cliffs. Take care as it's very narrow in places. On the way there are a number of lookout points with different views over the gorges, as well as some very picturesque hamlets.

The Richiusa footpath

This walking trail runs from Bocognano to the old restored chestnut mill by the River Gravona. The banks of the river are particularly pleasant in spring, when the Corsican scrub is at a minimum and the paths are clear. After crossing the river, another path leads to the slopes of Migliacello. This is a fantastic two-hour walk through Corsican scrubland, forest and stunning mountain scenery. The trail ends at the incredible Richiusa canyon (*Clue de la Richiusa*).

Swimming in the Richiusa canyon

The *Clue de la Richiusa*, a canyon with 200-ft (60-m) sheer walls, is unique in Corsica. The spectacle is majestic. It's a very popular spot for the comparatively new sport of canyoning, a combination of swimming, climbing and sliding down the canyon on your backside! (Not for the faint-hearted!) Experienced amateurs can attempt the descent of the canyon, but you must ensure that you're accompanied by a guide. Those of you who don't feel up to this sort of exertion can spend the day relaxing beside one of the delightful emerald pools that line the falls. It's safe to swim in these waters, providing you don't get too close to the Aval waterfalls (*Cascades d'Aval*).

A Muntagne Corse In Liberta (guided walks), 2, Avenue de la Grande-Armée, 20000 Ajaccio ☎ 04 95 20 53 14

The icy heights of the Busso glacier

Above 5,200 ft (1,600 m), the unusual Névé du Busso glacier has snow even in summer – the winter and spring avalanches pack this narrow corridor, forming a very thick layer of ice. This is the largest area of perennial snow in Corsica. There's an easy walk starting from a little path on the side of the road, halfway between Bocognano and the Clue de la Richiusa (near the small power station). The trail is marked with arrows to Névé du Busso. You won't find any cafés or souvenir shops here – you're at one with winter nature, even in the height of summer. From the top of the Névé du Busso there's a superb view of Corsica's central mountain ridge. However, don't forget to wrap up warm because even in the middle of August, it's still extremely cold here.

Spotcheck
B3

Things to do

- Rural cuisine
- Walk to the Busso glacier
- Richiusa walking trail

With children

- Swimming in Richiusa canyon

Within easy reach

Vanaco (pp. 142-143)
Ghisoni Inzecca (pp. 156-157)
Bastelica (pp. 184-185)
Cargèse and Sagone (pp. 98-99)

Tourist office

Corte:
☎ 04 95 46 26 70

Venaco and Vizzavona forest
the heart of the Corsican Alps

The Forêt de Vizzavona marks the geographical and cultural boundary between rich northern Corsica and poorer southern Corsica. This mountainous and sparsely populated area (only 50 inhabitants in Vizzavona and less in Venaco) has a majestic wildness. A short walk in the forest, at the foot of Monte d'Oro, will soon convince you of that.

Clifftop villages

The road between Corte and Vizzavona winds through valleys and clearings, before the villages of Venaco and Vivario suddenly appear on the horizon, clinging to the slopes at the heart of the 'Corsican Alps'. Beneath the villages you can see the full expanse of the Tavigno

valley and its gushing river. The region is renowned for its fine trout and wonderful cheeses. It's well worth stopping here.

Mountain walks

A number of paths suitable for family walks begin at Venaco and Vivario. They take you through the forest and the

gorges towards the chestnut mills, *pagliaghji* (hay-drying sheds) and *aghje* (wheat-threshing barns) that are still dotted around the region. Maps showing all the paths are available from campsites, restaurants and also from the national forest service (Office National des Forêts, ☎ 04 95 32 81 90). Vizzavona is also very popular with hikers on the GR 20 (p. 85), which passes close by. The grocery in the station restaurant is a good place to have a bite to eat (open daily until 7pm, sometimes later).

The little Venaco train

In Corsica, even a few houses perched on the mountainside are enough to justify a train stop. Venaco station has four services a day and is a popular starting point for walkers who intend to walk just half of the GR 20 trail. Vizzavona is also popular as it's the only place in the area where you can buy food, and is also notable for its extremely long tunnel, which extends for

2.5 miles (4 km). For those who are not too keen on walking, the train leaving four times a day for Bastia or Ajaccio is an alternative way to see the beauty of the region.

Canaglia
9 miles (15 km)
S of Venaco
The Manganellu gorges
This easy walking trail through the Gorges de Manganellu is one of the most beautiful footpaths in Corsica. From the little hamlet of

Rotondo. The climb is not too difficult and can be undertaken without a guide. However, remember that you're in the mountains, so take all the necessary precautions (see p. 80).

Vizzavona
11.5 miles (18.5 km)
S of Venaco
A view of Italy
Although it's not an easy walk, you don't have to be a mountaineer to climb Monte d'Oro. The most difficult part is the section after the sheepfolds and the pine forest, where you have to climb up stone steps cut into the rock. It's fine as long as you're not too scared of heights and it really is worth the effort. At the summit (7,838 ft/2,389 m) is one of the most beautiful views in Corsica, with Ajaccio on one side and the Italian coast on the other. The climb itself is also very beautiful, with views of the Cinto and

Spotcheck
B2

Things to do
• Walking and swimming in the Manganellu gorges
• Little train from Venaco
• Climb up Monte d'Oro

With children
• Picnic at the English falls

Within easy reach
Bocognano (pp. 140-141)
Fiumorbo valley (pp. 156-157)
Corte (pp. 132-135)
Niolo (pp. 136-139)

Tourist office
Corte:
☎ 04 95 46 26 70

CASCADE DES ANGLAIS ('ENGLISH FALLS')
It's a mystery why this spot is so called, but it makes a good family outing, and the river-side location is perfect for a picnic. From Vizzavona, follow the 'bridges' path' (*Chemin des Ponts*) and then the Gorges de l'Agnone to the foot of Monte d'Oro. All along the path, small waterfalls prepare you for your wild destination.

Canaglia, follow the path that runs northwest through the Forêt de Cervello. You then follow the river until you reach the GR 20 trail. From there, press on to the superb Tolla sheepfolds. If you are feeling energetic, you can continue to the Lac de Rotondo, ideal for a quick, refreshing swim, and then head for the summit of Monte

Incudine peaks. Here you're right in the centre of Corsica, and you can see practically the whole island. If you need to stop overnight somewhere, head for the shepherds' huts at Puzzatelli. The route to Monte d'Oro is mapped out at the Vizzavona train station, but you should also arm yourself with an IGN map in case you get lost.

Castagniccia
the chestnut kingdom

This region is the home of the 'tree of life' – the chestnut. But the chestnut tree is not just a symbol of northern Corsica's agricultural prosperity, it also marks a period of occupation and servitude, as it was the Genoese who planted these immense forests back in the 16thC. Today, Castagniccia is still an ocean of green, punctuated here and there by church steeples and mountainside hamlets.

Walking and hiking

Between the small lakes of Biguglia and Diane, from the foothills of Corte to the resorts of the east coast, Castagniccia is a vast, mostly unspoilt, walkers' paradise. The northern *Mare a mare* trail, between Moriani and Cargèse, and the *Mare e monti* trail, a bit further south, are the area's most famous walks (pp. 82-83). However, the region is also criss-crossed by numerous **country paths**, excellent for one-day walks. You can go from the Carcheto falls to the cliffs by the old convent of Orezza, or from the little forest hamlets of Haute Castagniccia (San Damiano, Casta and Croce) to the sheepfolds of San Giulian and Ortale in the south. The choice is yours. A brochure detailing the routes and walk durations (two to five hours) is available from the information centre in Castagniccia (Syndicat d'Initiative, ☎ 04 95 35 82 54) and from most other tourist offices, hotels, gîtes and restaurants.

Chestnuts

The chestnut tree is the soul and symbol of the Castagniccia region. For many years, the valleys of the region were terraced with chestnut orchards and you can still see the traces of these huge plantations, which were often up to 3,300 ft (1,000 m) high on the slopes, so that the trees

could develop a solid root structure. Nowadays many of these plantations are not actively managed and the trees and surrounding land have been left to run wild. In the early 19thC., the tree provided the region's staple food. Chestnuts were used to make flour, bread, tarts and soufflés and in hundreds of other ways. They were a valuable commodity and were traded with the Balagne region, in return for olive oil and wine, and with Sartène for wine and cheese. However, agricultural diversification, rural exodus and disease (especially the infamous 'ink disease', which caused the sap to run out of the roots and therefore completely dehydrated the trees) led to a decline in the importance of the chestnut tree and less interest in its cultivation. Nevertheless, chestnuts remain highly valued by Corsicans and tourists alike. Some old chestnut mills

they are still very popular in playgrounds everywhere for playing conkers!). If there are several fruit in the husk, however, they are chestnuts and in Corsica, these are the most common variety that are produced.

Piedicroce
Baroque church
Piedicroce is one of the Castagniccia region's most picturesque villages. The splendid Baroque **Saint-Pierre et Saint-Paul church** is evidence of the region's rich past. Clinging to the safety of the mountainside, overlooking a green valley of chestnut trees, Piedicroce is a pleasant place to stop.

A room with a view
Hôtel-restaurant
Le Refuge
Piedicroce
☎ **04 95 35 81 13**
Open all-year round.
Closed evenings in Nov.
Last orders 9.30pm.

remain and there's a good example of a restored one in Bocognano (p. 140).

Chestnut, sweet chestnut or horse chestnut?
It's very simple – if there is only one fruit in the husk, it's a sweet chestnut. The sort of chestnut trees you find in towns yield horse chestnuts, which are inedible (although

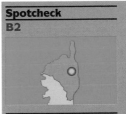

Spotcheck
B2

Things to do
• Piedicroce walks
• Horse riding in Poggio di Croce
• Loreto di Casinca local cuisine
• Orezza pipes

Within easy reach
Cervione (pp. 148-149)
Moriani (pp. 150-151)
Corte (pp. 132-135)
Bastia (pp. 102-105)

Tourist office
Piedicroce:
☎ 04 95 35 82 54

Verdese village

You'll find the best chestnut-based cooking at the Raffali family restaurant, Le Refuge. At this beautiful rustic restaurant, you'll be offered a wonderful selection of mountain charcuterie and a delicious game dish with a sumptuous sauce (about 100F per person). It's also a hotel (open Easter-end Oct.), with a few double rooms with exceptional views of the Castagniccia hills (300F per night).

Sparkling spring water, Orezza

number, you'll have no problem tracking them down – Valle d'Orezza only has about 30 inhabitants.

The view from Monte San Petrone

The walk to this lookout point starts in the hamlet of Campodonico, perched just above Piedicroce. From there, it takes about two hours to reach the ridge of Monte San Petrone, (5,800 ft/1,767 m), where the path winds steeply upwards, but presents it no real difficulty. However, you still need to take the necessary mountain precautions – sunhat, sunglasses, water and food. From the ridge, you'll have an extensive view of the whole of Castaniccia, the coast 20 miles away and, on a clear day, the island of Elba (to the left) and the Tuscany coast.

Orezza
*3.5 miles (6 km)
NE of Piedicroce*
Crystal clear spring water

You've probably already drunk the water of Orezza. In Corsica it's the most popular mineral water, with a unique, sparkling taste. The spring is located at the former thermal spa near the Valle d'Orezza. The crystal clear water gushes out beneath the trees and you can take just as much as you like because, for some reason, it's free.

Orezza valley's pipes

The pipes from Valle d'Orezza are famous everywhere on the island. Made from olive, heather and alder wood, these short pipes are carved and decorated by hand. They are true works of art. They come in a variety of designs – chimneys, hats, the map of Corsica

and some even shaped like a Moor's head. Even if you're not a pipe smoker, these hand made pipes still make excellent souvenirs. Expect to pay about 100F for one pipe. Moracchini and Lucien Colombani are craftsmen

with magic fingers. Although there's no address or telephone

Poggio di Croce
*12.5 miles (20 km)
N of Piedroce*
Castagniccia on horseback
**Centre Équestre Soliva
Poggio di Croce
☎ 04 95 39 22 92
Open throughout the year.**

Relax into a rhythmic trot amid the shady chestnut trees. The region is just as beautiful on horseback and you'll see a

lot more than you would on foot. At the **Soliva horse riding centre** in Poggio de Croce, why not take up the offer of the excursion called the *totale* – two days full board in a guesthouse including four half-day treks on horseback. Centrally located, you can head off in any direction – the centre will give you details of a range of treks to choose from. This package costs about 700F per person. Book in advance as this guesthouse is very popular.

A CORSICAN FAMILY MEAL
U Rataghju
Loreto di Casinca
15.5 miles (25 km)
NE of Piedicroce
☎ 04 95 36 30 66
Open all-year round by reservation only. When you sit down at a table the Albertinis' restaurant in Loreto di Casinca you'll feel like you've been invited for dinner with a Corsican family rather than being just an ordinary paying guest in a restaurant. After a warm welcome, you'll be served a chestnut kir and some *lonzu*, *figatelli* and *coppa*, followed by wild-boar stew, *brocciu* cheese tart, chestnut fritters and chestnut liqueur. Don't plan on moving too far after dinner – the portions are huge. The rustic setting of the old chestnut drying-shed is beautiful. Expect to pay 130F per head (wine included). In summer, it's essential to book a few days ahead.

Morosaglia
9.5 miles (15.5 km)
NW of Piedicroce
Paoli's birthplace

Pasquale Paoli's funeral chapel, Morosaglia

Morosaglia
☎ 04 95 61 04 97
Open July and Aug. 9am-7pm. Out of season, 9am-noon and 1.5pm. Closed Feb. and Mar.
Admission charge.
The famous Corsican patriot, Pasquale Paoli was born in Castagniccia, at Morosaglia, above Croce. Although an enlightened and cultured man, the fighting spirit obviously ran through his veins, as his father was a Corsican general. The pretty hamlet, with its maze of narrow lanes, is worth visiting, but the main attraction is **Paoli's birthplace**. Here the reconstruction of traditional Corsican life will give you a real feel for the island's history and particularly the period that culminated in Corsica's proudest moment, the declaration of independence. Paoli twice went into exile in England, and finally died in London in 1806. Next to the house, Paoli's ashes, which were recovered from England at the end of the 19thC., are kept in a granite funeral chapel.

Cervione, a theatre by the sea

The village of Cervione, climbs the slopes of Monte Castello to a height of 3,600 ft (1,100 m) in horseshoe-shaped tiers, looking remarkably like an amphitheatre. The village overlooks superb olive and chestnut groves and vineyards and from the terrace of Saint-Erasme church, the view includes the long beaches of Port-di-Taverna and Prunete. Leading up to the church, a tortuous collection of arched stairways and narrow lanes liess buried between the tall, light-coloured houses. In short, Cervione is quite beautiful.

The Corsica of yesteryear
Musée de Cervione
☎ 04 95 38 12 83
Open all-year round, 10am-noon and 2.30-6pm. Closed Sun.
Exhibiting regional artefacts, especially from the Roman sites in Aléria and Mariana (p. 152), the **Cervione museum** gives an insight into the ancient life of Corsica. The museum's themes include diplsys on cheese production, the milling and various uses

for chestnuts, rustic furniture and agricultural practices. The museum also recounts why the short-lived king of Corsica, Théodore de Neuhoff, chose to locate his court in Cervione. This German-born adventurer demanded to be crowned king in exchange for gaining Corsica's independence from Genoa, but he failed and fled to England, where died in 1756. He is commemorated on a wall in St Anne's church in Soho, London.

Prunete

3 miles (5.5 km) E of Cervione
The Virgin of the fishermen
The superb 16th-C. statue, the *Madone des Pêcheurs*, is housed in the chancel of the Chapelle di a Scupiccia, just above Cervione (ask for the key at the town hall). The white marble Virgin was discovered by Prunete fishermen on the beach, following the shipwreck of a vessel that was taking the statue to Cordoue. From the chapel, a small winding path takes you across forest and scrubland to a raised plateau, the Bucatojo basin, where there are gushing

Corsica of yesteryear, Musée de Cervione

Romanesque frescoes, Chapelle Santa Cristina

waterfalls. Swimming is not advisable, however, as the current is very strong here. There's a wonderful view over southern Castagniccia, and in the afternoon, when the sun moves to the west, the wild vegetation makes for photogenic scenery. Just below Cervione, the Chapelle Santa Cristina (10thC.) boasts some beautiful Romanesque frescoes. Ask for the key at the Café des Platanes.

Eucalyptus beach
Eucalyptus trees are quite rare in Corsica, but in Prunete there's a large beach with a eucalpytus grove in the neighbouring campsite. You can swim at the beach, but note that there are no lifeguards and the waves are sometimes large, as is often the case on the east coast

where there are no rocks. Like aromatherapy, the smell of the eucalyptus, carried by the light westerly breeze, will send you peacefully to sleep in the sun.

PICNIC AND A SWIM
Valle-di-Camploro
NE exit from Campoloro
Located between the sheltered marina and the heights of Cervione, the Valle-di-Campoloro area is a lovely place for a walk. Above, Monte Castellu d'Osari overlooks a pretty church, the Église Sainte-Christine. You might not stop here for long, but a picnic in the shade of the olive trees is a tempting thought. The diving club at Campoloro port (☎ 04 95 38 00 50), open in the summer season, offers beginners' lessons (tanks and flippers provided), enabling you to discover the mysteries of the underwater world. Prices start from 200F per person.

Pruno
20 miles (32 km) NW of Cervione
Gourmet treats
In Pruno, on the way up from Cervione towards Bastia, there are two acclaimed farmhouse inns. At **Antionette Don Simoni**, you can enjoy an aperitif in the shade of the hazelnut trees, which provide the main ingredient of a delicious tart. Make sure you try a slice after the *brocciu* cannelloni or the rabbit and olive stew. **Joseph Nasi**'s restaurant specialises in fish. The olive-oil coated trout with almonds is really special. Expect to pay 100-150F per head at both restaurants.

Antoinette Don Simoni
20264 Pruno
☎ 04 95 36 92 01
Open June-Sept.
Reservation only.

Joseph Nasi
U Travone, 20213 Pruno
☎ 04 95 36 98 98
Open all-year round.
Reservation only.

Moriani
take to the water

A large seaside resort, Moriani is a place for sunbathing, swimming, strolling along the seafront and sipping aperitifs in one of the many terraced bars. The sea is clear, the sand is fine, the beach is safe and the surrounding mountains shelter the town from the north and west winds.

Take a dip

From just south of Bastia to the outskirts of Porto-Vecchio, the east coast is one immense beach, separated from the countryside at various points by sand dunes (p. 76). On the minus side, the east coast lacks the inlets, deep coves and rocks of the west, however, the beaches are never overcrowded. Just south of Moriani, the large Plage de l'Alistro, which ends at the lighthouse of the same name, is 9 miles (14 km) long. Make sure you don't lose your children! Beyond Alistro is a area of holiday villages, rather packed together.

Have a drink!

The bars that line the seafront are only a stone's throw from the beach. In the summer heat, you'll appreciate a cool, refreshing drink or a bite to eat at **Pota Marina**

(☎ 04 95 38 53 13. Open 1 Apr.-30 Sept. Try the seafood set menu, 70-90F).

'I'll be back!'

These were the defiant words of Pasquale Paoli on 9 July 1739, when he left Moriani to go into exile on the island of Elba, along with his parents, who headed the

THE TAVAGNE FESTIVAL

Settembriu di Tavagnu is one of the few festivals held on the east coast. It's also one of the most varied. On the agenda are painting and sculpture exhibitions, discussion groups, debates and food tastings (local products, including all the chestnut-based delicacies). The whole of the Tavagne region, from Casinca to the outskirts of Moriani, comes together to celebrate. Corsican folk musicians and other artists from the continent put on special evening entertainment in various restaurants and bars on the coast and in the surrounding area. Others play in the village squares in the afternoons. The **Tavagna Club**, in Talasani, is probably the liveliest restaurant concert venue. The festival takes place every year throughout August and September. Further information is available from the tourist offices in Bastia (p. 103) or Castagniccia (p. 144).

Spotcheck
C2

Things to do

• Alistro beach
• San Nicolao chestnut walk
• Tavagne September festival

Within easy reach

Castagniccia region (pp. 144-147)
Cervione (pp. 148-149)
Aléria (pp. 152-153)

Tourist office

Moriani:
☎ 04 95 38 41 73

first Corsican revolts and were prominent in the movement when Corsica was declared independent in 1734. Pasquale Paoli did in fact return, on 16 June 1755. On 14 July of the same year, he was named General of the Corsican nation. There's a commemorative plaque honouring him in Moriani (on the side of a house near the beach). His exile was perhaps not one of the most decisive events in Paoli's life, but the plaque bears witness to the islanders' wish to lose

no opportunity to pay homage to this great patriot.

San Nicolao
6 miles (10 km)
SW of Moriani
Chestnut trees of San Nicolao

This tiny granite village seems lost in the interior, gleaming in the middle of a shady chestnut wood in the Castagniccia valleys. For lovers of old stone buildings, San Nicolao has a pretty 18th-C. Baroque church and two slightly worn Romanesque chapels. It's worth taking a look at these buildings, and perhaps a photo or two. Then, make your way down to San Giovanni di Moriani, just to the west. The small restaurant Cava is a good find. For less than 100F, wine included, you can tuck into goat in sauce and have your fill of *migliacci* (brocciu cheese fritters rolled in chestnut leaves).

Cava
☎ 04 95 38 51 14.
Open July and August, reservation required.

Roman Aléria
archaeology and sandy beaches

T his town is famous for two things – the Roman archaeological site and museum, and the large sandy beaches, which are very popular with the people of Bastia.

A look back at modern history

In summer 1975, the peaceful town of Aléria was suddenly the focus of the world's news cameras, the scene of one of the bloodiest episodes in the island's recent history. On 21 August, Edmond Simeoni and a group of Corsican separatists occupied a wine cellar, to draw attention to the plight of Corsican wine growers, who had been financially ruined by the bankruptcy – in murky circumstances – of a company on the French mainland that marketed Corsican wines. Following an assault by the police, two policemen were killed. Simeoni negotiated his comrades' freedom, in return for his own surrender.

The archaeological museum
Musée Jérôme Carcopino
Fort de Matra
☎ 04 95 57 00 92

Open daily 8am-noon and 2-7pm, May-Oct. Rest of the year, 8am-noon and 2-5pm. Closed Sun.
Admission charge (includes archaeological site visit).
In the medieval setting of the Matra fort (1494), about 20 rooms around the castle's interior court display relics from the archaeological site of the ancient town. These represent nearly 1,000 years of Corsican history. One room is entirely dedicated to Roman

Corsica. It's not Pompei or Athens, but people interested in archaeology will enjoy the visit. Well worth seeing.

Ancient Aléria
Same hours as the archaeological museum.
Admission charge (includes museum).

Whether you have a serious interest in archaeology or you're just curious, you really must visit this site (pp. 44-45). Located right next to the

Matra fort, in the small hamlet of Cateraggio, the remains of this Roman city, with a temple and forum, covers around 1 sq mile (2 km square). There are two parallel porticos, one of which contains the ruins of ancient town shops. This well preserved and maintained site also includes ponds and houses. Archaeologists are now beginning to uncover remains of the ramparts that once surrounded the town.

Welcome breaks
L'Ernella
R N 200, 20270
☎ 04 95 48 82 06
Open all-year round. Reservation essential for groups.

Spotcheck
C3

Things to do
• Tavignano river rafting, hydrospeed, canoeing and kayaking
• Swimming beaches
• Mavela distillery

With children
• L'Ernella donkey rides

Within easy reach
Fiumorbo valley (pp. 156-157)
Venaco (pp. 142-143)
Cervione (pp. 148-149)

Tourist office
Aléria: ☎ 04 95 57 01 51

Bungalows Marina d'Aléria
Route de la Mer, 20270
☎ 04 95 57 01 42
Fax: 04 95 57 04 29

Aléria and the coastal beaches get very crowded in summer. Although there's plenty of accommodation especially at the campsites, as with the rest of Corsica (particularly on the east coast in the summer) it's advisable to book several weeks in advance.
Here are two options at different prices. **L'Ernella**, on the outskirts of Tavignano on the Corte road, is an open-air campsite, simple, clean, with a friendly welcome. The young guests guarantee a good atmosphere, even if the place is quiet. It costs around 1,000F per person per week. The **Marina d'Aléria** bungalows are more expensive (1,200-4,400F per week, depending on the time of year), but the four-star benefits are superb. Partly shaded by pine trees beside the beach, with a restaurant, tennis courts, windsurfing boards and mountain bikes for hire, these luxury seaside bungalows can accommodate up to five people.

The Diane lake water farm
Ferme Aquatique d'Étang de Diane

Oyster lovers take note – this is the only place you'll find on Corsica that farms oysters. These oysters are not the delicately-flavoured kind, but they taste stronger and are slightly fattier than usual all-year round. They are, however, still quite delicious. The flat, watery landscape is also well worth seeing. You can savour excellent shellfish dishes served in the restaurant next to the lake. The delicious seafood platter with wine will set you back no more than 200F.

The Mavela estate distillery
Distillerie du Domaine Mavela
U Licettu
(2 miles/3 km S of Aléria),
20270 Aléria
☎ 04 95 56 60 30

In a huge vaulted cellar, you can visit an authentic and traditional distillery which uses wild berries from the Corsican scrub, including strawberry and myrtle, and traditional Corsican fruits such as plums, chestnuts and lemons. You can explore the copper stills, the maturing room, with its oak casks, and the shop, where you can taste the best of Corsica's liqueurs, accompanied by some traditional charcuterie. This is an excellent opportunity to pick up some gourmet gifts to take home. Here you'll find olive oil and chestnut flour, as well as an excellent choice of honeys and jams.

RAFTING AND CANOEING
Base Nautique de l'Ernella
Route de Corte 20270
☎ 04 95 57 05 03
Open all-year round. The Ernella water sports centre offers hydrospeed and rafting out of season, and guided walks and kayaking and canoeing expeditions in summer on the Tavignano river. Open to all, including beginners.

Solenzara
family beaches

To be honest, there are more attractive places to visit in Corsica, but contrary to popular opinion, Solenzara has more to offer than its aerodrome and old garrison.

In fact, it's a pretty little east coast resort, with a lively shopping area. Although this marshy region was once rife with mosquitoes and malaria, the whole of the eastern plain was sprayed with DDT in 1944 and is now perfectly safe.

The beautiful beach at Canella cove, near Solenzara

aubergines stuffed with brocciu, *figatelli*, pancetta and Corsican beans. Delicious, though not a good choice for slimmers. The tables on the terrace are perfect for May evenings in the fresh air. Around 150-200F per head, including wine.

The beaches

The beaches of Solenzara, close to the water's edge and bordered by hotels, have their fans. Families like them because they are safe places for children to play. There are breaking waves, but the current is generally not very strong. All the same, keep away from the mouth of the Solenzara river, which runs straight down from the Bavella range. The counter-current, which brings a sudden rise in the water level, as well as broken bits of branches and debris, make the area unsuitable for swimming. Instead, make the most of the Italian-style lido, located in front of the station.

Dine in comfort
**A Mandria
di Sabatien
Pont de Solenzara
20145
☎ 04 95 57 41 95**
Open all-year round except early autumn.
At the exit to Solenzara, on the Bastia road, stop at this restaurant located in a restored sheepfold. The setting is rather special in this region, where concrete and plastic chairs are the norm. The dining area has stone walls, oak tables, comfortable chairs and a quiet atmosphere – a big change from the bars on the beach. The food is excellent. The menu includes traditional charcuterie, grilled meats,

A charming little port

This port is not as small as it used to be! It's one of the few to have a marina large enough for pleasure yachts and it's a really fun place to be. Take a stroll and enjoy the lively atmosphere, before having a Pietra chestnut beer or an ice cream in the main street, with its many bars.

Favone
**7.5 miles (12 km)
S of Solenzara**

A beach cove

Favone has a large beach like all the others on the east

This pretty cove has crystal clear water and is much calmer than the main beach.

A beautiful tour by car

The little Bavella road is treacherous, with all its twists and turns, potholes and bumps. But it is very pretty, climbing gradually up to one of Corsica's most beautiful sites, the **Bavella needles** (*Aiguilles de Bavella*, p. 178). These rock formations are very popular with climbers. There are some easy climbs, often used to train beginners, as well as plenty more technical climbs. From Solenzara, the route runs

A tranquil swimming spot in the Solenzara gorges

coast, battered by rollers when the wind blows from the east (be careful when swimming in high easterly winds). The main road runs alongside the beach. What makes Favone unique is **Anse de Canella** (2.5 miles/4 km to the north).

alongside the river and, as the waters become more turbulent, the little bridges are succeeded by a series of hairpin bends. At this point you are already in deep forest, amid Laricio pines and firs, with mountains bordering the

Spotcheck
B3

Things to do
• Car trip to the Bavella needles
• A Mandria sheepfold restaurant

With children
• Canella cove beach

Within easy reach
*Alta Rocca (pp. 178-181)
Fiumorbo valley
(pp. 156-157)
Porto-Vecchio
(pp. 158-161)*

Tourist office
Solenzara:
☎ **04 95 57 43 75**

road. The large red granite cliffs, reminiscent of the Piana rocks, have an unusual charm. The nearer you get to the pass, the higher the road climbs into the firs. Along the way, many hiking trails, marked with wooden arrows, run deep into the forest towards the numerous **waterfalls**. The duration of each walk is signposted as well. Choose a path, taking your picnic along, before you rejoin the road to the pass. This is one of the few, really beautiful car trips you can take in Corsica.

Fiumorbo valley
Ghisonaccia and Ghisoni

Ghisonaccia, at the bottom of the valley, is a typical east-coast resort – a main street lined with shops and open-air bars that leads to a large beach and the Mediterranean sea. Climbing the valley you come to Ghisoni, a small and peaceful mountain village with a grocery, a bar-tabac and a winding road that leads to the Verde pass and Monte Renoso.

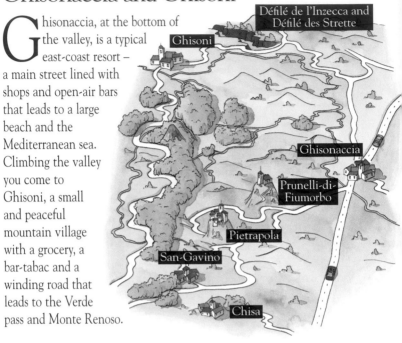

Défilé de l'Inzecca and Défilé des Strette

Ghisoni

Ghisonaccia

Prunelli-di-Fiumorbo

Pietrapola

San-Gavino

Chisa

A trip to the Inzecca and Strette gorges

The Défilé de l'Inzecca and the Défilé des Strette are narrow gorges cut into the red and grey cliffs that tower 1,000 ft (300 m) over a small, rushing river, which reflects the unique green Fiumorbo rocks. The car journey through the gorges is

spectacular, but keep your eyes on the road, because it's very narrow and the bends are tight. The road climbs to Ghisoni, following the river (from Ghisonaccia, head for the station and then carry straight on), the narrowness of the gorge giving you the impression that you are actually driving inside the canyon. In places, the road digs right into the canyon wall, which forms an arched roof over your head. There are only about three or four places to stop in Inzecca – recesses on the right-hand side where you can park. With the slope in your favour, the walk down to the river is easy, but you will have to climb past some fallen rocks. The trail is not signposted but is accessible. Past the Inzecca dam, the road widens a little, then joins with

the Strette gorge, which is even deeper and more hemmed in than the Inzecca gorge. From there, continue straight on and you will arrive at Ghisoni.

Prunelli di Fiumorbo
8 miles (12.5 km) W of Ghisonaccia
Village with a view
From Prunelli di Fiumorbo, there's an extensive view of the eastern plain beyond Aléria and Urbino and Diane lakes. A small path climbs

Fiumorbo valley from Prunelli village

gradually from Prunelli to the **Église de Saint-Jean l'Évangéliste**. The scenery on the way to the church is very photogenic. The walk starts at the entrance to the village, on the left before the

Chapelle San Giovanni. You can't miss it – it's the only side road.

Pietrapola
3 miles (5 km) SW of Prunelli, on the D 45
Roman thermal spas

Pietrapola is a tiny village worth visiting for its tall grey buildings perched on the rocks and for its **panoramic view**. The site was popular with the Romans for its excellent thermal spas. In the basement of the Hôtel des Thermes (open 15 Apr.-15 Dec., rooms from 260F per night in season, ☎ 04 95 56 70 03) there are 19th-C. baths (admission free outside treatment hours). Below Pietrapola, there are many delightful **walks** along the Abatesco river

The Fiumorbo footpaths
There is a network of some 15 **country walks** (marked clearly with orange signposts) in Fiumorbo and the surrounding area. There are many other mountain walks, for which you must be in good physical condition. The country walks vary in length from one to six hours and are accessible for all levels of walkers. Topographic maps of the trails are available in all the tourist offices (including Ghisonaccia tourist office, RN 198, Open June-Sept. 9am-noon and 4-9pm). One of the most beautiful circuit walks is the *Chisa à Chisa* walk (from the D 645,

Spotcheck
B3

Things to do
• Trip to the Inzecca and Strette gorges
Fiumorbo footpaths
U Sampolu gourmet stop

Within easy reach
Bocognano (pp. 140-141)
Vénaco (pp.142-143)
Aléria (pp. 152-153)
Solenzara (pp. 154-155)

Tourist office
Solenzara:
☎ **04 95 57 43 75**

15 miles/24 km SW of Ghisonaccia), which takes you to the **Bovile sheepfolds** via the Bocca di Manigoli. Emerging from thick forest, you arrive at the banks of the Travo river, where you take a refreshing and invigorating **swim**. Expect the walk to take you about five hours or a bit longer if you stop for a picnic or a dip. The circuit which starts and finishes at San Gavino (on the D 945) is a bit shorter. This takes you to the **Macini waterfall** (*Cascades de Macini*) and gives you a wonderful view of the Abatesco valley. A section of the path is at altitude, but the climb is very gentle.

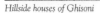
Hillside houses of Ghisoni

Porto-Vecchio
the number one tourist town

Beaches, restaurants, nightclubs, hiking trails, leisure activities and plenty of accommodation – Porto-Vecchio and the surrounding area has everything for a stimulating holiday.

A picture postcard view

The road crosses the mountain, winds its way through the Laricio pines of the Forêt de l'Ospedale, dips down to the lake and then, turning a corner, you suddenly come across **Porto-Vecchio bay** laid out 3,000 ft (1,000 m) below. This is one of the most beautiful views in the whole of Corsica. It makes a superb photo opportunity and

it would be a shame to miss it. There's just one hitch – there's nowhere to park. Rather than going on to the next hamlet and then having to walk back up on foot, it's best to find a parking space before you get there. When you see the sign marked 'Le Refuge' on the right-hand side of the road, slow down and park on the verge a little further on.

The lanes of the upper town

Information from the tourist office
**Rue du Déput-Camille-de-Rocca-Serra,
BP 92, 20137
Porto-Vecchio Cedex
☎ 04 95 70 09 58
Fax: 04 95 70 03 72**
Guided tour.
Porto-Vecchio may not be one of the prettiest towns in Corsica, but the old town,

Citadel and upper town of Porto-Vecchio

centred around the citadel, is well worth a visit. The twisting narrow lanes, tall houses, gateways, and shops nestled in the stone walls are attractive and shady. Don't miss the ramparts of the old fortified town, which are still standing to this day.

Sip an aperitif on the terrace

The marina is in the modern part of town and the most fashionable place to be. It welcomes some of the biggest yachts you can imagine and is a great place for a midday aperitif in one of the many

sun-kissed terraces of the bars. The marina's restaurants really come alive at night. This is a great place to indulge in a dozen oysters, but you should never have to pay more than 60F.

Reliable dining

Le Passe-Temps
Rue du Comandant-L'Herminier
☎ 04 95 72 10 88
Le Bistrot du Port
Le Port
☎ 04 95 70 22 96
There are many restaurants here, of varying quality. However, two reliable gems are **Le Passe-Temps**, which specialises in pizzas (from 40F) and **Le Bistrot du Port**, just opposite the marina, which has an 85F set menu at lunchtime (and à la carte dining in the evening).

Shopping for local produce

L'Orriu
5, Cours Napoléon
☎ 04 95 70 26 21
Open Mon.-Sat.
9am-12.30pm and
3 8.30pm (summer),
3-8pm (out of season).
Closed Nov. and
15 Feb-25 Mar.
To find genuine Corsican charcuterie, tasty fresh local cheese or good myrtle liqueur, L'Orriu is the best place in Porto Vecchio. Here you'll find all the best **traditional local specialities**, organically produced without the use of preservatives or chemicals. These are high quality products but you'll find that you pay a little bit more here than you would if you bought them from a producer in the countryside (around 150F for 2.2 lbs/1 kg of two-year matured whole ham). It's worth noting that L'Orriu is part of the 'taste trail' (*Route des Saveurs*), which about says it all.

Spotcheck
B4

Things to do

• Water sports and swimming at Palombaggia and Santa Giulia beaches
• Walking and swimming in the Ospedale forest
• Buy local produce at L'Orriu

With children

• Ponies on Palombaggia beach

Within easy reach

Figari Sotta (pp. 168-169)
Bonifacio (pp. 162-165)
Alta Rocca (pp. 178-181)
Sartène (pp. 154-155)

Tourist office

Porto-Vecchio:
☎ 04 95 70 09 58

A night on the town

Via Notte,
Route de Porra
☎ 04 95 72 02 12
Open daily in season,
11pm-5am.
Closed Sept.-June.
Via Luna
Route de Saint-Cyprien, Lecci
☎ 04 95 71 64 26
Open Sat. Oct.-May,
11pm-5am.
Like all seaside resorts, Porto-Vecchio is as lively at night as during the day. The attractive bars and restaurants of the old town and port certainly pull in the crowds. Don't find yourself stuck in an overpriced and dull venue. Instead, head for **Via Notte** (in season) or **Via Luna** (Saturday, out of season).

A Corsican coral workshop

Taillerie du Corail
Route de Bonifacio
☎ **04 95 70 21 21**
Fax: 04 95 70 92 76
Open Mon.-Sat.
9am-1pm and 3-8pm
in summer. 9am-noon
and 3-7pm in winter.
At this workshop in Porto-Vecchio, you'll find real
Corsican coral – the reddest
in the world – though it's
crafted in Italy. Mark Robbez-Masson exhibits a very pretty
collection here. The coral
pieces are all mounted on gold
and are original in design,
making **wonderful gift ideas**
or additions to your own
jewellery collection. A team
of divers works throughout the
year, collecting coral for the
workshop. The little clenched
fist symbol is a Corsican
speciality, which is said to
ward off evil spirits. Corsicans
normally give these as a
christening present, but their
powers of protection still work
whatever your age.

Take to the saddle

A Staffa horse treks
Route de Palombaggia
☎ **04 95 70 47 51**
An alternative and very
enjoyable way to discover
Corsica and the beaches of
Porto-Vecchio is in the saddle
of a horse. Near the town,
A Staffa organises various
trips – into the Corsican
scrubland and to Palombaggia
and Santa Giulia beaches.
These treks are suitable for
riders of all levels of
experience. The horses walk
slowly most of the time, so
the rides are quite easy-going.

The company will also take
care of your children to give
you a bit of a rest. They can
take a pony trek with a
qualified instructor, leaving
you free to go for a ride
without them.

Palombaggia beach

Palavesa

3 miles (5.5 km)
NW of Porto-Veccio
Araghju castle
The Torréene ('tower')
civilisation ruled the island
4,000 years ago. Remains
of their ancient civilisation
include the Castellu
d'Araghju, 3.5 miles (6 km)
north of Porto-Vecchio on
the D 559. There's a pleasant
short walk around the old
fortress. The path is in good
condition and you can admire
the well-preserved ramparts
while imagining just how

*The ancient remains
of Araghju castle*

these ancient warriors
defended this fortified town
in 2,000 BC.

Santa Giulia

3.5 miles (6 km)
S of Porto-Vecchio
Dream beaches
Santa Giulia
watersports
Route de Moby Dick
20137 Porto-Vecchio
☎ **04 95 70 58 62**
Closed 15 Oct.-early June.
Porto-Vecchio owes its
popularity to the two beaches
of Palombaggia and Santa
Giulia, which used to belong
to Club Med. The beaches
are signposted from the port,
on the Route de Bonifacio.
The **Plage de Palombaggia** is
an immense white expanse,
dotted with round, pink rocks.
The **Plage de Santa Giulia** is

DIVE RIGHT IN

Ospedale forest pool

*12 miles (19 km)
NW of Porto-Vecchio*
Information and map from Porto-Vecchio tourist office.
A pure, deep, emerald green forest pool, fed by a 160-ft (50-m) waterfall that gushes from the mountainside. This paradise is the *Piscia di Gallu* – but you'll have to earn your swim in its heavenly waters. Coming from Porto-Vecchio, the path begins half a mile (1 km) after the dam, marked by a small rock plaque and a refreshments stall. The two-hour walk will take you through the pine trees and rocky country of the Forêt de l'Ospedale. It's a pleasant walk, well signposted and not too difficult, although the path does become steep towards the end. Still, it's really worth it.

Both beaches are sunny and sheltered but get crowded in summer. Try not to arrive and leave at the most popular times.

Bitalza

*21.5 miles (35 km)
SW of Porto-Vecchio*
The Bitalza sheepfolds
After crossing the Bacinu pass (Col du Bacinu) and passing through a surreal landscape where wild, arid zones alternate with forests of Laricio pines and cork oaks, you'll arrive at the Bitalza sheepfolds – among the island's most extraordinary buildings. These shepherds' huts are embedded in the light-coloured rock. They are still used as sheepfolds, but also as second homes.

Sotta

*6 miles (10 km)
SW of Porto-Vecchio*
A charming village
Sotta is on the plain, but looks like a mountain village. The village is made up of several hamlets, as pretty as each other, with tangled houses of ochre rock, narrow alleys and pointed roofs. From the hamlets of **Vacca** and **Piscia**, two paths head towards Mount Cagna. As you climb, an enormous rock balanced on a narrow granite base, the extraordinary **Uomo di Cagna**, which dominates the plain, watches you from above. You won't get to the top of Cagna – it was one of the last Corsican mountains to be conquered. However, you can get quite close, allowing you to take a low-angle photo and pretend to your friends you made it – after all, the camera never lies!

also a natural haven, with stunning turquoise waters. It has an excellent watersports club, which organises many activities, including windsurfing, sailing, catamarans and canoes.

Bonifacio land's end

Many consider Bonifacio to be Corsica's most beautiful town. You'll almost certainly be taken in by the charm of this fortified city, its ramparts perched on the lofty cliffs. However, to fully appreciate the delights of Bonifacio, try to avoid the crowds and spend several days exploring the place at your leisure. Only then will you really have time to savour the atmosphere at twilight in the naval cemetery or the freshness of a morning walk around the old town.

A Mediterranean fjord

Bonifacio's business and pleasure port, known as **La Marine**, looks like a beautiful Scandinavian fjord. Between the old town, the citadel and the tall limestone cliffs you'll discover pontoons lined with fishing boats, sharing their moorings with some of the Mediterranean's most beautiful yachts. On the quayside you'll see fishermen mending their nets and, on the terraces, the townsfolk meeting up for their ritual late afternoon pastis and olives. At nightfall, the marina remains a lively place. Indeed, it's the best place in town for busy and atmospheric nightlife and can remain a hub of activity until the early hours of the morning. Don't worry if you get waylaid at the aperitif stage – the restaurants take orders until midnight and there are plenty of spots to choose from.

Late-night dining

A great place to try if you're thinking of taking a late meal is **Quatre Vents** (open Wed.-Mon., 29, Quai di Brando di Ferro, ☎ 04 95 73 07 50). This restaurant is unique, offering Alsatian cuisine as well as the traditional Corsican fare. Expect to pay around 150F a head.

THE SEA CAVES BY BOAT

The limestone cliffs of Bonifacio are unique. The sea is gradually eroding away the base of the cliffs and local experts are trying to find ways to halt the damage and save the houses most at risk. Departing from the marina, many boats will take you to see the caves, rocky inlets, beaches and islands that give the Bonifacio coast its surreal look. These trips are particularly pleasant in the late afternoon. **Sdragonato cave** (Grotte de Sdragonato) is particularly impressive. When the boat stops under the cliff, you can see clearly how the outline of the island itself appears on the roof of the cave, contrasting sharply with the surrounding blue. Two-hour boat trip around 50F. In season it's not worth reserving, but out of season you may have to wait until a certain number of places have been sold before setting off.

Tours of the town on foot or by train

Take the steps (all two hundred of them!) that lead to the upper town, the *ville haute*.

You are now in the real heart of Bonifacio. The overhead arches that link the old houses were designed by the town's first settlers, the Pisans, to circulate rainwater between the houses, an early version of domestic running water.

The houses, which were once only entered by ladders, which could be removed when enemy boats approached, now have short, steep staircases. The best way to get to know this district of Bonifacio is by taking a peaceful stroll armed with a pocket guide (available from the tourist office, Bonifacio town hall, ☎ 04 95 73 11 88. Open 9am-8pm in season). Children will love the little train that threads its way between the houses of the upper town, and it's a relaxing way of taking in some of the sights.

Bonifacio miniature train

(40-minute ride)
Departs from the port car park
Admission charge.

Spotcheck
B4

Things to do

• Quad biking in the Corsican scrub
• Petit Sperone bay
• Water sports at Santa Manza bay
• Scuba diving at the Lavezzi islands

With children

• Sea trip to the Lavezzi islands
• Train trip around the old town.
• Boat trip to the sea caves

Within easy reach

Figari Sotta (pp. 168-169)
Porto Vecchio (pp. 160-161)
Sartène (pp. 170-173)

Tourist office

Bonifacio:
☎ 04 95 73 11 88

L'Archivolto, a restaurant decorated with old curiosities

Ancient houses

The **Maison des Podestats**, opposite the church of Sainte-Marie-Majeur, is one of the oldest and most beautiful houses in Bonifacio. The Podestats were the magistrates who used to preside over the town and protect the keys. Unfortunately, the building is not open to visitors, but take a look at the facade, with its friezes and arches and the decorated coat of arms of the Republic of Genoa. Taking Rue du Palais and the Rue Longue, you'll be able to admire the **Maison du Comte Philippe Cattalaccio**. It has a door with a splendid Renaissance lintel. Keep an eye out for the **Maison Passano**, where Napoleon lived in 1793, while he was preparing his expedition to Sardinia.

The king of Aragon's stairway

Admission charge.
From the sea, you'll notice a huge stairway that climbs the cliff just below the old town. Legend has it that in 1420 this steep stairway was built in one night by the king of Aragon's men, in order to invade the

town after a siege that had lasted for five long months. However, the truth is that the stairway was almost certainly built by the people of the area, to enable them to stock up on food and water at night during the siege. From high up on the cliff, the stairway goes right down to the small shingle beaches. Be careful as you make your way down – the king's stairway is very steep and there are 187 steps in all.

Eating in style
L'Archivolto
Rue de l'Archivolto
☎ **04 95 73 17 58**
Open daily. Closed Sun. in season and Oct.-end Mar. The name of this restaurant, located in the upper town, evokes the town's many archways. At L'Archivolto Delphine and Henri serve **typical Corsican fare**,

including a courgette gratin, grilled lamb, goat in sauce, and a good chestnut beer. The decor is charming, with plenty of antiques and bric-à-brac, including wooden toys, and paintings that give the place an old-fashioned atmosphere. The terrace is bathed in sunshine, but you'll almost certainly prefer the cosy wood-panelled interior. Expect to pay around 150F per head.

Make a date for Easter

Easter is a magical time in Bonifacio. Six religious brotherhoods stage a morning procession on Good Friday, carrying the treasures and relics – some weighing more than half a ton (500 kg) – of the patron saints of their churches. In this manner the saints are celebrated and honoured, including Sainte-Marie-Majeure, Sainte-Croix, Saint-Jean-Baptiste, Saint-Barthélémy, Sainte-Marie-Madeleine and Saint-Érasme. Those participating in the procession dress in tunics representing the colours of their church. In the evening, the festival gets really lively.

(*cimetière marin*) is something special and is a fascinating place to explore. Its tiny square has the feel of a Tunisian medina and the tombs and mausoleums, built like miniature houses, stand side by side in an almost anarchic fashion, their tiled roofs reflecting the sunlight. The view stretches as far as the Lavezzi islands and the coast of Sardinia. Follow the cliff road to the headland and opposite you'll find the **Madonetta lighthouse** (*Phare de la Madonetta*), which flashes red and indigo lights at sunset, as the last boats make their way back to the port. This is the place to take the best photo of the holiday.

Idyllic beaches

This area is full of white sandy beaches and secret coves washed by the transparent sea. On the Route de Sartène, La Tonarra bay (*Baie de la Tonarra*) is a focal

Outside the Easter period you can still visit the churches where the relics and treasures are kept. If you only plan on seeing one, make sure it's the Église Sainte Marie-Majeure in the old town, a Romanesque church, restored in the 18thC.

An unmissable photo opportunity

A graveyard may not at first seem the most inspiring destination for a walk, but Bonifacio's clifftop naval cemetery

point for **windsurfers** and **sailing dingies**. The water-sport specialists love this

The Madonetta lighthouse keeping watch over Bonifacio

stretch of sea because of its exposure to the wind. However, the coastline undulates, so you can always find a sheltered spot in which to relax, protected from the elements. In the other direction, on the Route de Porto-Vecchio, it's a short trip to Santa-Giulia beach (p. 160), where you can satisfy your craving for some sun, sea and warm sand. Park the car on the Piantarella slipway (*Cale de Piantarella*, signposted on the road) and head towards Bonifacio. A 15-minute walk along the coastal creeks brings you to **Petit Sperone**, the island's prettiest bay, with pearly-white sand and clear azure water – like a gem embedded in the limestone rocks. If you have a boat, the secluded beaches of the Îles Lavezzi are another possibility (p. 167).

A walk to the Pertusato lighthouse

This is a peaceful walk from the old abattoirs in Bonifacio along the coastal cliffs. Be careful, though, as you're on a precipice and there are no

exposed to high winds and don't have any lifeguards, so it's wiser to give them a miss. From the lighthouse (not open to the public), there's a magnificent panoramic view of the sea, the islands and Bonifacio itself.

Windsurfing, surfing and jet ski
Tam-Tam
(water sports rental)
Route de Santa Manza,
20169 Bonifacio
☎ 04 95 73 11 59
If you like water sports, you'll be spoilt for choice here. Everything is available for hire in Bonifacio: windsurfers, surfboards, flippers and snorkels and jet skis (take note of the rules and regulations). A word of advice for beginners

Diving at Bonifacio
Barakouda Club
Avenue Sylvère-Bohn,
20169 Bonifacio
☎ 04 95 73 13 02
The coast boasts a vast array of marine life, with colourful fish, sea urchins and many different types of marine algae. With just a mask and snorkel, you can get an glimpse of this wonderful underwater world. However, the most beautiful dive sites are at a depth of 65-100 ft (20-30 m), located around the Lavezzi archipelago. The Mérouville site takes its name from the shoals of grouper fish (*mérous*) which gather here, and Les Bouches has one of the most beautiful coral gardens in the whole of the Mediterranean. The **Barakouda Club** organises regular diving courses for beginners and intermediates.

The Bonifacio Ripcurl classic
The 'Ripcurl Bonifacio Classic' is the third leg of the French funboard championship, which is a mixture of windsurfing and acrobatics. The competition takes place over five days in May, in the glorious Santa Manza bay, a windy site which is perfect for acrobatic wave jumping. This is a spectacle that no one will forget and is an absolute must for funboarding fans.
For further information:
☎ 04 95 73 11 89
Fax: 04 95 73 17 12.

barriers. The Phare de Pertusato is at Corsica's southernmost point. You'll notice the strange rock, which the Corsicans call the 'helm of Corsica' because of its shape and location. The beaches beneath the lighthouse are

– don't head westwards, the winds are much stronger there. A day windsurfing from the creeks of Petit Sperone to Santa Manza will certainly give you a new perspective on Corsica's beautiful Mediterranean coastline.

Sémillante pyramid commemorates the victims of a shipwreck on the Lavezzi islands in the middle of the 19thC.

Santa Manza

6 miles (10 km)
NE of Bonifacio

A walk in the bay of Santa Manza

Funboard enthusiasts and sun worshippers love the Golfe de Santa Manza. But if you're neither of these, don't worry, there are also a number of pretty walks around the bay's characteristic scrub, with two or three straw hut restaurants where you can have lunch with your feet in the sand. Watch out, though – you'll pay for the privilege.

The Lavezzi islands

Don't leave Bonifacio without visiting the Lavezzi archipelago, a group of around 10 islands that form a protected paradise, blessed with turquoise waters and sculpted rocks. The main island, Île Lavezzi, has a strange charm – an amazing entanglement of rocks,

rounded by the wind and weather, with a sheltered bay popular with sunseekers. It has lovely scenery and tempting pools, and is also the site of a cemetery for over 750 victims of a shipwreck, the Sémillante, in 1855. Although you can't disembark at Île Cavallo, you'll still be able to see the splendid villas, built between the rocks. The Corsicans will discreetly tell you the island is owned by 'Italian investors'. In the past, when livestock was moved to fresh pastures, the cattle would swim to these islands to fill up on the famous salted grass that grows here. But don't attempt the swim yourself – the currents are strong and many boats use the channel. There are a number of boat services to the islands, but not all allow enough time to really take in the splendour

of the islands. Try **Rocca Croisières**, in the port of Bonifacio, ☎ 04 95 73 13 96.

Figari, gateway to southern Corsica

Figari is synonymous with the airport – the only quick way to reach southern Corsica, but this low-lying region, opening onto a deep bay, does have other attractions. There are plenty of easy, attractive walks and some of southern Corsica's finest restaurants. Figari wine is highly respected and the hamlets are charming.

San Quilico chapel, Montilari

Exploring Figari's hamlets

The commune is known as Figari but, originally, none of the hamlets that make up the group had this name. Today, Figari is the official name for the hamlet of **Tivarello**. **Montilari** is without question the prettiest village in the commune, and is home to one of Corsica's most beautiful pre-Romanesque chapels. The **Chapelle San Quilico** (signposted on the right on the Route de Sotta from Figari), surrounded by vineyards, certainly makes a good photo opportunity. Built around 1150, the chapel still retains its *teghie* roof. *Teghie* are thin granite tiles, balanced expertly one on top of the other to form a covering that's as solid as a rock.

Figari bay

Deep and sheltered, the Golfe de Figari is a sort of *calanche* – not as tall as those of Piana, but with a rocky scarp descending into the crystal clear azure water. It also has some very pleasant sandy coves protected from the wind, and some little islands that are easily reached by swimming. Figari bay is a lovely place to visit and surprisingly

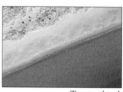

Tonnara beach

unpopular with tourists, who seem to prefer the larger but windier beaches of Tonnara bay (Golfe de la Tonnara), 8 miles (13 km) further south. Tonnara bay is a popular meeting place for seasoned windsurfers.

FARMHOUSE INN

Pozzo di Mastri farmhouse inn
Route de Sotta,
20114 Figari
☎ 04 95 71 02 65
Open daily.
Reservation essential.
Everything on the menu comes from the vegetable garden, the farmyard or is made in the farmhouse kitchen. To start with, you can select your own choice of crudités (raw vegetable salad), with the homemade olive oil. Then, you will be served some home-produced charcuterie, followed by veal, goat or wild boar for your main course, usually served in a sauce. For the rest of the meal, the local theme continues with polenta, goat's and ewe's cheeses and chestnut fritters, all homemade. The restaurant has a delightful rustic setting and with an aperitif and liqueur, you'll pay no more than 200F.

Sotta
7 miles (11 km)
N of Figari
Rock shelters
These shelters are almost troglodytic in style, embedded and integrated into the rock

itself. They were the dwellings of the first inhabitants of Sotta, who came here in the 18thC. and made their homes in these cool, sheltered recesses to escape the arid heat of this flat area. In fact, Sotta is very rare when it comes to Corsican regions in that it doesn't have a coastline. From **Vacca**, one of the region's hamlets, a path climbs to Mount Cagna. If you want to try the walk to the **Uomo di Cagna** rock, follow the slope that's used by all vehicles, which will lead you almost to the foot of this curious balancing stone.

Mount Cagna
3.5 miles (6 km)
N of Figari

Spotcheck
B4

Things to do
• Naseo sheepfolds walk
• Tonnara beach windsurfing
• Pozzo di Mastri farmhouse inn

Within easy reach
Bonifacio (pp. 162-167)
Porto-Vecchio
(pp. 158-161)
Surtène (pp. 170-173)
Santa-Lucia (pp. 182-183)

Tourist office
Bonifacio:
☎ 04 95 73 11 88

A walk through the Naseo sheepfolds
Along with the Bitalza sheepfolds located a little further north (p. 161), these are some of the most beautiful and best-preserved shepherds' huts in Corsica. The area, a vast meadow surrounded by

forest, is also well worth seeing. You can take a walk here from the path that climbs to the Montagne de Cagna – it should take you no more than 30 minutes to reach the Naseo site. If you prefer, you can take a route that's a little less strenuous, which departs from the hamlets of Vacca and Piscia. This is a very beautiful walk across woodland and rocky terrain (around four hours round trip). Interestingly enough, certain unusually powerful and aromatic plants could be found growing around the sheepfolds of Naseo and Bitalza until recently. The local police didn't take too kindly to this, however, and soon put a stop to it – not too surprising really!

The amazing balancing rock of Uomo di Cagna

Sartène
'the most Corsican town in Corsica'

So said Mérimée, the famous French writer. The island's traditional culture and way of life is certainly much in evidence in this peaceful town, well off the beaten track. And as you stroll around the streets, lined with the town's tall, grey buildings, you'll soon feel that you have discovered the true heart of Corsica.

Sartène's festivities

The Passage Bradi and the pretty Place Maghju lead to the old Genoese citadel, from where you can see far over the Sartène vineyards, which have the best reputation on the island. The tourist office (6, Rue Borgo, ☎ 04 95 77 15 40; open 9am-noon and 2-6.30pm) offers a detailed tour of the old town with commentary. Each year, around 15 June, Sartène hosts a **comedy festival** (*Festival du Rire*), with stand-up comedians, impressionists and clowns. It all seems quite peculiar in this austere town and it's a great opportunity to see the local people laughing at themselves... and foreigners. Another festival worth seeing is the **three-day craft fair** (*Trois Jours de l'Artisanat*), held in early August. Producers of charcuterie, cheese, honey and ceramics, and wood, leather and glass specialists clog the town's narrow streets with their stalls. You can find some good bargains, but be warned – the busier it gets, the higher the prices. Sartène tourist office has information on dates and programmes.

Retreat to the convent

Make sure you visit the hilltop **Saint-Damien convent**, for a panoramic view taking in the whole of the Rizzanese basin,

Saint-Damien convent church

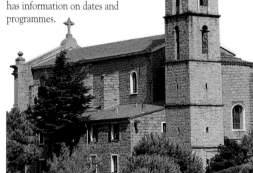

Valinco bay and the town. The best time to take photos is at the end of the afternoon, when the sun has disappeared behind the hill. If you're struck by curiosity or are suffering from a lack of spirituality, then note that you can stay at the convent for the modest sum of 50F per night (Couvent de Saint-Damien, ☎ 04 95 77 06 45). This is a popular retreat so, if you're coming in summer, it's wise to book in the spring.

The orange tree garden hotel
Jardin des Orangers
Route de Propriano
☎ **04 95 77 01 80**
Double rooms from 300F per night.
Closed Oct.-end Mar.
If the convent is full, head for the Jardin des Orangers. There's a hotel here,

comprising a number of small, ochre houses lost in a vast and magnificent garden. It's a splendid sight and as for the smells… peppery figs and pines, the sweet fragrances of the orange trees and lemony pomegranates. With the chattering cicadas in the background, under a clear blue sky, you couldn't possibly ask for more.

Fishing for limpets
In midsummer, Roccapina beach is extremely popular, but a short walk across the scrub and rocks will take you to some deep and very pretty isolated coves. Take the path to the right of the lion rock. The walk is about 1-2 miles (2-3 km) and fine for children. You'll feel completely

detached from the world. This area is famous for its limpets (which you can prise off the rocks with a knife). If you fancy trying this delicacy, simply break the point of the shell with a mallet and cook the limpets on a

Spotcheck
B4

Things to do
• Walk to the 'stone man'
• A Madudina horse treks
• Swimming at Roccapina beach

With children
• A Madudina pony rides
• Limpet fishing at Roccapina
• Palaggiu's megalithic stones

Within easy reach
Propriano (pp. 174-177)
Santa-Lucia (pp. 182-183)
Figari (pp. 168-169)
Alta Rocca (pp. 178-181)

Tourist office
Sartène:
☎ 04 95 77 15 40

A BEACH WITH ITS OWN LION
It may be a mountain village, but Sartène's land extends as far as the coast, making this commune of 4,000 souls the biggest in France. The huge **Plage de Roccapina** is picture-postcard material. The beach has warm, white sand, clear turquoise waters and is watched over by a giant lion-shaped rock, a naturally eroded sculpture that resembles a huge stretching cat. There are no lifeguards, but the bay is safe. If you're feeling peckish, head for **Chez Caralli**, above the beach (open daily in season, ☎ 04 95 77 05 94), where you can enjoy salads, charcuterie, grilled meats and regional wine for less than 100F – enough to satisfy even a lion's appetite!

grill, with the cone pointing downwards, sprinkle with coarse salt, and taste. Don't take limpets that are stuck to each other – these are families, and remember that over-zealous limpet fishing can seriously damage the limpet population, so go easy.

Giuncheto
5 miles (8 km)
S of Sartène
Sample some English cooking
Ferme-Auberge d'Acciola
Route de Bonifacio
☎ 04 95 77 14 00
Restaurant and shop open 15 June-30 Sept., service all day.

The Anglo-Corsican couple who display their fine culinary skills at this farmhouse inn are known as *Les Anglais* ('the English') by the locals. The hostess' strong English accent (when she speaks French) earned them this nickname and you'll have no difficulty detecting the English flavour to the menu, with its delicious fruit tart dessert. They also serve a wonderful selection of cheeses and a fine drop of fresh wine from the vineyards

SADDLE UP FOR AN ADVENTURE
A Madudina (horse riding centre)
Route de Propriano
☎ 04 95 73 40 37
Open 1 July-15 Sept.

There's nothing more pleasant than getting to know Corsica on horseback, and it's also perfectly secure. The horses are mild mannered and the environment is safe. Just sit back and take in the glorious scenery. At the A Madudina centre, all the family can earn their spurs. The adults ride on small, valiant Corsican horses – the same breed that Christopher Columbus took to the New World – and youngsters can trot alongside on calm little ponies. There are a variety of trips, ranging from a simple **one-day walk** to the **adventure trek**, during which you spend the night in tents or hostels. Around 3,000-4,000F for a week's adventure trekking.

of Sartène. To crown this delightful occasion you can sit out on the terrace while admiring the beautiful sunset over the coast. You'll pay around 100F a person for the meal and you won't have to leave empty handed either, as you can stock up on a variety of local products in their shop.

Rare megalithic remains at Palaggiu

Giannuccio

5 miles (8 km) S of Sartène

A well-balanced man – Uomo di Cagna

Uomo di Cagna literally means 'the stone man'. This natural sculpture, shaped by wind and rain, has a tenuous human-like resemblance and its precarious site makes it a real curiosity. Just how does it keep its balance? If you decide to take a closer look – don't worry, the stone isn't going to fall just yet. From the little village of Giannuccio, the pleasant uphill walk to the stone takes four to five hours (don't forget to take plenty of water and a picnic). The walk is signposted from Monaccia d'Aullène and the last small section of the path is a bit tricky. The most beautiful view of the Uomo di Cagna and the surrounding region can be had from another rocky promontory, the Uomo d'Ovace, which is shaped like an egg. On a clear day you can even see the coast of Sardinia.

Roccapina

12 miles (19.5 km) S of Sartène

The Genoese towers

Built by the Genoese as lookout posts, these famous towers are scattered all around the island's coast. They are all within sight of one another so that a warning could be passed on, by trumpet or flare, if a suspicious boat was seen approaching the island. The best preserved is at Sartène, from which there's a wonderful romantic view of the calm sea and the broken coast.

Palaggiu

9.5 miles (15 km) SW of Sartène

Mysterious stones

With its 260 menhirs, all standing to attention in a line, Palaggiu has the largest collection of megalithic stones in the whole of the Mediterranean. Easily accessible, it's signposted from the road from Sartène to Tizzano. Stantari, which is closer to Sartène, also has about 20 stones, one of which is a dolmen – a real rarity in the Mediterranean. Like the ones in Brittany, the dolmen here marks a collective burial ground. However, although many theories abound, the precise origin of the menhirs remains unknown. The sites make interesting places to walk around, whatever their actual meaning may be.

Propriano sun-kissed waters

S quashed between the headlands of Porto-Pollo and Campomoro, Valinco bay is always as calm as a lake. Meanwhile, Propriano, at the end of the bay, is one of the island's most popular tourist destinations. Tens of thousands of holidaymakers alight from the ferries here every summer.

Open daily 8am-8pm (except Sun. afternoon) in season, 9am-noon and 2-6pm out of season. Closed Wed.

A lively place to visit

Propriano's fish restaurants, café terraces, busy jetties and lively streets are charming and certainly worth a half-day visit (maps and tour guides available from tourist office). Avenue Napoléon runs alongside the harbour and is packed with businesses and bistros, with virtually everything that you'd find in any coastal resort. The real charm of Propriano, however, is its naval cemetery.

Plentiful accommodation

In Propriano there's no shortage of places to stay, including hotels, guesthouses, campsites and other rental accommodation. Still, demand is always high, so book early in the spring if you're planning to come in the height of summer. The tourist office will be happy to send you a list of available accommodation.

Tourist office, Port de Plaisance, 20110 Propriano, ☎ 04 95 76 01 49, fax: 04 95 76 00 65

THE BATHS AT BARACI

Bains de Baraci
3.5 miles (6 km)
E of Propriano
Route de Baraci
☎ **04 95 76 30 40**
Open 9am-1pm
and 3-9pm in season,
9am-noon and 2-7pm
out of season.
Admission charge.
If you think the Mediterranean is cold, then these baths may be the perfect answer for you. Water cure enthusiasts and those with aching muscles will love the sulphurous waters in these ancient Roman spas. There are two natural swimming pools, at 100°F (38°C) and 108°F (42°C) respectively. Although very popular at the start of the 20thC, the baths were abandoned for many years until being re-opened only a few years ago to the delight of many. It's best to go on a Wednesday or a Saturday in season, when the baths are open at night. When the cold wind gets up in the bay, there's nothing better than a good soak in one of these hot tubs. Sit back and relax those tired muscles, just like the ancient Romans used to. When in Propriano...

Overlooking the town and Valinco bay, the cemetery is a disparate mix of white, cream and ochre mausoleums with pink-tiled roofs. It's best to walk there in the early morning or late afternoon, when the low-angled sunshine will clearly define every contour of the jumbled granite and limestone. Take your camera with you.

Tasty sea urchins

L'Hippocampe restaurant
Rue Pandolfi
☎ **04 95 76 11 01**
Late orders in season.
Closed out of season.
In the rosy twilight, indulge in an enormous platter of sea urchins, freshly caught that day and some fruity white Sartène wine, in the lively atmosphere of one of the port's cafés. This is a time for pure relaxation

after a taxing day on the beach! L'Hippocampe has delicious food and is one of the best value-for-money restaurants in Propriano. A meal should cost around 120F per head, all inclusive.

Dining under the stars

Le Lido restaurant
20110 Propriano
☎ **04 95 76 06 37**
Fax: 04 95 76 31 18
Service until 10.30pm.
Closed out of season.
To reach this restaurant, you may have to walk a little way along the warm sand of Lido beach, but nothing too strenuous. Le Lido restaurant, on the peninsular that extends from Avenue Napoléon, is one of the most pleasant places in Propriano. Enjoying your meal as night falls over the bay is a real pleasure, and one you won't easily forget in a hurry. Expect to pay around 130F per head. It's a short walk to paradise, and worth every step.

Spotcheck
B4

Things to do
• Baraci horse treks
• Walk and swim in Campomoro

With children
• Puraja and Scoglio beaches

Within easy reach
Sartène (pp. 170-173)
Santa-Lucia (pp. 182-183)
Alta Rocca (pp. 178-181)
Porticcio (pp. 96 and 97)

Tourist office
Propriano:
☎ **04 95 76 01 49**

(*Pointe de Porto-Pollo*). It takes about an hour to get to the white sands, or a little longer if you venture a bit further on to the immensely pretty Genoese tower in Capriona. On the way back, stop off at one of the open-air bars in the marina. Not as well known as Propriano, Porto-Pollo may be a good place to stay if you can't make your mind up between the Ajaccio and Valinco bays. Try **Eucalyptus**, an excellent hotel overlooking Valinco bay (☎ 04 95 74 01 52, Fax 04 95 74 06 56. Half-board costs from 640F per day for two people. Open 1 May-1 October).

Baraci

3.5 miles (6 km)
E of Propriano
Horse-riding in Baraci
Ferme Équestre de Baraci
Route d'Ajaccio, BP 65, 20110 Propriano
☎ 04 95 76 08 02 (horse riding centre)
☎ 04 95 76 19 48 (gîte)
Gîte open all-year round. Horse-riding centre in summer and for organised treks out of season.
This horse-riding centre, run by the Leandri family, is one of the best in Corsica. You can choose anything from a simple

Beaches to suit all tastes
Propriano's beaches have earned a good reputation throughout the island. The two largest beaches are **Capo Lauroso** and **Portiglioli**, both of which are popular with sunbathers because of their south-facing positions. Be warned, however, the waves and currents can be powerful and these beaches are not supervised. Families may prefer to visit the nearby **Puraja** beach, near Capo Lauroso, or **Scoglio**, which is smaller, has calmer waters and has lifeguards on duty. The long, west-facing **Baraci** beach is ideal for taking walks or watching the sunset, although the nearby road rather spoils its natural charm.

Porto-Pollo

12.5 miles (20 km)
NW of Propriano
Beautiful coves
If you thrive on solitude and like to take a walk, you'll love this trip to the small, pretty turquoise and white coves of the **Porto-Pollo headland**

one-day trek to a horseback tour right across the island lasting 17 days. Don't worry if you're a beginner – the horses go at a gentle pace on the long trails. The special thing about these treks is that you can see the snow-covered peaks of Cinto and Renoso, the scrubland of Rizzanese and the cliffs of Bonifacio, all in just a few days. The treks require special planning (tents, provisions and other equipment), so it's advisable to book several weeks in advance to avoid missing out. Francis Landri and his daughter are also in great demand as guides.

The Genoese bridge, Spin a Cavallu

However, if you just want to make the most of the beach and the moonlight, you can also sleep and eat at the farm for 140F half-board, and leave the trekking to others!

Spin a Cavallu
4.5 miles (7 km)
E of Propriano

A medieval Genoese bridge

This small Genoese bridge, at Spin a Cavallu, located a short distance from Propriano on the Route de Sartène, epitomises the high quality of 18th-C. Italian architecture. During the 20thC., several locals came up with plans to replace the medieval bridge, but all these attempts were thwarted and it still stands proudly to this day. Its triangular arch is used as the emblem of one of the best local wine producers. Stop for a while and after admiring the bridge, take a stroll along the Rizzanese river.

CAMPOMORO WALK
7.5 miles (12 km)
SW of Propriano

On your return from Campomoro, you have to retrace your steps back down the same path – but you shouldn't have too many reasons to complain. Campomoro is a pretty little fishing port at the southern-most point of Valinco bay. Its long beaches stretch right to the foot of one of the oldest and best-preserved Genoese towers in the whole of Corsica. The immense watchtower was built in the 16thC. and fortified with a star-shaped surrounding wall. It takes around an hour to climb the rocks that

enclose the bay, but from the top the view takes in the Roccapina rocks to the left (p. 173) and to the right, the old Coti Chiavari prison. Campomoro still has that old fishing village feel, with its houses made of ochre stone and its moored boats. Also, there are some pleasant open-air bars if you want to delay your trip back across the scrub. If you're around at the right time, you may be able to take part in a boules tournament organised by the proprietor of **La Mouette** (to the right of the beach, ☎ 04 95 74 22 26).

A view from the sea

From the sea, you get a different and impressive view of Valinco bay and the mountains of Sartène. On a half-day boat trip you can also discover the pretty little beaches of Cupabia bay (*Baie de Cupabia*) and the attractive village of Campomoro. On the Big Blue catamaran, you can have a drink or even buy a ticket to attend a rather bizarre underwater organ concert – a series of musical vibrations that is surprisingly enjoyable (prices from 140F). Information from **Évasion Nautic**, ☎ 04 95 76 04 26 (Easter-October).

Alta Rocca
wild sheep and spring flowers

The Alta Rocca area is extremely attractive. From the Bavella needles to the Cuscione plateau, from the high walls of Levie to the Zonza forests, this is a wild, savage landscape. The inhabitants of Alta Rocca include the island's last remaining wild sheep and stags that have recently been introduced back into the wild.

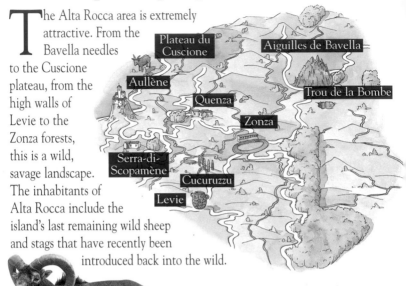

Plateau du Cuscione

Aiguilles de Bavella

Aullène

Quenza

Trou de la Bombe

Zonza

Serra-di-Scopamène

Cucuruzzu

Levie

Col de Bavella

18.5 miles (30 km) NW of Aullène

A panoramic view over Alta Rocca

From the Bavella pass (Col de Bavella) at 4,068 ft (1,240 m), the panoramic view of the granite peaks of the 'Bavella needles' (*Aiguilles de Bavella*) is impressive. The highest of the needles, the *Punta di u Furnellu*, is more than 2,900 ft (900 m) high. You can also admire the scenery from the terrace of the **Auberge du Col de Bavella** (☎ 04 95 57 43 87; open 15 June-15 Nov; lunch served; rooms from 80F per night). On the path from the guesthouse to the top of the mountain there's a small church, the destination of the 'snow pilgrimage' (*pèlerinage des neiges*) every 5 August

Statue of the Virgin and the Bavella needles

BOMBS AWAY!

This is possibly the most dramatic viewpoint in the Corsican mountains. From the pass, take the GR 20 trail (by the statue of the Virgin) to the *Funtana di u Cannone* ('gun carriage'). From there, an easy, signposted path takes you to the unusual site of the *Trou de la Bombe* ('bomb hole'). This huge arch opens into a sinkhole some 1,600 ft (500 m) deep! Although the path is wide and used regularly by tourists, you do need to be careful.

(p. 11). There are other walking trails from the pass, including one starting on the left side of the statue of the Virgin that leads to the base of the needles. Looking towards Solenzara, a track on the right, suitable for vehicles, climbs into the forest to a viewpoint over the whole of the Alta Rocca range. It's simply an unforgettable sight.

Zonza

13 miles (21 km) SE of Aullène

Zonza's racecourse

As you round the bend on the Route de Santa-Lucia from Tallano to Zonza, you'll see an astonishing sight. Below, in a large clearing in a forest of Laricio pines, is the Zonza racecourse. Not surprisingly, this is the only racecourse in the area. Horse races are still organised regularly in summer, especially around 14-15 August. Have a flutter – you may not win a fortune, but you can participate in the electric atmosphere that grips the racecourse. You'll be in the best possible position to see your horse romp home, as the stands are right next to the racetrack. Information and programme: **Alta Rocca tourist centre**, 20170 Levie ☎ 04 95 78 41 95. Open 9am-noon and 2-7pm, July and August only.

Zonza, Théodore, Mohammed and Hassan

King Theodore I of Corsica declared Zonza a tax-free haven when he arrived here in 1736. However, unfortunately for the locals, the French later withdrew the privilege. In 1953, while their own country was in a state of upheaval, King Mohammed V of Morocco and his son Hassan spent five months here, staying at the Hôtel du Mouflon d'Or, before moving to Île Rousse in the winter. This hotel is now a prime holiday centre, with a wide variety of accommodation options (☎ 04 95 78 67 34).

Spotcheck
B3-B4

Things to do
• Horse trekking in Alta Rocca
• White-water rafting around Quenza
• Bavella pass walk

Within easy reach
Sartène (pp. 170-173)
Santa-Lucia (pp. 182-183)
Propriano (pp. 174-177)
Porto Vecchio (pp. 158-161)

Tourist office
Levie:
☎ 04 95 78 41 95

Zonza is a great place to stay and makes an excellent base for exploring the dramatic, rugged landscape of the surrounding area.

A peaceful walk in Aullène

Aullène is a charming and tranquil village, some 3,000 ft (900 m) above sea level, and it's one of the few places in Corsica to remain quiet in mid-August. Take a pleasant stroll around the tall, grey houses of the village. The surrounding forest, granite peaks and clear blue sky makes for the perfect blend of fresh

The steep streets in the village of Aullène

air and freedom. The owner of the **Hôtel de la Poste** (☎ 04 95 78 61 21; closed Oct.-Apr; double rooms from 200F) will provide you with a very precise guide to all the area's trails, which he wrote himself. Report back after your walk and have a meal in the hotel restaurant, which serves spit-roasted pork. There are set menus at 95F and 120F.

Plateau du Cuscione

6 miles (10 km)
N of Aullène
Eagles and wild pigs
This high-altitude plateau is dry and wild in summer and snow-covered with frozen ponds in the winter. Mountain lovers regard this as a magical place, because of the mysterious quality of the evening light, as it casts shadows over the

surrounding area. The plateau comprises vast expanses of *maquis* scrub, sharp granite rocks and peaks, and wild marshland. Mouflons (wild sheep) live on the plateau, though you'll be very lucky to see one, and there are also wild pigs and other rare fauna, including bearded vultures, kites and eagles.

The area also contains the sources of two of the most beautiful Corsican rivers, the Taravo and the Rizzanese, which descend to the southern plain. It takes two hours to walk to the plateau from Quenza. Maps are available from Quenza town hall (open 9am-noon and 2-6pm, ☎ 04 95 78 62 11). The walk is splendid, but don't spoil your enjoyment by forgetting to bring water, a picnic and a pair of binoculars.

Quenza

8 miles (13 km)
E of Aullène
Alta Rocca horse treks
Centre Equestre
Gîte d'Étape
Hameau de Jalicu
☎ 04 95 78 63 21
The landscape of Alta Rocca seems made for horse trekking. The animals cope easily with the steep paths and being led across the rocky, scrubland terrain is great fun. Heading towards Cuscione from Quenza, you can't miss the hamlet of Jalicu, site of Pierre Millani's refuge. This is a walking shelter, a guesthouse and a horse riding centre all in one as well as the ideal place to spend two or three days getting to know Alta Rocca. Prices start at 550F per day per person for full-board accomodation, with horse trekking included. Pierre Millani knows Cuscione better than anyone else and talks passionately about the area. Reservations are essential, especially in summer.

SERRA DI SCOPAMENE GÎTE

5 miles (8 km)
S of Aullène
Recently refurbished, this guesthouse in the Scopamene range couldn't be more comfortable. However, the highlight of your stay is likely to be the evening meal. If you're here in spring, you may

be served the famous *figatelli*, which the owner, Henri, makes himself. These Corsican sausages taste absolutely heavenly. The other traditional dish served here – a wild boar stew – always goes down a treat with famished walkers and no one ever leaves the table hungry. However, it's advisable to book, especially for groups wanting to stay together in a dormitory. Half board costs 160F per person. For information: ☎ 04 95 78 64 90.

Canyoning and white-water rafting

I Muntagnoli Corsi
☎ 04 95 78 64 05
Open all-year round. There's certainly no shortage of water here. **Canyoning** enthusiasts love the Alta Rocca rapids. If it's your first descent, the I Muntagnoli team will advise you on how to begin and treat you to all the thrills and spills of the rapids in complete safety. The association also runs a gîte at Quenza and you can take full advantage while in the area. A delightful meal of spit-roasted wild boar and a

quilted bed costs about 500F per person, equipment hire included (half board compulsory in summer).

Cucuruzzu

8 miles (13 km)
S of Aullène
Cucuruzzu archaeological site

Tours 1 Apr.-30 Oct.
Open 9am-6pm
(8pm in July and Aug.).
Admission charge.
This archaeological site dates from the Bronze Age, 2000 BC. The tall, intact spirals of stone lead to a circular promontory with a view over the whole of southern Corsica, from

Monte Incudine to Bonifacio. On arrival, you'll be handed a tape-recorded commentary that will guide you around the site. A short distance away, there's another village from the same period, named Capula (maps available at the entrance to Cucuruzzu). Capula was actually inhabited until the Middle Ages.

Levie

16 miles (26 km)
SE of Aullène
'The Lady of Bonifacio'

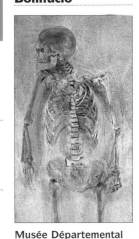

Musée Départemental de Levie

☎ 04 95 78 47 98.
Open daily 10am-6pm in season, 10am-noon and 2-4.30pm out of season.
Closed Sun. and Mon.
Admission charge.
The Levie museum illuminates 10,000 years of Corsican history. The artefacts exhibited here include tools, pottery fragments and cooking utensils from the nearby prehistoric sites of Cucuruzzu, Capula and Calec. You can also see Corsica's most important archaeological find – the legendary *Dame de Bonifacio*, who is almost 9,000 years old. These human remains are the oldest ever discovered in Corsica.

The breathtaking Costello de Cucuruzzu site

Santa-Lucia-di-Tallano
the spirit of the mountains

S anta-Lucia-di-Tallano preserves the pastoral spirit of the early-20thC. mountain dwellers, with its tall, granite houses, arched streets and little squares where the villagers get together at the end of the day to unwind, watch a game of boules and enjoy a glass of pastis or two. This is the true mountain lifestyle.

The Saint François convent

In 1492 Christopher Columbus, who is thought to have hailed from Calvi, discovered America. In the same year, Count Rinuccio della Rocca, who was brought up in Santa-Lucia, established the **Saint-François convent** (Couvent de Saint-François), which dominates the south-western part of the town. The convent's cloister boasts a magnificently realistic painting of Christ's Crucifixion (restored in Ajaccio in 1999), which was donated to the convent by the Rocca family. The painting is the work of the Spanish artist Castelsardo. The convent also offers a wonderful view of the sunset over Propriano. To get into the convent, you'll need to obtain the key from the town hall (*mairie*). Don't forget to return the key after your visit.

A charming place to stay
U Fragnonu guesthouse
20112 Santa-Lucia-di-Tallano
☎ 04 95 78 82 67 or 04 95 78 82 56
Open all-year round.
U Fragnonu, which literally means 'the big mill', is an old oil-mill, restored using the original 19th-C. stone. The rooms are big and beautiful, with two to four beds, and are popular with walkers and non-walkers just passing through the village. Your friendly and informative hosts, Carlo and Palma, can tell you all about the best family walks around the gîte. Half board from around 180F a night. The guesthouse is always full in summer, so book well in advance or time your visit in the spring. It's worth coming just for Palma's chestnut-flour tart and the lasagne with spinach and brocciu cheese – simply delicious.

IN SEARCH OF THE WHITE DIAMOND

The quarries closed over 20 years ago and now there's hardly any diorite left in Alta Rocca, although occasionally a lucky walker stumbles upon an example of this rare precious stone. Deposits of this grainy, volcanic rock are extremely rare; there's just a small deposit in Australia, but it's nowhere near as pure as the Corsican diorite. Diorite was once highly prized for its white or grey colour, speckled with black spots, which gave monuments, such as the Medici funeral chapel in Florence, a unique charm.

At **Mme Renucci** (next to the Hôtel Leandri), you can still buy a piece of this precious rock to take home and proudly display on your mantlepiece (prices start from 50F). However, you'll find the most beautiful example at the Serra di Scopamène gîte (p. 181). This heavy diorite slab was discovered by Henri found during one of his walks in the Corsican scrub in 1997.

Spotcheck
B4

Things to do

• Thermal baths at Caldane
• Walks from the U Fragnonu guesthouse
• Searching for diorite

Within easy reach

Propriano (pp. 174-177)
Sartène (pp. 170-173)
Porto-Vecchio
(pp. 158 161)

Tourist offices

Levie: ☎ 04 95 78 41 95
Propriano: ☎ 04 95 76 01 49

Mela

3 miles (5 km) E of
Santa-Lucia-di-Tallano
Picture-perfect

Views of this pretty village adorn the front of nearly all the tourist brochures. Below the road from Santa-Lucia to Levie, the tangled buildings of Mela, huddled around a charming little square, the shining stones of the cobbled streets and the mountainous backdrop makes a picture-perfect view. The best time and place to take a photo is around 9am, when the sun is still high above Zonza and Levie, from one of the tortuous bends that overlook the hamlet

Caldane

6 miles (10 km) S of
Santa-Lucia-di-Tallano
Open-air thermal spa
Bains de Caldane
Open 8am-midnight.
Admission charge.

The Baraci baths (p. 175) are more appealing, but the sulphurous Caldane spa will certainly relax any aching muscles and alleviate any rheumatic pain you may have. The water's therapeutic

qualities are unquestioned, even if their grey and muddy appearance doesn't tempt you to linger in your restorative bath. Note that the place is not well signposted. Don't miss the D 148 turn, around 2.5 miles (4 km) from Santa-Lucia, heading towards Sartène.

Mela village

Bastelica
home of Sampiero Corso

Sampiero Corso,
revolutionary hero
of the Genoese
occupation

Sampiero Corso, one of the greatest Corsican revolutionaries, was born here in 1498. Staunchly opposed to Genoese rule, Corso managed to convince the king of France to intervene against Genoa. From 1560, he operated a group of guerrilla rebels, inflicting considerable damage on the occupying forces.

Bastelica walking trails

Bastelica is a rustic mountain village that makes a good base for walks to the **Renoso and Niello mountains**. For winter tours, the nearby small Val d'Ese resort, recently reopened by Stéphane Léonetti, is one of the best equipped on the island, along with the Ghisoni refuge. If walking's not really your thing, just take a short stroll to the hamlet of Costa to take in the panoramic view over the whole of the Renoso range. Don't miss this opportunity – the view is quite breathtaking in both winter and summer alike.

Gourmet shopping

**François Urbani
Quartier Stazzona,
20119 Bastelica
☎ 04 95 28 71 83**
Open daily
(ring the bell
if no one is there).
Bastelica is a prime location for Coriscan charcuterie. As in the neighbouring town of Niolo, the animals enjoy good mountain air and excellent

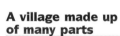

pasture and the flavour of the meat really benefits. At François Urbani's shop you can try all the charcuterie for which Bastelica is famous, including fresh *prisuttu* and smoked *coppa*.

A village made up of many parts

Bastelica, made up from six pretty hamlets hidden away in a chestnut forest, is one of the highest villages on the island (2,600 ft/800 m above sea level). Surrounded by

KEEP YOUR EYE ON THE SKI LIFT

This is a lovely summer walk. From the small ski station at the Ese pass (Col d'Ese), follow the largest ski lift to Coperchiata (6,361 ft/ 1,939 m). This is a short and gentle climb through a shady beech forest and it's suitable for all the family (two hours round trip). From Coperchiata there's one of the best views of the valley's highest summit, Monte Renoso (7,700 ft/ 2,350 m). It's a perfect spot to enjoy a picnic. Why not buy some goodies from François Urbani's shop before setting off

mountains, it's an enchanting location. In summer, the village is delightfully cool compared to the stifling coastal resorts, and has become very popular. Many Corsicans holiday here, and they have renovated the tall old houses with their outside staircases. Sampiero Corso's house is located in the hamlet of Dominicacci, at the very top of the hill.

Local auberge cuisine

U Castagnetu restaurant

Bastelica 20119
☎ 04 95 28 70 71
Closed Nov. and Dec.
Stop here for a fine selection of charcuterie, an invigorating wild pig stew or a potato and brocciu omelette, a good bottle of wine from the slopes

of Ajaccio and some chestnut fritters (*frittelli a gaju frescu*). Then round off this delicious meal with a refreshing nap in the shade of the chestnut trees on the surrounding hills. The auberge has one of the best restaurants in the village, much acclaimed by various gastronomic associations. It's located right next to the statue of Sampiero Corso – a real gem of a place. Allow around 150F per head, including wine.

The Prunelli and Val d'Ese gorges

This car trip should not be missed. Take the D3 from Ajaccio, which climbs straight to the small village of Bastelicaccia, where there's a wide panorama of Ajaccio bay. Then follow the winding **Gorges de Prunelli**, stopping along the way to see the valley and the reservoir, and don't miss the majestic Bocca di Mercuio ring of mountains. Afterwards, you may want to stop at the village of Tolla, clinging to the dizzy heights of the cliff. Without stopping in

Bastelica (you'll return there later), continue along the **Ese valley** (Val d'Ese) on the D27, another road that offers impressive views. However, make sure you drive carefully as the road is very narrow. There are a number of lookout points opposite the magnificent Renoso and Niello mountains. Having enjoyed the spectacular views, just make your way back down the same road to Bastelica. If you want to return to Ajaccio, follow the D27 on the other side of the gorges for more splendid views, including some stunning waterfalls.

Spotcheck
B3

Things to do

• Prunelli gorges by car
• François Urbani's charcuterie
• Renoso mountain walks

Within easy reach

Ajaccio (pp. 92-95)
Fiumorbo valley (pp. 156-157)
Venaco and Vizzavone forest (pp. 142-143)

Tourist office

Ajaccio:
☎ 04 95 51 03 53

This guide was written by OLIVIER GOUJON, with the help of FRÉDÉRIC OLIVIER, FRANÇOISE PICON and AUDE SARRAZIN

Illustrations: PASCAL GINDRE

Illustrated maps: RENAUD MARCA

Cartography: © IDÉ INFOGRAPHIE (THOMAS GROLLIER)

Translation and adaptation: Y2K TRANSLATIONS (Email: info@y2ktranslations.com)

Additional design and editorial assistance: SOFI MOGENSEN, SIMON TUITE, JANE MOSELEY and CHRISTINE BELL

Project manager: LIZ COGHILL

We have done our best to ensure the accuracy of the information contained in this guide. However, addresses, telephone numbers, opening times etc. inevitably do change from time to time, so if you find a discrepancy please do let us know. You can contact us at: hachetteuk@orionbooks.co.uk or write to us at Hachette UK, address below.

Hachette UK guides provide independent advice. The authors and compilers do not accept any remuneration for the inclusion of any addresses in these guides.

Please note that we cannot accept any responsibility for any loss, injury or inconvenience sustained by anyone as a result of any information or advice contained in this guide.

Distributed in the United States of America by Sterling Publishing Co., Inc. 387 Park Avenue South, New York, NY 10016-8810

A CIP catalogue for this book is available from the British Library

ISBN 1 84202 100 1

Hachette UK, Cassell & Co., The Orion Publishing Group, Wellington House, 125 Strand, London WC2R 0BB

Printed in France by I.M.E. - 25110 Baume-les-Dames

Handy words and phrases

• •

Over the next few pages you'll find a selection of very basic French vocabulary and many apologies if the word you are looking for is missing. For those struggling with French menus, there is more help at the back of the book in the detailed menu decoder.

Let us begin, however, with a very basic guide to some French grammar: All French nouns are either masculine or feminine and gender is denoted as follows: 'the' singular is translated by le (m), la (f) or l' (in front of a word beginning with a vowel or mute 'h'; 'the' plural = les (whatever gender and in front of a vowel or mute 'h'). 'A' = un (m), une(f) (no exceptions for vowels or mute 'h').

There are two forms of the word 'you' – tu is 'you' in the singular, very informal and used with people you know, vous is 'you' in the singular but is used in formal situations and when you don't know the person, vous is also the plural form. Young people often address each other as 'tu' automatically, but when in doubt and to avoid offence, always use 'vous'.

Adjectives agree with the gender of the accompanying noun. For a singular masculine noun there is no change to the adjective, but to indicate the masculine plural, an 's' is added to the end of the adjective; an 'e' is usually added for a feminine noun and 'es' for the plural. If you are not very familiar with French don't worry too much about gender agreement when talking (unless you wish to perfect your pronunciation, as 'e' or 'es' usually makes the final consonant hard), we have used feminine versions where applicable simply to help with the understanding of written French. These are either written out in full or shown as '(e)'. Finally, if you do not know the right French word try using the English one with a French accent – it is surprising how often this works.

The verb 'to be'

• •

I am	je suis
you are (informal/sing.)	tu es
he/she/it is	il(m)/elle(f)/il est*
we are	nous sommes
you are (formal/plural)	vous êtes
they are	ils(m)/elles(f) sont*

When you are in a hurry gender can complicate things – just say le or la, whichever comes into your head first and you will sometimes be right and usually be understood.

* The most common forms use the masculine: 'it is' = il est, 'they are'= ils sont. C'est = 'that is' or 'this is', and is not gender specific.

Essential vocabulary

• •

Yes/No	Oui/Non
OK	D'accord
That's fine	C'est bon
Please	S'il vous plaît
Thank you	Merci
Good morning/Hello	Bonjour (during the day)

Good evening/night/Hello	Bonsoir (during the evening)
Hello/Goodbye (very informal)	Salut
Goodbye	Au revoir
See you soon.	bientôt
Excuse me	Excusez-moi
I am sorry	Je suis désolé(m)/désolée(f)
Pardon?	Comment?

Handy phrases

••

Do you speak English?	Parlez-vous anglais?
I don't speak French	Je ne parle pas français
I don't understand	Je ne comprends pas
Could you speak more slowly please?	Pouvez-vous parler moins vite s'il vous plaît?
Could you repeat that, please?	Pouvez-vous répéter, s'il vous plaît?
again	encore
I am English/Scottish/ Welsh/Irish/American/ Canadian/Australian/ a New Zealander	Je suis anglais(e) /écossais(e)/ gallois(e)/ irlandais(e)/ américain(e)/ canadien(ne)/ australien(ne)/ néo-zélandais(e)
My name is ...	Je m'appelle ...
What is your name?	Comment vous appelez-vous?
How are you?	Comment allez-vous?
Very well, thank you.	Très bien, merci.
Pleased to meet you.	Enchanté(e).
Mr/Mrs	Monsieur/Madame
Miss/Ms	Mademoiselle/Madame
How?	Comment?
What?	Quel (m)/Quelle (f)?
When?	Quand?
Where (is/are)?	Où (est/sont)?
Which?	Quel (m)/Quelle (f)?
Who?	Qui?
Why?	Pourquoi?

Essential words

••

good	bon/bonne
bad	mauvais/mauvaise
big	grand/grande
small	petit/petite
hot	chaud/chaude
cold	froid/froide
open	ouvert/ouverte
closed	fermé/fermée
toilets	les toilettes/les w.c.
women	dames
men	hommes
free (unoccupied)	libre
occupied	occupé/occupée
free (no charge)	gratuit/gratuite
entrance	l'entrée
exit	la sortie
prohibited	interdit/interdite
no smoking	défense de fumer

Time and space

••

PERIODS OF TIME

a minute	une minute
half an hour	une demie-heure
an hour	une heure
a week	une semaine
fortnight	une quinzaine
month	un mois
year	un an/une année
today	aujourd'hui
yesterday/tomorrow	hier/demain
morning	le matin
afternoon	l'après-midi
evening/night	e soir/la nuit
during (the night)	pendant (la nuit)
early/late	tôt/tard

TELLING THE TIME

What time is it?	Quelle heure est-il?
At what time?	A quelle heure?
(at) 1 0'clock/2 0'clock etc.	(à) une heure/deux heures etc.
half past one	une heure et demie
quarter past two	deux heures et quart
quarter to three	trois heures moins le quart
(at) midday	à midi
(at) midnight	à minuit

Getting around

••

by bicycle	à bicyclette/en vélo
by bus	en bus
by car	en voiture
by coach	en car
on foot	à pied
by plane	en avion
by taxi	en taxi
by train	en train

IN TOWN

map of the city	un plan de la ville
I am going to ...	Je vais à.....
I want to go to....	Je voudrais aller à ...
I want to get off at...	Je voudrais descendre à
platform	le quai
return ticket	un aller-retour
single ticket	un aller simple
ticket	le billet
timetable	l'horaire
airport	l'aéroport
bus/coach station	la gare routière
bus stop	l'arrêt de bus
district	le quartier/l'arrondissement
street	la rue
taxi rank	la station de taxi
tourist information office	l'office du tourisme
train station	la gare
underground	le métro

bag/handbag	le sac/le sac-à-main
case	la valise
left luggage	la consigne
luggage	les bagages

DIRECTIONS

Is it far?	Est-ce que c'est loin?
How far is it to...?	Combien de kilomètres d'ici à ...?
Is it near?	Est-ce que c'est près d'ici?
here/there	ici/là
near/far	près/loin
left/right	gauche/droite
on the left/right	à gauche/à droite
straight on	tout droit
at the end of	au bout de
up	en haut
down	en bas
above (the shop)	au-dessus (du magasin)
below (the bed)	au-dessous (le lit)
opposite (the bank)	en face (de la banque)
next to (the window)	à côté (de la fenêtre)

DRIVING

Please fill the tank (car)	Le plein, s'il vous plaît
car hire	la location de voitures
driver's licence	le permis de conduire
petrol	l'essence
rent a car	louer une voiture
unleaded	sans plomb

In the hotel

I have a reservation	J'ai une réservation
for 2 nights	pour 2 nuits
I leave	Je pars .....
I'd like a room	Je voudrais une chambre
Is breakfast included?	le petit-déjeuner est inclus?
single room	une chambre à un lit
room with double bed	une chambre à lit double
twin room	une chambre à deux lits
room with bathroom	une chambre avec salle de bains
and toilet	et toilette/W.C.
a quiet room	une chambre calme
bath	le bain
shower	la douche
with air conditioning	avec climatisation

1st/2nd floor etc	premier/deuxième étage
breakfast	le petit-déjeuner
dining room	la salle à manger
ground floor	le rez-de-chaussée (RC)
key	la clef
lift/elevator	l'ascenseur

PAYING

How much?	C'est combien, s'il vous plaît?/ Quel est le prix?
Do you accept credit cards?	Est-ce que vous acceptez les cartes de crédit?
Do you have any change?	Avez-vous de la monnaie?

(in) cash	(en) espèces
coin	le pièce de monnaie
money	l'argent
notes	les billets
price	le prix
travellers' cheques	les chèques de voyage

Eating out

If you are having trouble understanding the rather complicated-looking menu which is put before you, then turn to p.x for the menu decoder. In the meantime, the following phrases should be useful when you are trying to communicate with the waiter or waitress.

GENERAL
Do you have a table?	Avez-vous une table libre?
I would like to reserve a table	Je voudrais réserver une table.
I would like to eat.	Je voudrais manger.
I would like something to drink	Je voudrais boire quelque chose.
I would like to order, please	Je voudrais commander, s'il vous plait.
The bill, please.	L'addition, s'il vous plait.
I am a vegetarian.	Je suis végétarien (ne).

MEALS AND MEALTIMES
breakfast	le petit-déjeuner
cover charge	le couvert
dessert	le dessert
dinner	le dîner
dish of the day	le plat du jour
fixed price menu	la formule/le menu à prix fixe
fork	la fourchette
knife	le couteau
lunch	le déjeuner
main course	le plat principal
menu	le menu/la carte
(Is the) service included?	Est-ce que le service est compris?
soup	la soupe/le potage
spoon	la cuillère
starter	l'entrée/le hors-d'oeuvre
waiter	Monsieur
waitress	Madame, Mademoiselle
wine list	la carte des vins

COOKING STYLES
baked	cuit/cuite au four
boiled	bouilli/bouillie
fried	à la poêle
grilled	grillé/grillée
medium	à point
poached	poché/pochée
rare	saignant
steamed	à la vapeur
very rare	bleu
well done	bien cuit

MEAT, POULTRY, GAME AND OFFAL
bacon	le bacon
beef	le boeuf
chicken	le poulet
duck	le canard

frogs' legs	les cuisses de grenouilles
game	le gibier
ham	le jambon
kidneys	les rognons
lamb	l'agneau
meat	la viande
pork	le porc
rabbit	le lapin
salami style sausage (dry)	le saucisson-sec
sausage	la saucisse
snails	les escargots
steak	l'entrecôte/le steak/le bifteck
veal	le veau

FISH AND SEAFOOD

cod	le cabillaud/la morue
Dublin bay prawn/scampi	la langoustine
fish	le poisson
herring	le hareng
lobster	le homard
mullet	le rouget
mussels	les moules
oysters	les huîtres
pike	le brochet
prawns	les crevettes
salmon (smoked)	le saumon (fumé)
sea bass	le bar
seafood	les fruits de mer
skate	le raie
squid	le calmar
trout	la truite
tuna	le thon

VEGETABLES, PASTA AND RICE

cabbage	le chou
cauliflower	le chou-fleur
chips/french fries	les frites
garlic	l'ail
green beans	les haricots verts
leeks	les poireaux
onions	les oignons
pasta	les pâtes
peas	les petits pois
potatoes	les pommes-de-terre
rice	le riz
sauerkraut	la choucroute
spinach	les épinards
vegetables	les légumes

SALAD ITEMS

beetroot	la betterave
cucumber	le concombre
curly endive	la salade frisée
egg	un oeuf
green pepper/red pepper	le poivron/poivron rouge
green salad	la salade verte
lettuce	la laitue
tomato	la tomate

FRUIT

apple	la pomme
banana	la banane

blackberries	les mûres
blackcurrants	les cassis
cherries	les cerises
fresh fruit	le fruit frais
grapefruit	le pamplemousse
grapes	les raisins
lemon/lime	le citron/le citron vert
orange	l'orange
peach	la pêche
pear	la poire
plums	les prunes/les mirabelles (type of plum)
raspberries	les framboises
red/white currants	les groseilles
strawberries	les fraises

DESSERTS AND CHEESE

apple tart	la tarte aux pommes
cake	le gâteau
cheese	le fromage
cream	la crème fraîche
goat's cheese	le fromage de chèvre
ice cream	la glace

SUNDRIES

ashtray	un cendrier
bread	le pain
bread roll	le petit pain
butter	le beurre
crisps	les chips
mustard	la moutarde
napkin	la serviette
oil	l'huile
peanuts	les cacahuètes
salt/pepper	le sel/le poivre
toast	le toast
vinegar	le vinaigre

DRINKS

beer	la bière
a bottle of	une bouteille de
black coffee	un café noir
coffee	un café
with cream	un café-crème
with milk	un café au lait
a cup of	une tasse de
decaffeinated coffee	un café décaféiné/un déca
espresso coffee	un express
freshly-squeezed lemon/ orange juice	un citron pressé/une orange pressée
a glass of	un verre de
herbal tea	une tisane/infusion
with lime/verbena	au tilleul/à la verveine
with mint	à la menthe
with milk/lemon	au lait/au citron
milk	le lait
(some) mineral water	de l'eau minérale
orange juice	un jus d'orange
(some) tap water	de l'eau du robinet
(some) sugar	du sucre
tea	un thé
wine (red/white)	le vin (rouge/blanc)

Shopping (also see 'Paying')

••

USEFUL SHOPPING VOCABULARY

I'd like to buy...	Je voudrais acheter…
Do you have…?	Avez-vous …?
How much, please?	C'est combien, s'il vous plaît?
I'm just looking, thank you	Je regarde, merci.
It's for a gift	C'est pour un cadeau.

SHOPS

antique shop	le magasin d'antiquités
baker	la boulangerie
bank	la banque
book shop	la librairie
cake shop	la pâtisserie
cheese shop	la fromagerie
chemist/drugstore	la pharmacie
clothes shop	le magasin de vêtements
delicatessen	la charcuterie
department store	le grand magasin
gift shop	le magasin de cadeaux
the market	le marché
newsagent	le magasin de journaux
post office	la poste/le PTT
shoe shop	le magasin de chaussures
the shops	les boutiques/magasins
tobacconist	le tabac
travel agent	l'agence de voyages

expensive	cher
cheap	pas cher, bon marché
sales	les soldes
size (in clothes)	la taille
size (in shoes)	la pointure
too expensive	trop cher

TELEPHONING

telephone/phone booth	le téléphone/la cabine téléphonique
phone card	la carte téléphonique
post card	la carte postale
stamps	les timbres

Months of the year

••

January	janvier
February	février
March	mars
April	avril
May	mai
June	juin
July	juillet
August	août
September	septembre
October	octobre
November	novembre
December	décembre

a year	un an/une année
a month	un mois

Days of the week

....

Monday	lundi
Tuesday	mardi
Wednesday	mercredi
Thursday	jeudi
Friday	vendredi
Saturday	samedi
Sunday	dimanche

Colours

....

black	noir/noire
blue	bleu/bleue
brown	brun/brune
green	vert/verte
orange	orange
pink	rose
red	rouge
white	blanc/blanche
yellow	jaune

Numbers

....

enough	assez
zero	zéro
one; first	un/une; premier/première
two/second	deux/deuxième
three/third	trois/troisième
four/fourth	quatre/quatrième
five/fifth	cinq/cinquième
six/sixth	six/sixième
seven/seventh	sept/septième
eight/eighth	huit/huitième
nine/nineth	neuf/neuvième
ten/tenth etc	dix/dixième etc
eleven	onze
twelve	douze
thirteen	treize
fourteen	quatorze
fifteen	quinze
sixteen	seize
seventeen	dix-sept
eighteen	dix-huit
nineteen	dix-neuf
twenty	vingt
twenty-one	vingt-et-un
twenty-two/three etc	vingt-deux/trois etc.
thirty	trente
forty	quarante
fifty	cinquante
sixty	soixante
seventy	soixante-dix
eighty	quatre-vingts
ninety	quatre-vingt-dix
hundred	cent
thousand	mille

Menu decoder

À point medium rare
Abats offal
Abricot apricot
Acarne sea-bream
Affiné(e) improve, ripen, mature (common term with cheese)
Africaine (à l') african style: with aubergines, tomatoes, ceps
Agneau lamb
Agrumes citrus fruits
Aigre-doux sweet-sour
Aiguillette thin slice
Ail garlic
Aile (Aileron) wing (winglet)
Aïoli mayonnaise, garlic, olive oil
Algues seaweed
Aligot purée of potatoes, cream, garlic, butter and fresh Tomme de Cantal (or Laguiole) cheese
Allemande (à l') German style: with sauerkraut and sausages
Alsacienne (à l') Alsace style: with sauerkraut, sausages and sometimes foie gras
Amande almond
Amandine almond-flavoured
Amer bitter
Américaine (à l') Armoricaine (à l') sauce with dry white wine, cognac, tomatoes, shallots
Amuse-gueule appetizer
Ananas pineapple
Anchoiade anchovy crust
Anchois anchovy
Ancienne (à l') in the old style
Andouille smoked tripe sausage
Andouillette small chitterling (tripe) sausage
Aneth dill
Anglaise (à l') plain boiled
Anguille eels
Anis aniseed
Arachide peanut
Arc-en-ciel rainbow trout
Artichaud artichoke
Asperge asparagus
Assaisonné flavoured or seasoned with; to dress a salad
Assiette (de) plate (of)
Aubergine aubergine, eggplant
Aumônière pancake drawn up into shape of beggar's purse
Auvergnate (à l') Auvergne style: with cabbage, sausage and bacon
Avocat avocado pear
Baba au rhum sponge dessert with rum syrup
Baguette long bread loaf
Baie berry
Baigné bathed or lying in
Banane banana
Bar sea-bass
Barbeau de mer red mullet
Barbue brill

Basilic basil
Basquaise (à la) Basque style: Bayonne ham, rice and peppers
Baudroie monkfish, anglerfish
Bavette skirt of beef
Béarnaise thick sauce with egg yolks, shallots, butter, white wine and tarragon vinegar
Béchamel creamy white sauce
Beignet fritter
Belle Hélène poached pear with ice cream and chocolate sauce
Berrichonne bordelaise sauce
Betterave beetroot
Beurre (Échiré) butter (finest butter from Poitou-Charentes)
Beurre blanc sauce with butter, shallots, wine vinegar and sometimes dry white wine
Beurre noir sauce with brown butter, vinegar, parsley
Bière à la pression beer on tap
Bière en bouteille bottled beer
Bifteck steak
Bigarade (à la) orange sauce
Bisque shellfish soup
Blanc (de volaille) white breast (of chicken); can also describe white fish fillet or white vegetables
Blanchaille whitebait
Blanquette white stew
Blé corn or wheat
Blettes swiss chard
Blinis small, thick pancakes
Boeuf à la mode beef braised in red wine
Boeuf Stroganoff beef, sour cream, onions, mushrooms
Bombe ice-cream
Bonne femme (à la) white wine sauce, shallots, mushrooms
Bordelaise (à la) Bordeaux style: brown sauce with shallots, red wine, beef bone marrow
Boudin blanc white coloured sausage-shaped mixture; pork and sometimes chicken
Boudin noir black pudding
Bouillabaise Mediterranean fish stew and soup
Bouillon broth, light consommé
Bouquet garni bunch of herbs used for flavouring
Bourguignonne (à la) Burgundy style: red wine, onions, bacon and mushrooms
Bourride creamy fish soup with aioli
Brandade de morue salt cod
Bretonne sauce with celery, leeks, beans and mushrooms
Brioche sweet yeast bread
Brochet pike
Brochette (de) meat or fish on a skewer
Brouillé scrambled
Brûlé(e) toasted
Bruxelloise sauce with asparagus, butter and eggs

Cabillaud cod
Cacahouète roasted peanut
Cacao cocoa
Café coffee
Caille quail
Cajou cashew nut
Calmar (Calamar) inkfish, squid
Campagne country style
Canard duck
Caneton (Canette) duckling
Cannelle cinnamon
Carbonnade braised beef in beer, onions and bacon
Carré chop
Casse-croûte snack
Cassis blackcurrant
Cassolette small pan
Cassoulet casserole of beans, sausage and/or pork, goose, duck
Cèpe fine, delicate mushroom
Cerise (noire) cherry (black)
Cerneau walnut
Cervelas pork garlic sausage
Cervelle brains
Champignons (des bois) mushrooms (from the woods)
Chanterelle apricot coloured mushroom
Chantilly whipped cream with sugar
Charcuterie cold meat cuts
Charcutière sauce with onions, white wine, gherkins
Chasseur sauce with white wine, mushrooms, shallots
Chateaubriand thick fillet steak
Chaussons pastry turnover
Chemise (en) pastry covering
Chicon chicory
Chicorée curly endive
Chipiron see calmar
Choix (au) a choice of
Chou (vert) cabbage
Choucroute souring of vegetables, usually with cabbage (sauerkraut), peppercorns, boiled ham, potatoes and Strasbourg sausages
Chou-fleur cauliflower
Chou rouge red cabbage
Choux (pâte à) pastry
Ciboule spring onions
Cidre cider
Ciboulette chive
Citron (vert) lemon (lime)
Citronelle lemon grass
Civet stew
Clafoutis cherries in pancake batter
Clou de girofle clove (spice)
Cochon pig
Cochonailles pork products
Cocotte (en) cooking pot
Coeur (de) heart (of)
Coing quince
Colin hake
Compote stewed fruit
Concassé(e) coarsely chopped
Concombre cucumber
Confit(e) preserved or candied
Confiture jam
Confiture d'orange marmalade
Consommé clear soup

Coq (au vin) chicken in red wine sauce
Coque (à la) soft-boiled or served in shell
Coquillage shellfish
Coquille St-Jacques scallop
Coriandre coriander
Cornichon gherkin
Côte d'agneau lamb chop
Côte de boeuf side of beef
Côte de veau veal chop
Côtelette chop
Coulis de thick sauce of
Courge pumpkin
Couscous crushed semolina
Crabe crab
Crécy with carrots and rice
Crème cream
Crème anglaise light custard sauce
Crème brûlée same, less sugar and cream, with praline (see Brûlée)
Crème pâtissière custard filling
Crêpe thin pancake
Crêpe Suzette sweet pancake with orange liqueur sauce
Cresson watercress
Crevette grise shrimp
Crevette rose prawn
Croque Monsieur toasted cheese or ham sandwich
Croustade small pastry mould with various fillings
Croûte (en) pastry crust (in)
Cru raw
Crudité raw vegetable
Crustacés shell fish
Cuisse (de) leg (of)
Cuissot (de) haunch (of)
Cuit cooked
Datte date
Daube stew (various types)
Daurade sea-bream
Décaféiné decaffeinated coffee
Dégustation tasting
Diane (à la) pepper cream sauce
Dieppoise (à la) Dieppe style: white wine, cream, mussels, shrimps
Dijonaise (à la) with mustard sauce
Dinde young hen turkey
Dindon turkey
Dorade sea-bream
Doux (douce) sweet
Échalotte shallot
Écrevisse freshwater crayfish
Émincé thinly sliced
Encre squid ink, used in sauces
Endive chicory
Entrecôte entrecôte, rib steak
Entremets sweets
Épaule shoulder
Épice spice
Épinard spinach
Escabèche fish (or poultry) marinated in court-bouillon; cold
Escalope thinly cut (meat or fish)
Escargot snail
Espadon swordfish
Estouffade stew with onions, herbs, mushrooms, red or white wine (perhaps garlic)

Estragon tarragon flavoured
Farci(e) stuffed
Farine flour
Faux-filet sirloin steak
Fenouil fennel
Fermière mixture of onions, carrots, turnips, celery, etc.
Feuille de vigne vine leaf
Feuilleté light flaky pastry
Fève broad bean
Ficelle (à la) tied in a string
Ficelles thin loaves of bread
Figue fig
Filet fillet
Financière (à la) Madeira sauce with truffles
Fines de claire oyster (see Huîtres)
Fines herbes mixture of parsley, chives, tarragon, etc.
Flageolet kidney bean
Flamande (à la) Flemish style: bacon, carrots, cabbage, potatoes and turnips
Flambée flamed
Flamiche puff pastry tart
Foie liver
Foie de veau calves liver
Foie gras goose liver
Fond d'artichaut artichoke heart
Fondu(e) (de fromage) melted cheese with wine
Forestière bacon and mushrooms
Four (au) baked in the oven
Fourré stuffed
Frais fresh or cool
Fraise strawberry
Fraise des bois wild strawberry
Framboise raspberry
Frappé frozen or ice cold
Friandise sweets (petits fours)
Fricassée braised in sauce or butter, egg yolks and cream
Frisé(e) curly
Frit fried
Frites chips/French fries
Friture small fried fish
Fromage cheese
Fromage de tête brawn
Fruit de la passion passion fruit
Fruits confits crystallised fruit
Fruits de mer seafood
Fumé smoked
Galette pastry, pancake or cake
Gamba large prawn
Ganache chocolate and crème fraîche mixture used to fill cakes
Garbure (Garbue) vegetable soup
Gâteau cake
Gauffre waffle
Gelée aspic gelly
Genièvre juniper
Gésier gizzard
Gibelotte see Fricassée
Gibier game
Gigot (de) leg of lamb; can describe other meat or fish
Gingembre ginger
Girofle clove
Glacé(e) iced, crystallized, glazed
Glace ice-cream
Gougère round-shaped, egg and cheese choux pastry
Goujon gudgeon
Goujonnettes (de) small fried pieces (of)
Gourmandises sweetmeats; can describe fruits de mer
Graisse fat
Gratin browned
Gratin Dauphinois potato dish with cheese, cream and garlic
Gratin Savoyard potato dish with cheese and butter
Gratiné(e) sauced dish browned with butter, cheese, breadcrumbs, etc.
Gravette oyster (see Huîtres)
Grenouille (cuisses de grenouilles) frog (frogs' legs)
Gribiche mayonnaise sauce with gherkins, capers, hardboiled egg yolks and herbs
Grillade grilled meat
Grillé(e) grilled
Griotte (Griottine) bitter red cherry
Gros sel coarse rock or sea salt
Groseille à maquereau gooseberry
Groseille noire blackcurrant
Groseille rouge redcurrant
Gruyère hard, mild cheese
Hachis minced or chopped-up
Hareng herring
    à l'huile cured in oil
    fumé kippered
    salé bloater
    saur smoked
Haricot bean
Haricot blanc dried white bean
Haricot vert green/French bean
Hollandaise sauce with butter, egg yolk and lemon juice
Homard lobster
Hongroise (à la) Hungarian style: sauce with tomato and paprika
Huile oil
Huîtres oysters
    Les claires: the oyster-fattening beds in Marennes terrain (part of the Charente Estuary, between Royan and Rochefort, in Poitou-Charentes).
    Flat-shelled oysters: *Belons* (from the river Belon in Brittany)
    Gravettes: from Arcachon in the South West); both the above are cultivated in their home oyster beds.
    Marennes are those transferred from Brittany and Arcachon to *les claires*, where they finish their growth.
    Dished oysters (sometimes called *portugaises*): these breed mainly in the Gironde and Charentes estuaries; they mature at Marennes.
    Fines de claires and *spéciales* are the largest; *huîtres de parc* are standard sized. All this lavish care covers a time span of two to four years.
Hure (de) head (of); brawn, jellied
Île flottante unmoulded soufflé of beaten egg with white sugar
Imam bayeldi aubergine with rice, onions, and sautéed tomatoes
Infusion herb tea
Italienne (à l') Italian style: artichokes,

mushrooms, pasta
Jalousie latticed fruit or jam tart
Jambon ham
Jambonneau knuckle of pork
Jambonnette boned and stuffed (knuckle of ham or poultry)
Jarret de veau stew of shin of veal
Jarreton cooked pork knuckle
Jerez sherry
Joue (de) cheek (of)
Julienne thinly-cut vegetables: also ling (cod family)
Jus juice
Lait milk
Laitue lettuce
Lamproie eel-like fish
Langouste spiny lobster or crawfish
Langoustine Dublin Bay prawn
Langue tongue
Lapereau young rabbit
Lapin rabbit
Lard bacon
Lardons strips of bacon
Laurier bay-laurel, sweet bay leaf
Léger (Légère) light
Légume vegetable
Lièvre hare
Limaçon snail
Limande lemon sole
Limon lime
Lit bed
Lotte de mer monkfish, anglerfish
Loup de mer sea-bass
Louvine (Loubine) grey mullet, like a sea-bass (Basque name)
Lyonnaise (a la) Lyonnais style: sauce with wine, onions, vinegar
Mâche lamb's lettuce; small dark green leaf
Madeleine tiny sponge cake
Madère sauce *demi-glace* and Madeira wine
Magret (de canard) breast (of duck); now used for other poultry
Maïs maize flour
Maison (de) of the restaurant
Maître d'hôtel sauce with butter, parsley and lemon
Manchons see Goujonnettes
Mangetout edible peas and pods
Mangue mango
Manière (de) style (of)
Maquereau mackerel
Maraîchère (à la) market-gardener style; velouté sauce with vegetables
Marais marsh or market garden
Marbré marbled
Marc pure spirit
Marcassin young wild boar
Marché market
Marchand de vin sauce with red wine, chopped shallots
Marengo tomatoes, mushrooms, olive oil, white wine, garlic, herbs
Marennes (blanches) flat-shelled oysters (*see* Huîtres)
Marennes (vertes) green shell oysters
Marinières see Moules
Marmite stewpot

Marrons chestnuts
Médaillon (de) round piece (of)
Mélange mixture or blend
Ménagère (à la) housewife style: onions, potatoes, peas, turnips and carrots
Mendiant (fruits de) mixture of figs, almonds and raisins
Menthe mint
Merguez spicy grilled sausage
Merlan whiting (in Provence the word is used for hake)
Merlu hake
Merluche dried cod
Mesclum mixture of salad leaves
Meunière sauce with butter, parsley, lemon (sometimes oil)
Meurette red wine sauce
Miel honey
Mignon (de) small round piece
Mignonette coarsely ground white pepper
Mijoté(e) cooked slowly in water
Milanaise (à la) Milan style: dipped in breadcrumbs, egg, cheese
Mille-feuille puff pastry with numerous thin layers
Mirabeau anchovies, olives
Mirabelle golden plums
Mitonée (de) soup (of)
Mode (à la) in the manner of
Moelle beef marrow
Moelleux au chocolat chocolate dessert (cake)
Montmorency with cherries
Morilles edible, dark brown, honeycombed fungi
Mornay cheese sauce
Morue cod
Moule mussels
Moules marinières mussels cooked in white wine and shallots
Mousseline hollandaise sauce with whipped cream
Moutarde mustard
Mouton mutton
Mûre mulberry
Mûre sauvage (de ronce) blackberry
Muscade nutmeg
Museau de porc (de boeuf) sliced muzzle of pork (beef) with shallots and parsley with vinaigrette
Myrtille bilberry (blueberry)
Mystère a meringue desert with ice-cream and chocolate; also cone-shaped ice cream
Nature plain
Navarin stew (usually lamb)
Navets turnips
Nid nest
Noilly sauce based on vermouth
Noisette hazelnut
Noisette sauce of lightly browned butter
Noisette (de) round piece (of)
Noix nuts
Noix de veau topside of leg (veal)
Normande (à la) Normandy style: fish sauce with mussels, shrimps, mushrooms, eggs and cream
Nouille noodle
Nouveau (Nouvelle) new or young

Noyau sweet liqueur from crushed stones (usually cherries)
Oeufs à la coque soft-boiled eggs
Oeufs à la neige see Île flottante
Oeufs à la poêle fried eggs
Oeufs brouillés scrambled eggs
Oeufs cocotte eggs cooked in individual dishes in a bain-marie
Oeufs durs hard-boiled eggs
Oeufs moulés poached eggs
Oie goose
Oignon onion
Ombrine fish, like sea-bass
Onglet flank of beef
Oreille (de porc) ear (pig's)
Oreillette sweet fritter, flavoured with orange flower water
Origan oregano (herb)
Orléannaise Orléans style: chicory and potatoes
Ortie nettle
Os bone
Osso bucco à la niçoise veal braised with orange zest, tomatoes, onions and garlic
Pain bread
Pain complet/entier wholemeal
Pain de campagne round white loaf
Pain d'épice spiced honey cake
Pain de mie square white loaf
Pain de seigle rye bread
Pain grillé toast
Pain doré/Pain perdu bread soaked in milk and eggs and fried
Paleron shoulder
Palmier palm-shaped sweet puff pastry
Palmier (coeur de) palm (heart)
Palombe wood pigeon
Palomête fish, like sea-bass
Palourde clam
Pamplemousse grapefruit
Panaché mixed
Pané(e) breadcrumbed
Papillote (en) cooked in oiled paper or foil
Paquets (en) parcels
Parfait (de) mousse (of)
Paris-Brest cake of *choux* pastry, filled with butter cream, almonds
Parisienne (à la) leeks, potatoes
Parmentier potatoes
Pastèque watermelon
Pastis (sauce au) aniseed based
Pâte pastry, dough or batter
Pâte à choux cream puff pastry
Pâte brisée short crust pastry
Pâté en croûte baked in pastry crust
Pâtes fraîches fresh pasta
Pâtisserie pastry
Paupiettes thin slices of meat or fish, used to wrap fillings
Pavé (de) thick slice (of)
Pavot (graines de) poppy seeds
Paysan(ne) (à la) country style
Peau (de) skin (of)
Pêche peach
Pêcheur fisherman
Pèlerine scallop
Perche perch
Perdreau young partridge

Perdrix partridge
Périgourdine (à la) goose liver and sauce *Périgueux*
Périgueux sauce with truffles and Madeira
Persil parsley
Persillade mixture of chopped parsley and garlic
Petit gris small snail
Pétoncle small scallop
Picholine large green table olives
Pied de cheval large oyster
Pied de mouton blanc cream coloured mushroom
Pied de porc pig's trotter
Pigeonneau young pigeon
Pignon pine nut
Piment (doux) pepper (sweet)
Pintade (pintadeau) guinea fowl (young guinea fowl)
Piperade omelette or scrambled eggs with tomatoes, peppers, onions and sometimes ham
Piquante (sauce) sharp tasting sauce with shallots, capers and wine
Pissenlit dandelion leaf
Pistache green pistachio nut
Pistou vegetable soup bound with *pommade* (thick smooth paste)
Plateau (de) plate (of)
Pleurote mushroom
Poché(e), pochade poached
Poêlé fried
Poire pear
Poireau leek
Pois pea
Poisson fish
Poitrine breast
Poitrine fumée smoked bacon
Poitrine salée unsmoked bacon
Poivre noir black pepper
Poivron (doux) pepper (sweet)
Polonaise Polish style: with buttered breadcrumbs, parsley, hard-boiled eggs
Pomme apple
Pommes de terre potatoes
   château roast
   dauphine croquettes
   frites chips
   gratinées browned with cheese
   Lyonnaise sautéed with onions
   vapeur boiled
Porc (carré de) loin of pork
Porc (côte de) loin of pork
Porcelet suckling pig
Porto (au) port
Portugaise (à la) Portuguese style: fried onions and tomatoes
Portugaises oysters with long, deep shells (see Huîtres)
Potage thick soup
Pot-au-feu clear meat broth served with the meat
Potimarron pumpkin
Poularde large hen
Poulet chicken
Poulet à la broche spit-roasted chicken
Poulpe octopus
Poussin small baby chicken

Pré-salé (agneau de) lamb raised on salt marshes
Primeur young vegetable
Profiterole puffs of *choux* pastry, filled with custard
Provençale (à la) Provençal style: tomatoes, garlic, olive oil, etc.
Prune plum
Pruneau prune
Quenelle light dumpling of fish or poultry
Queue tail
Queue de boeuf oxtail
Quiche lorraine open flan of cheese, ham or bacon
Raclette scrapings from specially-made and heated cheese
Radis radish
Ragoût stew, usually meat but can describe other ingredients
Raie (bouclée) skate (type of)
Raifort horseradish
Raisin grape
Ramier wood pigeon
Rapé(e) grated or shredded
Rascasse scorpion fish
Ratatouille aubergines, onions, courgettes, garlic, red peppers and tomatoes in olive oil
Réglisse liquorice
Reine-Claude greengage
Rémoulade sauce of mayonnaise, mustard, capers, herbs, anchovies
Rillettes (d'oie) potted pork (goose)
Ris d'agneau lamb sweetbreads
Ris de veau veal sweetbreads
Riz rice
Robe de chambre jacket potato
Rognon kidney
Romarin rosemary
Rôti roast
Rouget red mullet
Rouget barbet red mullet
Rouille orange-coloured sauce with peppers, garlic and saffron
Roulade (de) roll (of)
Roulé(e) rolled (usually crêpe)
Sabayon sauce of egg yolks, wine
Sablé shortbread
Safran saffron
Saignant(e) underdone, rare
St-Jaques (coquille) scallop
St-Pierre John Dory
Salade niçoise tomatoes, beans, potatoes, black olives, anchovies, lettuce, olive oil, perhaps tuna
Salade panachée mixed salad
Salade verte green salad
Salé salted
Salmis red wine sauce
Salsifis salsify (vegetable)
Sandre freshwater fish, like perch
Sang blood
Sanglier wild boar
Saucisse freshly-made sausage
Saucisson large, dry sausage
Saucisson cervelas saveloy
Sauge sage
Saumon salmon
Saumon fumé smoked salmon
Sauvage wild
Scipion cuttlefish
Sel salt
Soja (pousse de) soy bean (soy bean sprout)
Soja (sauce de) soy sauce
Soubise onion sauce
Sucre sugar
Tapenade olive spread
Tartare raw minced beef
Tartare (sauce) sauce with mayonnaise, onions, capers, herbs
Tarte open flan
Tarte Tatin upside down tart of caramelized apples and pastry
Terrine container in which mixed meats/fish are baked; served cold
Tête de veau vinaigrette calf's head vinaigrette
Thé tea
Thermidor grilled lobster with browned béchamel sauce
Thon tuna fish
Thym thyme
Tiède mild or lukewarm
Tilleul lime tree
Tomate tomato
Topinambour Jerusalem artichoke
Torte sweet-filled flan
Tortue turtle
Tournedos fillet steak (small end)
Touron a cake, pastry or loaf made from almond paste and filled with candied fruits and nuts
Tourte (Tourtière) covered savoury tart
Tourteau large crab
Tranche slice
Tranche de boeuf steak
Traver de porc spare rib of pork
Tripoux stuffed mutton tripe
Truffade a huge sautéed pancake or galette with bacon, garlic and Cantal cheese
Truffe truffle; black, exotic, tuber
Truite trout
Truite saumonée salmon trout
Turbot (Turbotin) turbot
Vacherin ice-cream, meringue, cream
Vapeur (à la) steamed
Veau veal
Veau pané (escalope de) thin slice of veal in flour, eggs and breadcrumbs
Venaison venison
Verveine verbena
Viande meat
Vichyssoise creamy potato and leek soup, served cold
Viennoise coated with egg and breadcrumbs, fried (usually veal)
Vierge litterally virgin (best olive oil, the first pressing)
Vierge (sauce) olive oil sauce
Vinaigre (de) wine vinegar or vinegar of named fruit
Vinaigrette (à la) French dressing with wine vinegar, oil, etc.
Volaille poultry
Yaourt yogurt

© Richard Binns